EVALUATING AND VALUING IN SOCIAL RESEARCH

EVALUATING AND VALUING IN SOCIAL RESEARCH

Thomas A. Schwandt
Emily F. Gates

THE GUILFORD PRESS
New York   London

Library of Congress Cataloging-in-Publication Data
Names: Schwandt, Thomas A., author. | Gates, Emily F., author.
Title: Evaluating and valuing in social research / Thomas A. Schwandt,
    Emily F. Gates.
Description: New York : The Guilford Press, [2021] | Includes
    bibliographical references and index.
Identifiers: LCCN 2021000525 | ISBN 9781462547326 (paperback) |
    ISBN 9781462547333 (cloth)
Subjects: LCSH: Social sciences—Research. | Social sciences—Methodology.
Classification: LCC H62 .S357 2021 | DDC 300.72—dc23
LC record available at *https://lccn.loc.gov/2021000525*

Preface

This is a book about values, valuing and evaluating (i.e., answering evaluative questions) in the practice of social science research—particularly research done in applied fields, including program and policy evaluation, policy analysis, organizational and community development, business and nonprofit management, clinical sociology, social work, community psychology, international development, education, and public health. We address a broad multidisciplinary audience of social science researchers. Some of these researchers self-identify as professional evaluators. Others conduct evaluations of social programs and policies in these applied fields but define their professional identities as psychologists, sociologists, educational researchers, program analysts, and so on.

Research in applied fields is designed to be of use to policymakers, practitioners, and communities. It is often financially and politically commissioned and shaped by an array of stakeholder perspectives and interests, including those of funders and commissioners, social researchers themselves, and the institutions within which they work. This research is often committed to producing actionable results. As noted in the *Handbook of Applied Social Research Methods* (Bickman & Rog, 2009, p. x), the environment in which social researchers work is typically "complex, chaotic, and highly political, with pressures for quick and conclusive answers" to pressing problems. That environment is also infused with values and with decisions about what to value and how.

We side with those philosophers of social science and science practitioners who argue that the value-free ideal for social scientific research (and all research for that matter) is unrealistic. All social research is generated from some perspective, orientation, or viewpoint and is thus partial (i.e., there is no "view from nowhere"). At the same time, however, research-ers are committed to identifying and addressing biases, to preserving the ideal of objectivity (in the sense of a disciplined and transparent commit-ment to evidence), and to generating "useful" knowledge that contributes to improving the lives of individuals, communities, and societies.

In pursuit of an alternative to a value-free ideology for social science research, we argue for sustained, systematic reflexivity about what is val-ued in research, what values research promotes, how decisions about what to value are made and by whom, and how evaluating takes place. Reflexiv-ity about values, valuing, and evaluating is an essential dimension of robust inquiry. What matters is developing a judicious and critical understanding of (1) how valuing as reflected in professional behavior as well as in social policies, commissioning organizations, researcher stances, and public pref-erences influences the conduct of applied social research in legitimate and illegitimate ways, and (2) how evaluative questions can be effectively pro-posed and evaluative judgments legitimately defended.

We are fully aware of the ongoing discussion of whether there are differences between practices of social research and evaluation that truly make a difference. Some scholars argue that there is overlap between the practices, whereas others argue that each is unique (e.g., Mathison, 2008; Mertens, 2014; Scriven, 2016a; Vedung, 1997). We adopt the view that evaluators are explicitly concerned with a process of examining, apprais-ing, or weighing up some phenomenon (a program, policy, project, strat-egy, etc.) against some type of yardstick or criteria. In addition, evaluation typically has a goal of providing valid and useful information to inform decision making. Social researchers may, from time to time, wear this kind of evaluator's hat, as they systematically investigate and assess contexts, policies, and programs designed to address social problems (Rossi, Lipsey, & Henry, 2019). In that respect, what we have to say here about evaluating will likely be relevant to their work. In addition, evaluation knowledge pro-duced by both large (e.g., Mathematica, WestEd, Abt Associates, MDRC) and small research and evaluation firms as well as in academic research centers tends to overlap with other forms of social scientific knowledge pro-duction, including descriptive studies, theory building, performance mea-surement, and data science (Lemire, Nielsen, & Christie, 2018). We use the terms *evaluation* and *evaluation research* interchangeably.

DEFINITIONS

Values

The term *values* is not easily defined. Sociologists, philosophers, econo-mists, political scientists, and psychologists all have somewhat different ways of making sense of the concept. Value can refer to a core principle or belief, a preference for something, a quality or importance of something, and a measure. We routinely speak of a variety of types of values, including moral, cultural, scientific, political, personal, social, intrinsic, instrumental, and so on. For our purposes, the concept *value* includes both normative (i.e., relating to a standard) and emotive commitments to what individuals, groups, and societies esteem, cherish, and respect—for example, equal treatment under the law, veneration of family, equality, democratic deliberation, individuality, respect for human dignity, and so on—as well as perspectives on what is right or wrong, good or bad, important or unimportant, and so on (Makau & Marty, 2013). Individuals, organizations, and communities hold values implicitly and make them explicit only when challenged.

In this book, we do not treat values as stable notions defined in advance of their application or use, but rather as ideals we grapple with, formulate, and express in day-to-day activities (Dussage, Helgesson, Lee, & Woolgar, 2015). In other words, we do not regard values as fixed influences or off-the-shelf standards that determine a decision but rather as a critical dimension of decisions made in specific situations. Often, values are thought of as preferences or matters of taste or choice that are simply there waiting to be stated or revealed. Professor of political science and economics Charles Lindblom (1977, 1990) distinguished preferences or mere matters of taste from volitions—the latter understood as patterns of desires reflecting a combination of principle, appraisal, judgment, and opinion. Borrowing his idea, we regard values as analogous to volitions. They are created and are "complex choices on which deliberation is both possible and practiced" and "emergent acts of will" that express how things ought to be (Lindblom, 1977, p. 135). Values are more like thoughtful judgments and considered choices.

Valuing

The term *valuing* as opposed to values best captures this dynamic sense of how cherished and prized values are continually explained and examined as they are made plain in actions and practices. Valuing is a kind of practice that involves identifying, naming, considering, and holding or respecting something (an action, behavior, trait, idea, point of view, etc.) as important, beneficial, right to do, good to be, and so forth. For example, valuing occurs when a researcher decides how to integrate her economic goals and personal career ambitions with ethical and scientific considerations in the conduct of a given investigation. Valuing reveals distinct perspectives on what is considered important and significant and is manifest in applied social research in multiple ways.

• Researcher behavior involves valuing the importance and priority of moral values that express what is good or right in terms of researcher conduct, including honesty, truthfulness, respect for persons, and cultural sensitivity and fairness, along with cognitive or epistemic values such as a commitment to systematic inquiry and justified belief, empirical grounding of claims, and objectivity. Both kinds of values are typically represented in professional standards or codes for ethical conduct. However, those guidelines are not "how-to" manuals. The kind of valuing involved in professional conduct is something continually conceived and achieved by practitioners in their interactions with colleagues, research funders, and those involved in the research process.

• The activity of valuing is also found in the stakes (investments, motivations, interests, perspectives) that individuals or groups bring to some situation or set of circumstances. Quite often, those stakes are not only different but may conflict, and hence must be explored and negotiated. For example, policymakers may see the highest value in the relationship between financial investment in a policy and achievement of predetermined outcomes; practitioners responsible for operationalizing the policy might instead find greater value in the practicality of implementing its provisions and sustaining effects over time; researchers examining the program might place the highest value on technical matters, including the rigor of design and analysis.

• Moral and political valuing is embedded, and often explicitly stated, in the mission and vision statements of organizations and agencies employing or funding applied researchers. Oxfam, for example, states that it values empowerment, inclusiveness, and accountability; the United Nations Development Programme claims that it exemplifies integrity, accountability, transparency, professionalism, mutual respect, and results orientation in all that it does as an organization. The Consortium of Social Science Associations in its ongoing series of briefs "Why Social Science?" (*www. cossa.org/tag/why-social-science*) openly promotes the very value of social research itself to society—a contested political issue in recent years in the United States.

• The activity of valuing is reflected in the conceptual frameworks that shape research, policy, and practice in applied fields. For example, studies of global health problems and their solutions can be driven by the realization of different moral values, including humanitarianism, utilitarianism, equity, and rights.

• Valuing is manifest in researchers' epistemological, methodological, and moral-political commitments. Controversies among the merits of different research frameworks—experimentalism, participatory action research, feminism, critical and queer theories, activist anthropology, culturally responsive evaluation—are most often centered on valuing different kinds of commitments.

Evaluating

Values and valuing take on specific meaning and importance in applied social research devoted expressly to *evaluating*. Evaluating is a particular kind of empirical investigation often spoken of as appraising, weighing up, assessing, calculating, gauging, rating, and ranking, depending on the field or practice where it takes place. It involves answering evaluative questions that require judging the merits of some action, typically a project, program, policy, or strategy. In social science research, this includes questions such as, are children better off if parents who want a divorce stay together; will this intervention improve child survival in countries with a high burden of neonatal and child mortality; what makes for unhealthy housing in this community; what is the most effective media campaign to lower tobacco use? Moreover, many evaluative questions arise in research situations where the valuing done by affected parties (stakeholders) conflicts—for example, when farmers wish to draw water from a river to irrigate their crops, while conservationists want to preserve the endangered fish species residing in the river. Contested perspectives on valuing make evaluating a challenging undertaking.

Answering evaluative questions about projects, policies, programs, and strategies requires making evaluative judgments; that is, decisions about what is right, good, best, important, significant, meritorious, and so on. Those judgments, in turn, often rest on both explicit and implicit appeals to specific criteria such as effectiveness, efficiency, or sustainability. Criteria are expressions of valuing done by individuals and groups holding often differing motivations, interests, and perspectives on what is being evaluated. Understanding how and whose criteria should matter in addressing evaluative questions as well as how evaluative judgments are made and by whom is a critical professional responsibility of many researchers working in applied fields.

OUR AIM AND PERSPECTIVE

This book offers conceptual and practical guidance to social researchers and evaluators who intend to navigate the tangled and complicated terrain of values, valuing, and evaluating. We focus on understanding how these phenomena and associated practices are at work in social research, what investigators can and should do in dealing with such matters, and how their actions relate to long-standing concerns about objectivity, impartiality, the nature and use of evidence, and the purpose(s) of applied social research.

Our primary aim is to help researchers become more explicit about values, valuing, and evaluative judgments in their practices and to refine their capacity to engage in deliberative argumentation guided by standards of reasonableness.

Much applied research takes place as if there is no controversy over values and valuing or as if moral–political issues can be dealt with in a purely technical way. Data-driven mentalities such as evidence-based policy and practice, reliance on big data, social technologies (e.g., regulatory impact assessment, results-based management, performance management), and best practices tend to define what can be known, depoliticize the matter of valuing, and suggest that data alone can support decisions without the interference of values. Being more explicit about valuing not only serves as a corrective to these practices, but it also helps clarify thinking and can be a remedy against smuggling values on board the applied research vessel. Of course, declaration, explicitness, and transparency do not and cannot solve problems of value conflict. Conflicts about fundamental values, including moral disagreements, are permanent conditions of democratic politics and thus are not problems to be solved but situations to be addressed through dialogue and deliberation. In this book, we explore several means of using intentional values-based dialogue to engage value conflicts.

This book is a call for a morally centered and democratic form of the professional practices of social research and evaluation, one that steps deeper and with greater awareness and responsibility into the contested ethical and political worlds of community engagement, civic involvement, and deliberation. Elsewhere, following an idea first introduced by Martin Rein (1983), we identified this as a value-critical stance (Schwandt, 1997; Schwandt & Gates, 2016). To be value critical as a social researcher or evaluator in Rein's view is not only to present the empirical case for the consequences of pursuing alternative actions to solve social problems, but also to interpret what it is we are doing in society, why we are doing what we do, and what we might do differently given our puzzlement and worry about what we do. In our view, this stance redefines social inquiry and evaluation as dialogical and critically reflective processes of democratic discussion about desirable goals and actions in which we use deliberative methods to determine what we should do and structure our conversation to permit interaction and learning.

A value-critical stance as a social researcher or evaluator involves advocacy for this way of interrogating social action—bringing together fact-sensitive appraisals of social conditions and value-sensitive deliberations about the current state of affairs and possible social direction. Given the concern of much applied research for use in decision making, a value-critical stance might also involve advocating that decision makers most concerned about the findings of such investigations take action for the common good based on those findings. However, we distinguish this value-critical stance from that of the activist researcher who serves as a community organizer or mobilizes social movements (McBride, Casillas, & LoPiccolo, 2020; Neubauer & Hall, 2020). To be sure, these are needed roles in society, but we do not regard them as essential to the skill set or experiences of social researchers and evaluators. Moreover, such activities may preempt the difficult co-produced, deliberative activity of boundary setting and critique that in our view characterizes the professional responsibility of social researchers engaged in value-critical work.

A value-critical stance inevitably requires interrogating multiple values and perspectives held by professional inquirers themselves and those espoused by the individuals and groups that they work with and address. It also requires unwavering acceptance of the fact that any inquiry always requires setting boundaries on what values, perspectives, and evidence are swept into consideration in that inquiry and what is left out. In the following pages, we advocate for critical self-reflection, support of civic agency, dialogue, and deliberation as central professional responsibilities.

Writing from our positions as privileged members of elite universities advocating for these aspects of reasoned moral–political argumentation, we realize that some scholars and practitioners might read our perspective as an appeal to the "presumed neutrality of White European Enlightenment epistemology" (Sensoy & DiAngelo, 2017). Yet, in our view, deliberative argumentation means opening matters of values and valuing to critical analysis and negotiation that, in turn, invites transparency and accountability of research and evaluation practices to the plurality of groups involved and affected. Doing so provokes researchers and evaluators to wrestle with how to address normative and epistemological differences and justify choices made about what is valued within a given study and circumstances. This often means working to address power imbalances between groups and advancing the values and worldviews of minoritized and oppressed groups, such as in indigenous-led (Smith, 2012) and anti-racist research (Zuberi & Bonilla-Silva, 2008). Moreover, reasoned dialogue need not and should not exclude the play of emotions and the affective dimensions of deliberation, nor should it require privileging certain forms of knowledge (e.g., White, Eurocentric) over others. Moral emotions such as compassion and feelings of responsibility and justice play an important role in judging the ethical aspects of policies and programs designed to achieve social change (Helm, 2007). Neither must the idea of being civil in contentious dialogues equate to silencing marginalized voices. People who wish to maintain the status quo often view pushing back against taken-for-granted understandings and practices as being uncivil. Yet, orchestrating the terms of civility with parties to a dialogue ought to be part of deliberation rather than assuming all parties to the dialogue will simply respond to the majoritarian view of what civility ought to be.

OVERVIEW OF THE BOOK

Chapters 1 and 2 focus on values and valuing in terms of the responsibilities of social researchers in applied fields—responsibilities for both professional ethical behavior and knowledge generation. Some of these are moral responsibilities—duties or obligations to act in a certain way to which a professional is required, by some standard, to attend (Talbert, 2019). Standards or norms for behavior are acquired through the socialization of researchers into their respective fields of study; others are part of the general religious and secular discourses of societies; still others are role specific, for example, the moral obligations of the lawyer, the physician, the anthropologist, and so on. In the social sciences, talk of ethics, particularly applied, practical, or professional ethics (Jamieson, 2013), is more prominent than talk of morality. Yet the two terms are very closely related. One common view is that ethics is concerned with making decisions about what is right and wrong to do (or good or bad to be), whereas morality refers to a set of norms that inform ethical decisions. We abide by the convention of talking about social science research and evaluation ethics but could just as well be talking about morality in social science research and evaluation.

Throughout both chapters, we examine how the activity of valuing is visible not simply in terms of the personal value stances and decisions of investigators but also in social policies, commissioning organizations, and research frameworks. In daily practice, researchers usually do not neatly distinguish the kind of valuing involved in producing scientific knowledge from the kind of valuing that involves ethical reasoning. We separate the two here for analytic purposes, allowing a closer investigation of each.

Chapter 1, "Expanding the Conversation on Research Ethics," focuses on applied or practical ethics in researcher behavior and addresses valuing unfolding in the practical and policy issues related to responsible scientific conduct. Rather than focusing on the growing bureaucratization of research ethics and the tendency to view ethics as a matter of regulating professional behavior, we regard ethical research norms—honesty, openness, respect for colleagues, respect for persons, social responsibility, and so on, represented in professional codes of conduct—as something developed and resolved in specific situations. We emphasize that values typically valorized in professional conduct are interpreted and expressed differently depending on historical, social, cultural, organizational, and technological circumstances. This chapter also emphasizes the contrast between raising social researchers' awareness of ethical codes and principles and receiving instruction in ethical reasoning, and it offers some practical guidance on the latter.

Without rehearsing the extensive debates in the philosophy of social science surrounding the aims of the social sciences (vis-à-vis the natural sciences) and the notion of value neutrality, Chapter 2, "From Value Neutrality to Morally Informed Research," wades into the long-standing discussion of the role of facts and values in scientific research and the legitimate and illegitimate roles that values and valuing can and do play in research. It locates multiple sources of valuing and their potential influence on the conduct of research, including political, cultural, and social values and norms that tacitly, and in many cases explicitly, are represented in programs and policies that are the object of investigation; value positions held by institutions and agencies that commission research and evaluations; the honest broker and value-neutral stance of applied researchers as well as advocacy stances that may be openly ideological and promoting a particular moral and political point of view. We are particularly concerned with the relationship between moral commitments and factual discoveries and defend the idea of morally informed applied social science that does not take the form of preaching.

Chapters 1 and 2 discuss how valuing—understood as naming, considering, holding or respecting, and identifying what is good with respect to professional responsibility in human conduct and knowledge production—operates in the conduct of applied social science. With Chapter 3, we shift the focus to evaluating, the making of judgments of merit, worth, importance, and significance of policies, programs, projects, strategies, innovations, advocacy campaigns, and the like that must be justified and publicly defended (De Munck & Zimmerman, 2015). Chapter 3, "The Conventional Frame for Evaluating Social Interventions," presents the mainstream view of evaluating found in social science research. This is a traditional focus on the methodical, technical, instrumental activity of determining the value of planned interventions, policies, and projects. Chapter 3 describes the assumptions—for example, regarding the definition of social problems, the problem-solving process, the definition and role of stakeholders, the nature and use of evidence—characteristic of this frame that also serves as a mental model for many social researchers.

Chapter 4, "Expanding the Conventional Frame for Evaluating," looks at the work of Michael Scriven and other evaluation scholars who distinguish evaluating from social research. The emerging science of evaluating raises important issues about the criteria on which to base an evaluative judgment; how and to what extent evaluative judgments involve stakeholder considerations; how evaluation practice unfolds in a political policymaking milieu; and who precisely is responsible for making an evaluative judgment.

For analytic purposes, in Chapter 5, "An Emerging Alternative Frame for Evaluating," we contrast the conventional frame for evaluating in Chapter 3 with ideas raised in Chapter 4 and then contrast both of these accounts with an emerging alternative frame that is developing across several areas of evaluation as well as social research theory and practice. This alternative addresses the complexity of social problems and change processes and the necessity of evaluating interventions in ways that account for this complexity and support iterative and adaptive change efforts. In this alternative framing of evaluation, researchers, practitioners, citizens, and policymakers view social problems and situations as interconnected and fluid. In addressing these problems, these groups possess varying degrees of uncertainty about the definition and extent of the problem and often operate with incomplete knowledge and information. Evaluating interventions to address these social problems requires expanding beyond a point-in-time judgment of "How did we do?" based on chosen criteria, to an ongoing learning process among all stakeholders bringing together data and values to change a state of affairs, innovate, and adapt. Evaluating is thus less like gauging performance against a standard and more like an activity of practical reasoning in which participants address the question "Given what we know now, what should we do?"

However, in the day-to-day reality of on-the-ground practices of evaluation research, evaluating may not fall neatly within one of these frames. Despite establishing a contrast between ways of thinking about evaluating through the sequencing of Chapters 3, 4, and 5, we do not suggest that one set of ideas and practices totally replaces an earlier set of ideas and practices. Thus, in Chapter 6, "Evaluating as a Multifaceted Investigation of Value," we explore how the conventional and alternative frames for evaluating coexist and function in complementary ways both conceptually and within a specific case example. We argue that matters of determining the value of an intervention within a specific context play an important role in social policy and practice. Reaching ethically and technically defensible conclusions in such circumstances requires critical reflection and democratic deliberation about the underlying values and criteria that bound evaluative judgments. Without diminishing the importance of making such judgments, we argue that amidst complexity, questions of value are continually developing and often amplifying. We illustrate this coexistence of determining value (based on the expanded conventional frame) and developing value (based on the emerging alternative) in the case of a philanthropic initiative to transform the systems that shape health and well-being in the United States. The appendix to this chapter illustrates a variety of methods that are useful in developing value and that extend beyond what is traditionally in social researchers' toolkits.

Chapter 7, "Valuing, Evaluating, and Professional Responsibility," argues for a new form of professionalism in social research and evaluation. It explores the limits of professional researchers' theoretical and methodological expertise. We espouse a view of the responsibilities of social researchers aligned with notions of co-production and democratic professionalism. Here researchers serve the public less as outside experts and more as catalysts and collaborators. Citizens are not merely beneficiaries in receipt of expert knowledge but collaborators who contribute their knowledge, experience, skills, and capabilities to creating social innovation. We also make the case for moving applied scientific inquiry out of an adversarial and argumentative culture to one of dialogue and deliberation. We conclude with some implications for the training and education of social researchers.

Chapters 1 through 5 and 7 include an annotated "Important Resources" section as well as a "Bridge to Practice" section that encourages readers to engage issues raised in each chapter. Chapter 6 is unique in providing an extended case discussion that concludes with a briefly annotated Methods Appendix. A Glossary of select terms used in the book is also provided.

ACKNOWLEDGMENTS

Tom: I have been working on issues related to the place of moral inquiry and practical reasoning in the conduct and use of applied social science, particularly evaluation research, for more than 35 years, the last few years in fairly constant dialogue with Emily about these issues. This book is the latest statement of that evolving understanding emerging from my collaboration with Emily as coauthor, interlocutor, and tireless champion of new ways of thinking about evaluating. What we have to say here is, of course, not only the product of our joint efforts but reflects the thoughtful contributions that so many colleagues have made to our thinking. I am especially indebted to my good friend Peter Dahler-Larsen, and to Elliott Stern, Bob Stake, Mel Mark, Eleanor Chelimsky, Ernie House, Mike Morris, Martin Reynolds, Zenda Ofir, and Brad Cousins for their own work on issues in evaluation as well as for their insights into my work. Jennifer Greene's scholarship on a values-engaged approach to evaluation and her insistence that evaluation studies must contribute to democratic decision making have been particularly inspiring. I regard it is a major gift to have had the opportunity to be in scholarly conversation with all these colleagues for so many years. In recent years, beginning with an initial collaboration on a National Research Council committee examining the use of science as evidence in policymaking, I also had the good fortune of coming to know Ken Prewitt at Columbia University. Our conversations about the use value of social science research have been enlightening and invaluable. For her unwavering support and encouragement of my work, I am most grateful to my wife, Sherry. As a senior university administrator with extensive responsibilities for supporting faculty research across the social, behavioral, and natural sciences, she was invaluable to me as a source of insight on matters of the applied sciences. But, more importantly, she showed the patience of Job at countless dinner conversations when I worked out my ideas by talking them over with her, and she offered useful questions and comments that helped clarify my thinking. All the really clear aspects of what I have written I no doubt owe largely to her; the muddied parts are obviously my own usual creation. Finally, I confess that while writing, my mood oscillated between the excitement of perhaps offering some new work and depression on realizing that it might have all been said before and better by others. I shall leave that evaluative judgment to readers.

Emily: My perspective and inputs to this book are grounded in my evaluation work, training and influence by systems thinkers, and conversations with colleagues and friends working in this space as well as students. In no particular order, I acknowledge Jennifer Greene, Lizanne DeStefano, Robert Stake, and Melvin Hall for instilling a care and commitment to honoring values and multiple perspectives in myself and the field; to fellow systems thinkers Bob Williams, Martin Reynolds, Beverly Parsons, Tina Smith, Judy Oakden, Bobby Milstein, Pablo Vidueira, Michael Quinn Patton, Gerald Midgley, Mat Walton, and numerous others for sustaining the space for systemic evaluating; to dear friends Ayesha Boyce, Jori Hall, Rebecca Teasdale, Gabriela Garcia, Lorna Rivera, Maria Carolina Hidalgo Standen, Gizelle Gopez, and others for inspiring me in how you lead the next generations in equitable research and evaluation; and to my evaluation collaborators, particularly from ReThink Health, and students who bounced ideas and contributed examples. Finally, I thank my parents for their unconditional support.

From us both: We benefited greatly from the insightful comments of reviewers Tom Archibald, Robin Miller, Mike Morris, Anne Vo, and Deborah Wasserman, who helped us sharpen our focus and clarify our arguments. Finally, we are indebted to our editor, C. Deborah Laughton, not only for her enthusiastic support of this work, but for her wise counsel at all points in the preparation and production of the manuscript. She is a genuine joy to work with.

Contents

CHAPTER 1

Expanding the Conversation on Research Ethics

Ethics is not something that can be understood adequately
just by learning norms—indeed, the unchecked rigid
application of norms can lead to unethical practice; the
practical, social experience of relating to others in different
situations is an important source of ethical wisdom.
—SAYER (2011, p. 82)

INTRODUCTION

Why begin a book with a chapter on research ethics? The topic of ethics
is often buried near the end of research texts or course syllabi and cast
primarily as a matter of adhering to legal requirements and professional
ethical codes for social research. That is not the version of ethics we focus
on in this chapter. Rather, in the day-to-day conduct of being a social
researcher, each of us encounters ethical issues and choices whether or not
we see and consider them as such. Consider the context of the COVID-19
pandemic. As we were preparing this book, deaths from the COVID-19
virus were nearing 190,000 in the United States and 875,000 worldwide.
After a brief letup, the virus was again spreading rapidly throughout the
United States and in many other countries. Throughout the world, reopening (business, schools, churches, restaurants, sports arenas) had become a
highly charged political and scientific issue. But reopening also inescapably
presented ethical issues. Amidst the pandemic, some social, health, and
educational researchers quickly found themselves wrestling with unavoidable ethical questions as the results of studies were rapidly used in decision making about reopening and the ramifications of such decisions had
apparent life or death consequences. Other social researchers began halting

studies altogether, given more urgent personal needs or because they faced the infeasibility of in-person data collection and necessary social distancing and precautions. How are researchers to act responsibly amidst such apparent and consequential ethical matters? Clearly, they need guidance beyond what is found in professionally sanctioned ethical codes and procedures.

Box 1.1 illustrates what considering the ethical dimensions of reopening looked like within one framework that addressed such matters head-on. The framework considers ethical perspectives for evaluating policy options that define the process of reopening. The framework is particularly instructive for our purposes. It illustrates how social researchers and evaluators working in the real world of policy decision making face circumstances laden with multiple competing values; how social problem solving involves simultaneous considerations of political, ethical, and technical rationalities; and how acting ethically requires what sociologist Andrew Sayer (2011) calls a postdisciplinary perspective, extending beyond the concerns of any single discipline's (e.g., sociology, psychology, anthropology, political science, philosophy) perspective on ethical being.

Social researchers recognize that professional ethics is the study of the principles and standards that underlie a profession's responsibilities and conduct. Several widely understood aspects of the ethics of social research include the following:

• Social researchers working in education, community psychology, sociology, public health, or other applied fields of study are, by virtue of both their education and experience, familiar with ethical issues relating to matters of confidentiality, consent, disclosure, anonymity, conflict of interest, covert research, and research with vulnerable groups.

• University-based, as well as commercial, institutional review boards (IRBs) assess and monitor ethical concerns in research and evaluation involving human participants in accordance with the three primary principles of autonomy, beneficence, and justice as discussed in the Belmont Report and the U.S. Federal Policy for the Protection of Human Subjects (45 Code of Federal Regulations part 46), more familiarly known as the Common Rule.

• The Department of Health and Human Services Office for Human Research Protections (2019) revised the Common Rule emphasizing expanded exemption categories and consent form changes with a full compliance date of January 21, 2019. Ethical guidance provided by IRBs on interacting with human subjects is familiar to social and behavioral scientists who are required to complete training offered through the National Institutes of Health and the Collaborative Institutional Training Initiative (CITI), and a revised Common Rule course is now offered through CITI.

BOX 1.1. AN ETHICAL FRAMEWORK FOR EVALUATING POLICY OPTIONS DEFINING THE COVID-19 REOPENING PROCESS

From the Introduction

- Ethical decisions will not and should not be made based on either the science or economics alone. Rather, these decisions are best understood as a series of trade-offs that reflect many shared social values, including shared interests in health and economic flourishing as well as other aspects of well-being, and in liberty and justice. These values and how to think about them in concert are the subject of ethics.

- Ethical analysis of potential policies is not about finding the perfect course of action; there is no perfect course of action. Any policy we adopt will have morally significant costs that can neither be ignored nor fully justified. Ethical analysis helps to identify the trade-offs inherent in policy choices and to guide decisions as to which trade-offs to accept or reject. Such analysis also helps identify ways to modify policies to make them more ethically acceptable. There is no guarantee that all people will be satisfied with the conclusions reached through even the most careful ethical analysis.

Ethics Framework

Step 1: Select Policies and Consider Feasibility

- The clear identification of policies requires not only an articulation of the suite of policies that are simultaneously under consideration but also the proposed timing, duration, and sequencing of different measures.

- Consider the technological, economic, administrative, and political feasibility of the policy or set of policies.

- Recognize salient forms of uncertainty: Important public policy decisions often have to be made in the context of considerable uncertainty about the effects of alternative courses of action.

Step 2: Well-Being

- Assess how the policies identified as feasible will impact the well-being of all people in society.

- *Well-being concerns the kinds of conditions that are needed for people to lead a decent life.* Health, economic well-being, and social connection are all central to well-being for both individuals and communities. For many people, spiritual experience and fellowship, meaningful work, or learning are central to their well-being.

(continued)

- The relationship between policy choices and well-being is complex. It is a mistake to assume that social distancing policies are the best way to promote public health or that reopening policies are the best way to bolster the economy.
- A particular policy may have a variety of effects on many different dimensions of well-being—some good and some bad: For example, lifting shelter-in-place orders would provide many people with the opportunity to spend time with people they care about but would also inevitably risk an increase in COVID-19 cases and the accompanying harms to well-being—including death. For example, reopening businesses could promote health to the extent that the beneficial economic impact will prevent illnesses and death caused by unemployment or poverty. But the same policy could undermine the health to the extent that returning to the workplace exposes them to increased risk of infection and COVID-19 disease.

Step 3: Liberty

- Assess how potentially feasible policies address issues of liberty.
- Four kinds of fundamental liberties are particularly relevant to decisions about continuing, relaxing, or reinstituting social distancing and about the public health measures under consideration:
  - *Freedom of movement and association*—individuals have a fundamental interest in being free to travel and to gather with others in public and private spaces;
  - *Freedom of religion*—individuals have a fundamental interest in gathering for religious worship;
  - *Privacy*—individuals have a fundamental interest in choosing whether others can have access to their personal information; and
  - *Political participation*—individuals have a fundamental interest in participating in democratic processes, such as voting and census reporting. From an ethics perspective—independent of questions of constitutionality and legality—there must be a good reason to restrict these freedoms or violate privacy.

Step 4: Justice

- The third broad moral value to consider is justice. *Justice concerns whether the burdens and benefits of a policy are distributed fairly.* Justice is often analyzed in terms of the differential impacts of policies on different, ethically relevant groups.
- Importantly, when assessing the justness of a policy, we should also consider the benefits and burdens of implementing or enforcing that policy.
- The groups of particular moral concern in this pandemic include people who are low income, people of color (racial and ethnic minorities and native peoples), people in different stages of life, and essential workers. Other groups of

moral concern include rural communities, people living in congregate facilities such as incarcerated populations and some agricultural workers, and undocumented persons.

Step 5: Legitimacy

- The fourth moral value to consider is legitimacy. *Legitimacy refers to the appropriate authority to make governing decisions, issue guidelines, make recommendations, and enforce rules.*
- Legitimacy is relevant to an evaluation of not only the content of a given social distancing policy or reopening plan, but also the process by which a policy decision is reached, the perceived authority of the decision makers, and the ways in which the policy is implemented or enforced.
- There are four interconnected aspects of legitimacy: legitimacy of the process; legitimacy of knowledge and expertise; communicative legitimacy; and, enforcement legitimacy.

Step 6: Mitigation and Remedies

- Once a policy has been identified and evaluated according to Steps 1–5, decision makers must assess whether or to what extent it is feasible to blunt any of the negative impacts of policies still under consideration. To the extent this is possible, policies that are ethically problematic may become more ethically acceptable.
- Any policy or set of policies adopted in response to COVID-19 will have significant negative effects. These negative effects are likely to include increased health risks for some, loss of income for many, and lost opportunities of all sorts. Moreover, these negative impacts are often distributed unequally in ways that are unfair or that exacerbate existing injustice.

Step 7: Overall Assessment

- Reflect on the results from Steps 1–6 to determine which set of policies should be implemented. Taking into account the full set of potential benefits and burdens, their distribution across groups, liberty concerns, legitimacy concerns, along with feasible remedies, which set of policies is most justifiable all things considered?
- Some ethics frameworks structure this "all-things-considered" question as a matter of balancing the four kinds of considerations we've been considering: well-being, liberty, justice, and legitimacy.

Note. From Bernstein et al. (2020).

• Professional ethical codes abound, as illustrated in the examples provided in Table 1.1. While these codes may serve as prescriptions, recommendations, or directives for the professional behavior of researchers, the values represented in these codes generally function more as guidelines than as rules or standards.

• Professional codes across different social science disciplines broadly reflect a common set of values, including carefulness, competence, fairness, honesty, integrity, respect for persons, and social responsibility; see, for example, *Fostering Integrity in Research* (National Academies of Sciences, Engineering, and Medicine, 2017b) and *Responsible Conduct of Research* (Shamoo & Resnik, 2015).

Although these considerations are important to any understanding of research ethics, we choose not to retrace this rather familiar territory. Instead, we argue for an expansion of research ethics to take up additional matters that are central to how researchers reason and make choices when faced with ethically contentious circumstances. First, we emphasize that (1) the growing bureaucratization of research ethics leads to researchers

TABLE 1.1. Examples of Ethical Principles in Codes for Professional Conduct	
Professional association	**Principles**
American Sociological Association (ASA, 2019) *Code of Ethics*	Professional competence; integrity; professional and scientific responsibility; respect for people's rights, dignity, and diversity; social responsibility; and human rights
American Evaluation Association (AEA, 2018) *Guiding Principles for Evaluators*	Systematic inquiry; competence; integrity; respect for people; common good and equity
American Educational Research Association (AERA, 2011) *Code of Ethics*	Professional competence; integrity; professional, scientific, and scholarly responsibility; respect for people's rights, dignity, and diversity; social responsibility
United Nations Evaluation Group (2016) *Norms and Standards for Evaluation*	Evaluation must be conducted with the highest standards of integrity and respect for the beliefs, manners, and customs of the social and cultural environment; for human rights and gender equality; and for the "do no harm" principle for humanitarian assistance.
	Evaluators must respect the rights of institutions and individuals to provide information in confidence, United Nations Evaluation Group must ensure that sensitive data is protected and that it cannot be traced to its source and must validate statements made in the report with those who provided the relevant information. Evaluators should obtain informed consent for the use of private information from those who provide it. When evidence of wrongdoing is uncovered, it must be reported discreetly to a competent body (such as the relevant office of audit or investigation).

confusing compliance with ethical responsibility; (2) a focus on ethics in terms of the Responsible Conduct of Research, while necessary, is insufficient; (3) while values such as honesty, respect for persons, and transparency might be regarded as universal, how those values are interpreted and expressed varies in view of historical, social, cultural, organizational, and technological circumstances; and (4) ethical codes and lists of ethical principles are important resources, though researchers should pay more attention to how those principles are used in ethical reasoning. Second, we return to the example displayed in Box 1.1 as part of a discussion on expanding the idea of researchers' social responsibility.

CHALLENGING THE BUREAUCRATIZATION OF RESEARCH ETHICS

For the past decade or two, the effectiveness of IRBs and whether they overreach in their efforts to regulate research through the protection of human subjects have been matters of considerable debate. Discussion has been extensive, with opinions expressed in the communiques of professional societies (e.g., American Anthropological Association Statement on Ethnography and Institutional Review Boards, 2014) and scholarly organizations (e.g., American Association of University Professors, n.d.), as well as in opinions and viewpoints aired in the academic media (e.g., Aufderheide, 2016).

Overreach is also known as "ethics creep"—the expansion and intensification of ethical regulations to govern social science (Haggerty, 2004). While acknowledging the heavy workload of IRB members, some scholars claim that IRBs are often overwhelmed by a focus on documentation and procedure at the expense of thoughtful consideration of serious ethical issues (Gunsalus et al., 2006). This development has led other scholars to argue that the relevant ethical concerns shared particularly by field researchers are going unattended (Bosk, 2007). Researchers in social science fields, including anthropology, sociology, and organizational and educational research, have also criticized the appropriateness of relying on a biomedical model of research to inform approaches to obtaining informed consent, identifying and managing risks, and determining the benefits of research. They maintain that IRB members often render judgments about ethical protections in study designs without an adequate understanding of research approaches other than laboratory experimentation or clinical trials (e.g., focus groups, in-depth interviewing, oral history, ethnography, field observation, and participatory research; see Boser, 2007).

The growing bureaucratization of research ethics or what some researchers refer to as regulatory or institutionalized research ethics (Bozeman, Slade, & Hirsch, 2009; Dyck & Allen, 2012; Haggerty, 2004; Heimer & Petty, 2010; Martyn, 2003) can lead researchers to believe that ethical responsibility is largely a matter of compliance with rules and regulations promulgated by an IRB or independent ethics committees. To be sure, the composition, responsibilities, procedures, and effectiveness of IRBs are important issues in any discussion of the scope and conduct of ethical research. However, compliance with policies, laws, and regulations does not exhaust ethical responsibility. Compliance is reactive; exercising ethical responsibility is proactive. Compliance is a requirement; ethical responsibility is something one chooses to accept and enact. In this regard, a distinction raised by Brall, Maeckelberghe, Porz, Makhoul, and Schröder-Bäck (2017) is instructive. They identified "research ethics 1.0" as a framework focused primarily on the issue of informed consent and the relationship between researcher and research subject. They contrasted that with a framework of "research ethics 2.0" that places social scientific integrity in a broader "network of responsibilities"—different relations of moral responsibilities that researchers have with other stakeholders and actors. Research ethics 2.0 broadens the scope of ethical responsibility to include multiple ethical values as well as multiple actors.

The field of health policy and systems research offers insights into the importance of this research ethics 2.0 framework. The World Health Organization (2019) explains that it is difficult to interpret and apply principles of ethical conduct related to the research ethics 1.0 framework—that is, justice, informed consent, beneficence—given the following unique characteristics of health policy and systems research:

- It combines research, practice, and policy and thus involves collaboration with multiple policymakers and decision makers. Furthermore, given that the research is embedded in real-world contexts, it is not a simple matter to separate what should be governed by the ethics of health systems practice and policymaking and what should be governed by the ethics of research.

- Multiple stakeholders are involved when examining service delivery, complicating decisions about who is to be identified as the participants in the research and from whom informed consent should be attained—from patients? health providers? (Are hospitals, for example, nonhuman participants?)

- Given that beneficiaries of health policy and systems research (HPSR) are often communities, health care institutions, and hospitals, both group and institutional (and not simply individual) interests and perspectives are involved. How is permission acquired from such groups or institutions; who speaks on their behalf?

- Given that the goal of HPSR is to strengthen health systems, researchers may be obliged to ensure that health service interventions shown to be effective are adequately rolled out and are sustainable.

Research ethics 2.0 also challenges the conventional placement of the behavior of individual researchers at center stage when discussing matters of ethical conduct in scientific research. Researchers are part of a much larger ecosystem of ethical concerns—an integrated adaptive system of multiple agents and stakeholders (individuals and organizations) and their interactions that influences the creation, promotion (directly and indirectly), maintenance, revision, and, in some circumstances, enforcement of standards, norms, and practices of good scientific conduct. The system is depicted in Figure 1.1 (National Academies of Sciences, Engineering, and Medicine, 2017b). Education and training, systems of incentives and rewards, material and reputational interests of scientists, accountability pressures from

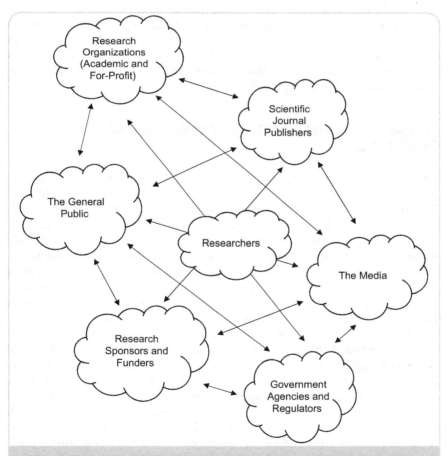

FIGURE 1.1. The research enterprise as adaptive system. Based on National Academies of Sciences, Engineering, and Medicine (2017b). Republished with permission of National Academies Press.

regulators, desires to protect scientific inquiry from political manipulation, as well as many other influences all affect researcher behavior in this inter-active environment. This system is dynamic and changing as new tech-nologies, research practices, sources of funding, sites of knowledge genera-tion, means of knowledge sharing, forms of research collaboration, and pathways of research to innovation are explored—each with implications for the ethically responsible conduct of research. Moreover, focusing on individual conduct in the context of a larger system of relationships helps shift the understanding of misconduct "from a focus on deviance stemming from a bad actor's rational set of choices to a more nuanced understand-ing of the multifactorial influences on human decision making" (National Academies of Sciences, Engineering, and Medicine, 2017b, p. 96).

While ethics is most certainly about the behavior of the individual researcher and her or his interactions and relationships with other human beings during a study, it is more than that. Criticisms of the work of IRBs and the notion of "research ethics 2.0" remind us that ethics is also about organizational behavior and that it extends to moral matters outside the scope of any given research study.

EXPANDING THE IDEA OF THE RESPONSIBLE CONDUCT OF RESEARCH

The responsible conduct of research is understood with reference to its antithesis, namely, "research misconduct," which the U.S. Office of Research Integrity (*https://ori.hhs.gov/definition-misconduct*) defines as "fabrication, falsification, or plagiarism in proposing, performing, or reviewing research, or in reporting research results." *Fabrication* is making up data or results and recording or reporting them. *Falsification* is manipu-lating research materials, equipment, or processes, or changing or omitting data or results in such a way that the research record does not accurately represent the research. *Plagiarism* is the appropriation of another person's ideas, processes, results, or words without giving appropriate credit.

The National Academies of Sciences, Engineering, and Medicine (2017b) expanded the idea of research misconduct to address additional threats to responsible scientific conduct. The Academies argued that many questionable practices, as well as damaging behaviors by researchers, research institutions, research sponsors, and journals, should be considered "detrimental research practices" that may cause damage to the research enterprise beyond that caused by research misconduct. The report of the Academies offered the following examples of detrimental research prac-tices: (1) detrimental authorship practices that may not be considered mis-conduct, such as honorary authorship, demanding authorship in return for access to previously collected data or materials, or denying authorship to those who deserve to be designated as authors; (2) not retaining or making data, code, or other information/materials underlying research results available as specified in institutional or sponsor policies, or standard practices in the field; (3) neglectful or exploitative supervision in research; (4) misleading statistical analysis that falls short of falsification; (5) inadequate institutional policies, procedures, or capacity to foster research integrity and address research misconduct allegations, and deficient implementation of policies and procedures; and (6) abusive or irresponsible publication practices by journal editors and peer reviewers (p. 74).

Despite this expanded view of what responsible researcher conduct as well as misconduct entails, philosopher of science Heather Douglas (2014a, p. 961) argues that framing research ethics in terms of the responsible conduct of research "clearly does not suffice as an account for the moral terrain of science." Fellow philosopher and professor of the history and sociology of science Robert Pennock (2015) claims that the responsible conduct of research is often perceived in terms of a quasi-legalistic, compliance-oriented, external control approach that focuses on eliminating research misconduct through policies of zero tolerance, whistleblower protections, oversight mechanisms, and education and training focused on establishing and maintaining rules for proper research conduct. Ethicist Stanley Joel Reiser (1993) adds that an ethos of concern for scientific misconduct has tended to dominate thinking about research ethics and that

> this focus is damaging because it turns the attention to seeking and finding wrong-doers and determining punishment rather than discussing generic issues of doing the right thing, preventing harms, seeking benefits, and understanding the right-making and wrong-making characteristics of actions. The focus on scientific misconduct makes ethical issues appear synonymous with legal issues and the search for ethical understanding synonymous with carrying out an investigation. (p. S84)

It is not difficult to see how university administrators and faculty can readily incorporate the definitions of research misconduct and detrimental research practices into a legalistic framing not only of individual ethical conduct but also of an ethical culture within a research institution or organization as well.

One alternative to a quasi-legalistic framing of research ethics is offered by Kenneth Pimple (2002), former director of the teaching research ethics programs at the Poynter Center for Ethics and American Institutions at Indiana University. He explained that there are three key questions to be asked and answered in addressing ethical issues in research: (1) Is it good science?; (2) Is it fair?; and (3) Is it wise? Good science is the domain of *scientific research integrity* and encompasses concerns about honesty, objectivity, respect for empirical evidence, and so forth. The three domains of fairness include *protection of human subjects,* along with *institutional integrity* and *collegiality.* The fifth domain is that of *socially responsible research.* Figure 1.2 displays these domains and key considerations. Thus, there is more to the responsible conduct of research than either the concept of research misconduct or human subjects' protection. As Pennock (2015) has argued, while scientists are researchers, they also are colleagues and mentors. They interact with other actors in other professions and other walks of life. They are citizens and human beings.

Conducting research responsibly is a multifaceted task extending beyond the protection of participants in a research study to include interactions with one's colleagues and the organizations in which one works. Doing good science also means attending to ethical values beyond those recognized as internal to the practice (e.g., objectivity, honesty). Once we broach the idea of socially responsible research, we inevitably must address ethical matters of justice, fairness, and the value of research to communities and society in general.

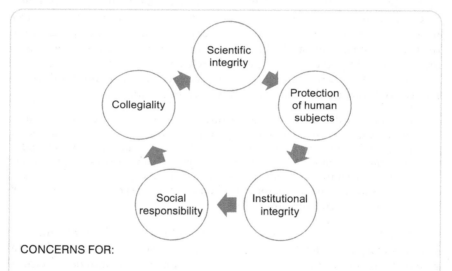

CONCERNS FOR:

- *Scientific integrity:* Technical competence, Data manipulation, Data falsification, Fabrication of data
- *Protection of human subjects:* Informed consent, Anonymity and confidentiality, Deceit, Debriefing, Research risks and benefits
- *Institutional integrity:* Conflict of interest, Regulatory compliance, Data retention and storage
- *Social responsibility:* Research priorities, Fiscal responsibility, Public service, Research advocacy
- *Collegiality:* Authorship, Plagiarism, Peer review, Mentorship

Note: Pimple includes a sixth domain of fairness, animal welfare, that has been omitted here.

FIGURE 1.2. Domains of research ethics. Based on Pimple (2002).

RECOGNIZING THE CONTEXTUAL DYNAMICS OF ETHICAL CONSIDERATIONS

A quasi-legalistic, compliance perspective on ethical conduct of research obscures the fact that values and valuing associated with professional responsibility are subject to change. "Doing" professional ethics is like witnessing moral values in action. That action requires both reflection and deliberation, and it unfolds in view of multiple considerations and trade-offs. For example, in the controversy over whether political scientists should involve communities in their research, one political scientist observes: "In practice, scholars are increasingly attempting to achieve both academic and policy relevance with their research, but, due to the large time investment of having a foot in both worlds, it is difficult to meet academic standards of promotion and tenure through research that attempts to cover both well" (Michelitch, 2018). Responsible ethical behavior is not a straightforward matter of literally implementing or applying a set of guiding principles or standards.

Values expressed as abstract concepts (consent, respect for persons, confidentiality, justice, etc.) informing responsible ethical behavior acquire concrete content in historical and cross-cultural perspectives. At the present time, awareness of the historical context of ethical principles and norms is perhaps no more acute than in concerns about social media-based and Internet-based research that includes the Internet and social media both as a venue for research (such as studying online behavior) and as a tool of research (i.e., a means of collecting data) (Harriman & Patel, 2014). Several applied researchers and ethicists (e.g., Burbules, 2009; Sugiura, Wiles, & Pope, 2017) argue that long-standing conceptions of the meaning of public versus private, freely given informed consent, and autonomy are inadequate as guides in this kind of research and that new ethical guidance is required. Nick Burbules (2009), a philosopher of education with special interest in research ethics, calls for a new understanding of research ethics in "networked environments" that requires attending to several conditions of this as a unique ethical sphere including its ubiquity, complexity and indeterminacy, uncertainty, and global character. These concerns became particularly critical in view of many types of research studies using Twitter datasets, Facebook data, and Google trend data during the COVID-19 crisis. The United Nations Children's Fund (UNICEF) (Berman, Powell, & Garcia Herranz, 2018), while pointing to the possible benefits of generating evidence via social media platforms to engage children and their communities (e.g., providing a voice for those least heard, providing real-time information), also discusses the considerable risks involved in such research and offers specific guidance for identifying those risks. Box 1.2 displays one perspective on ethical issues that arise in using social media in research.

Among many social researchers there is a more long-standing awareness of how cultural and cross-cultural understandings influence the ways

BOX 1.2. ETHICAL ISSUES TO BE CONSIDERED IN USING SOCIAL MEDIA FOR EVIDENCE GENERATION

Managing a Web Page; Using an App for Communication and Data Collection

1. Have you secured consent to the greatest extent possible, regarding:
   - The purpose of engagement?
   - Subsequent use of any data?
   - Who will have access to data, and in what form?
   - Any potential risks or privacy issues?
   - A landing page that participants must access in order to participate or register to sign up?

2. Will you be able to reach relevant populations, including the most disadvantaged or marginalized groups/individuals among them, considering:
   - The Internet coverage in your country?
   - The level of access to particular social media channels?
   - The cost of technologies?

   (If not, what are the implications for findings, and how will you ensure that findings clearly note this limitation? How will you address the lack of information from this/these cohort/s?)

3. Have you ensured as much as possible that information provided by participants is not personally identifiable information (PII)? If some form of PII is necessary, how will you safeguard this data and ensure its confidentiality? How is this built into the platform?

4. Have you provided cyber-safety advice about privacy and security settings to participants?

5. Do you have a process and the personnel to carefully curate content in forums or on webpages and to vet any offensive or harmful content?

6. Have you created opt-out provisions for participants to remove themselves and their information from your lists or forums to the greatest extent possible?

7. Have you made it clear, even if you remove individuals' content from social media platforms, that you cannot guarantee that this data will be removed from all databases and sites due to any unknown channels where information/data may be shared?

8. If you are working in a context where the government has had a history of imposing restrictions on and blocking messaging app usage, have you considered alternate arrangements/social media services or channels for information if the service used is regularly blocked, restricted, or monitored?

9. Have you considered means to verify findings from data collected?

10. Have you established clear channels to respond to participants' possible requests for help, support, or advice?

Note. Adapted from Berman, Powell, and Garcia Herranz (2018).

researchers and evaluators and the people whom they study understand and interpret values and how those understandings influence norms for ethical conduct. Scholars that are particularly attentive to underserved communities and indigenous and cross-cultural perspectives (e.g., Bledsoe & Hopson, 2009; Drugge, 2016; Smith, 2012) criticize the Eurocentric bias of the very idea of research itself as well as current institutional ethical practices that impinge on the legitimacy and use of indigenous knowledge. A particularly strong argument claims that much Western research practice has been situated within systems and ideologies that fundamentally destroy and dehumanize particular groups of people (Haslam & Loughnan, 2014; Smith, 2012). Another critical issue is how ethical processes and responsibilities ensure protection for the heritage and benefits that accrue to Indigenous peoples for their knowledge and not only to the researchers and their institutions (Battiste, 2008). Cultural geographer Nina Morris (2015) points to the danger of silencing indigenous ethics: For example, the conventional principle of informed consent assumes that research participants are autonomous individuals accustomed to notions of contractual relations with other human beings. Yet, in some non-Western societies and cultures, this principle can be perceived as an assault on the values of individuals who believe in the matrix of relationships and strong family, group, and community decision making. Box 1.3 displays a set of ethical principles that should guide research with Indigenous peoples.

Morris (2015) also advises that heightened attention to ethical principles for researchers and evaluators working with collaborators in international development contexts is important because it "reminds those working in privileged positions and in wealthier countries of the need to reflect not only on their own framework of thinking, but also on the implications of the very different mindsets and environments in which their research projects will be carried out," and "it can also draw attention to the risk of exploitation that might result from inequalities (e.g. financial, access to resources) between the project collaborators" (p. 212). The invisibility of local collaborators in much research originating in the Global North has come to the fore with new awareness in view of the COVID-19 crisis. A group of researchers with extensive experience in international development research (Dunia et al., 2020) point to the ethical consequences of the erasure from published texts of facilitating researchers in the Global South (those local researchers or so-called research assistants) who are engaged by contracting researchers from funding agencies in the Global North. They argue that this is an issue for funding agencies, research institutions, ethics review boards, and academic publishers. This echoes the view of Linda Tuhiwai Smith (2012, p. 10), who questions the extraction of knowledge from the Global South by researchers from the Global North without ever delivering it in ways understandable or valuable to those from who it was extracted. She advises researchers to ask: "Whose research is it? Who

BOX 1.3. EXAMPLE OF SPECIFIC ETHICAL PRINCIPLES FOR RESEARCH WITH INDIGENOUS PEOPLES

- **Principle 1.** Recognition of the diversity and uniqueness of peoples, as well as of individuals, is essential.

- **Principle 2.** The rights of Indigenous peoples to self-determination must be recognized.

- **Principle 3.** The rights of Indigenous peoples to their intangible heritage must be recognized.

- **Principle 4.** Rights in the traditional knowledge and traditional cultural expressions of Indigenous peoples must be respected, protected, and maintained.

- **Principle 5.** Indigenous knowledge, practices, and innovations must be respected, protected, and maintained.

- **Principle 6.** Consultation, negotiation, and free, prior, and informed consent are the foundations for research with or about Indigenous peoples.

- **Principle 7.** Responsibility for consultation and negotiation is ongoing.

- **Principle 8.** Consultation and negotiation should achieve mutual understanding about the proposed research.

- **Principle 9.** Negotiation should result in a formal agreement for the conduct of a research project.

- **Principle 10.** Indigenous people have the right to full participation appropriate to their skills and experiences in research projects and processes.

- **Principle 11.** Indigenous people who are involved in research, or who may be affected by research, should benefit from, and not be disadvantaged by, the research project.

- **Principle 12.** Research outcomes should include specific results that respond to the needs and interests of Indigenous people.

- **Principle 13.** Plans should be agreed on for managing the use of, and access to, research results.

- **Principle 14.** Research projects should include appropriate mechanisms and procedures for reporting on ethical aspects of the research and complying with these guidelines.

Note. From Australian Institute for Aboriginal and Torres Strait Islander Studies (2012).

owns it? Whose interests does it serve? Who will benefit from it? Who has designed its questions and framed its scope? Who will carry it out? Who will write it up? How will its results be disseminated?" Table 1.2 is an example of specific legal and ethical guidance for researchers working in cross-cultural settings.

Lastly, "doing" research ethics often means situating research practice in comprehensive, extensive, formally adopted cultural ethical frameworks. For example, the 1975 Treaty of Waitangi and its 1985 amendment in New Zealand (Hudson & Russell, 2009) situate both researchers' purposes and their behavior in the context of Indigenous peoples' rights. Evaluation scholars and practitioners have explored the extent to which their professional work aligns with the Calls to Action of the Truth and Reconciliation Commission of Canada (Bremmer, 2018).

Consideration of the contextual dynamics of ethics heightens social researchers' understanding of their social responsibility. Research using social media and digital data, for example, raises new challenges around consent, traceability, authenticity, dealing with illicit activity, and anonymity. Awareness of issues in cross-cultural, international, and indigenous research point to the risk and costs of unethical behavior not simply as it impacts the individual researcher and the people he or she studies, but as it reflects on the very enterprise of social research.

FOCUSING ANEW ON ETHICAL REASONING

Learning ethical principles, while an important aspect of social scientists' education, is not the same as learning ethical reasoning, that is, how to reach reasonable, warranted judgments about right and wrong human conduct. Generally, we do not lack awareness of core ethical principles, as is evident from the proliferation of codes of ethics for researchers noted earlier. Petteri Niemi (2016, p. 1018), writing in the journal *Science and Engineering Ethics,* argues that the very proliferation of moral intuitions, values, codes, and theories presents a challenge to ethical conduct: "How can we ever obtain clear and unanimous answers from such chaotic-looking diversity?" Pluralism in ethical theories, however, is the rule rather than the exception, and no single ethical code or collection of principles can cover all cases. The central problem is not pluralism per se but, rather, turning ethics into a matter of conformity to a routine, for example, of completing an IRB application.

Researchers can counteract the tendency to reduce ethical behavior to a customary behavior by attending to the development and cultivation of the moral imagination and by learning how to apply ethical principles and theories in situations where one faces an ethical dilemma (Sternberg, 2012). Ethical dilemmas are situations in which the decision maker must

TABLE 1.2. Collaborative, Cross-Cultural Social Research: Important Ethical Considerations and Practical Guidance

Legal and ethical guidance

- Do individual researchers or the research project require official approval before the work commences?
- Does the researcher hold a position of power or authority over research subjects?
- Does the institution with which you are affiliated hold a position of power or authority over research subjects?
- Are research participants truly free to grant consent related to the research (e.g., for an interview or granting access to property)?
- Do any of the sponsors claim proprietary rights to intellectual property or to data collected through the research?
- What steps are required to gain permissions for access to field site(s)?
- What are the rules that govern the field site(s)?
- Will research objectivity or independence be compromised in return for financial or nonfinancial benefits to the researcher, a relative, or a friend?

Guidance for the rights of human subjects

- Is the research subject capable of understanding what is involved in the study?
- Is sufficient detail about the study provided and in an appropriate format?
- Will research subjects understand (1) the risks involved, (2) that they can withdraw from the study, (3) whom to contact in the event that they are unhappy with the conduct of the study or the researchers?
- Will promises to not use names be sufficient to protect confidentiality?
- Will other people beyond the researcher have access to the data?
- Will feedback, and the opportunity to edit responses, be given to respondents?
- Will steps be taken to ensure that individuals are not spatially identifiable?
- Is the research part of an international collaboration that will involve the transfer of personal data overseas? If so, does the receiving country have adequate data protection regulations, or has appropriate contact been made with the recipient of the data which specifies the data protection requirements that must be upheld?
- Will the explicit consent of the participants to be quoted verbatim be obtained during data collection, and will they be made aware that their email address may be identifiable?
- Will participants be advised that research data given in confidence does not enjoy legal privilege and may be liable to subpoena by a court?
- Does the funding body require the archiving of data? Will the participants be informed of this when giving consent?

Guidance regarding harm, discomfort, or stress for research participants

- Will the research address sensitive issues? If so, what steps will be taken to ameliorate distress?
- Will the researchers approach research subjects with sensitivity to cultural differences?
- Will the researchers approach the community or area in which research is undertaken with sensitivity to cultural differences? What steps will be taken to minimize the effects of disruption?
- Will the research involve foreseeable physical discomfort or harm? What steps will be taken to minimize or ameliorate these effects?
- Will distressful questions be asked that are only incidental to the research?
- Will the true purpose of the research be concealed from the participants? If yes, what information will be concealed and why?
- What remedies will be available to those who feel harmed or impacted upon by the research?

Note. Adapted from the Ecosystem Services for Poverty Alleviation (ESPA) Program, *ESPA ethics principles and procedure*; available at *www.espa.ac.uk/files/espa/Ethics%20Guidelines.pdf.*

make a choice between two desirable principles or values, neither of which is unambiguously preferable, each suggesting a different course of action. The principles or values present themselves in a mutually exclusive way, such that following one would result in violating the other. If a choice is not required—that is, the situation merely makes one feel uncomfortable—then it is not an ethical dilemma. For example, each of the following questions poses an ethical dilemma: "Does the principle of beneficence take precedence over the principle of autonomy of the research participant in certain circumstances?"; "When is being honest unkind?"; "Is something less than fully informed consent or even deception justified in the pursuit of scientific knowledge?" Moral imagination can be cultivated through the study of cases as well as through exercises where researchers (both practicing and in training) identify ethical principles central to their work and describe in detail how and when they will be applied (Niemi, 2016). That process of application, so to speak, is the subject of perspectives on ethical reasoning. A summary of what ethical reasoning involves and how it can be done is provided in Box 1.4.

Focusing anew on ethical reasoning means going beyond knowledge of ethical principles to developing researchers and future researchers' capacities to engage with ethical dilemmas and build ethically defensible arguments. Such a process is not one and done. There is an open texture to ethical life; that is, ethics is a continual dialogical process between researchers and the world and the people in that world that they study. In that life, we could always act differently and perhaps in some circumstances unethically (Sayer, 2011).

EXPANDING THE UNDERSTANDING OF RESEARCHERS' SOCIAL RESPONSIBILITY

Stephanie Bird (2014), ethics consultant and coeditor of the journal *Science and Engineering Ethics*, argues that a focus on the ethical behavior of individual researchers must be complemented by a broader focus on social responsibility. In her view, the focus on ethical behavior is largely a "micro-ethical" issue "addressed within the everyday context of research through education, explicit policies developed by laboratory and department heads, university administrators, disciplinary societies, and in the relationships between individuals" (p. 1). With regard to the focus on social responsibility, Bird writes:

> The social responsibilities of researchers arise not simply because research is funded (directly or indirectly) by the public. Research is carried out in the

(continued on page 24)

BOX 1.4. NOTES ON ETHICAL REASONING

Literature on moral psychology explains that ethical reasoning unfolds on two different levels (Kimmel, 2015). Intuitionism claims that ethical reasoning or moral judgment is an intuitive, automatic process linked to personal knowledge and experience. This view received considerable popular attention through the publication of Jonathan Haidt's (2012) *The Righteous Mind*, where he argued that people are fundamentally intuitive, and that reason works less like an impartial judge weighing evidence for and against a given view or action and more like a defender justifying to others the view one already holds. In contrast, rationalism promotes a critical-evaluative perspective wherein judgments should be forthcoming from a careful, strategic reasoning process taking account of ethical principles and moral theories and considering which specific behaviors should be judged good or bad according to which ethical principles. For example, consider a situation where a community researcher received informed consent from a household in which a language other than English was spoken and the adults of the household had limited English-language skills and then later learned that the family did not really understand what the researcher was talking about. A critical appraisal would involve examining what values, principles, moral rules, and so forth are involved in this situation, what conflicts exist between them, and how best to weigh them. It would require examining different grounds for moral arguments such as consequentialism—whether an action is good or bad is determined by the outcome of the action and whether it has positive or negative consequences—or principlism—whether an action is good or bad is determined not by the outcome of action but by the action itself, that is, whether it conforms to or upholds a principle; for example, it is wrong to disregard the views of X because it violates the golden rule.

Defenders of the rationalist, critical-evaluative approach argue that it can illuminate ordinary, intuitive moral judgments and improve them (e.g., Kitchener, 1984), as shown in Figure 1.3. Strong intuitionists, on the other hand, like Haidt (2012) are deeply skeptical of reason as a guide to moral judgment. He argues that "intuitions come first, strategic reasoning second" and that "moral thinking is more like a politician searching for votes than a scientist searching for truth" (p. 106). In other words, in his view, we most often employ strategic reasoning to justify positions we already hold rather than subject them to critical scrutiny. Strong rationalists, on the other hand, argue that an intuitionist approach is insufficient because it is based on factors subject to emotional influences and cognitive distortions (Rogerson, Gottlieb, Handelsman, Knapp, & Younggren, 2011).

A middle ground approach on this matter is prudent. On the one hand, as psychologist Karen Kitchener (1984, p. 44) argued, "immediate moral feelings are critical to everyday ethical decisions . . . [and] we ought not feel apologetic about having a firm set of ethical beliefs which allow us to take immediate action." On the other hand, Kitchener points out, one cannot deny that ethical intuition is not always enough—not only is it the case that "not all individuals have moral intuitions that lead them to defensible ethical choices, but some cases may be so unusual "that we have no ordinary sense of which direction to take" (1984, p. 44) Thus, it seems wise to submit the everyday intuitive judgments we make to scrutiny

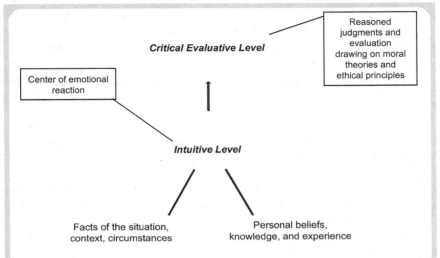

FIGURE 1.3. A stage model of ethical reasoning. Based on Kitchener and Kitchener (2012). Adapted with permission from Sage Publications.

from time to time and to cultivate the capacity to engage in more systematic ethical reasoning.

There are multiple points of view on how to engage in ethical reasoning. Psychologist James Rest's (1986, cited in Johnson, 2018) widely known framework of the four requirements for moral action includes:

- Moral sensitivity (recognition)—Consideration of how one's behavior affects others, identification of possible courses of action, and determining the consequences of each potential strategy. Empathy and perspective skills are essential to this component of moral action.
- Moral judgment—Decisions about what it is right (or wrong) to do in the situation at hand.
- Moral focus (motivation)—Willingness to follow through on one's chosen course of action, even while acknowledging a conflict of values.
- Moral character—The courage to act, prudence, and integrity.

Psychologist Robert Sternberg (2012) lists eight steps, each requiring specific skills and abilities:

1. Recognize that there is an event to which to react.
2. Define the event as having an ethical dimension.
3. Decide that the ethical dimension is significant.
4. Take personal responsibility for generating an ethical solution to the problem.

(continued)

5. Figure out what abstract ethical rule(s) might apply to the problem (including any codes of ethics relevant to the situation).

6. Decide how these abstract ethical rules actually apply to the problem so as to suggest a concrete solution.

7. Prepare to counteract contextual forces that might lead one not to act in an ethical manner.

8. Act.

The logic of ethical reasoning as seen from the perspective of critical thinking (Paul & Elder, 2013) involves asking the following questions:

- Considering my own rights, needs, and obligations as well as those of others in this situation, my *purpose* should be . . . (To act so as to help rather than harm.)

- The key ethical *questions(s)* I am trying to answer is/are . . . (How should I act so as to help rather than harm?)

- The most important *information* I will need to answer this ethical question is . . . (What are the options for action, especially information that helps avoid harming others?)

- The key ethical *concepts and principles* that should guide my thinking are . . .

- The main *assumptions* I am using in reasoning through this ethical issue are . . .

- The *points of view* I need to consider before coming to conclusions about this ethical issue are . . .

- The main *inferences/conclusions* I am coming to in reasoning through this ethical issue are . . .

- If I come to the conclusions stated in number seven above, some of the important *implications/consequences* for myself and others are . . .

A significant alternative to these kinds of step-by-step procedures for ethical reasoning is a method called reflective equilibrium, which involves drawing on common-sense moral judgments (deMaagt, 2017; Rawls, 1999; Shouten & Brighouse, 2015; Thacher, 2006). Those judgments, in turn, are generated by examining a case or ethical dilemma and reflecting on general principles (e.g., being fair, being honest), moral theories (e.g., we should do X because it is our professional responsibility), and basic intuitions. One reflects on all three levels in order to develop a coherent view. Where levels of moral thinking conflict, an adjustment is made. Coherence is achieved when the moral judgment in question—that is, "what is the right thing to do in this situation?"—aligns with our beliefs about similar cases and our beliefs about a broader range of moral and factual issues. The method "rests on the idea that we try to criticize, clarify, and improve our existing views about normative ideals by reflecting on the implications they have for other convictions" (Thacher, 2006, p. 1647). Figure 1.4 offers a visual representation of this process of moral reasoning. What is distinctive about this approach to ethical reasoning is

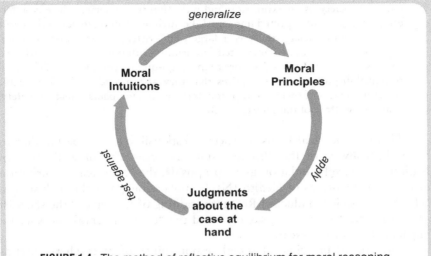

FIGURE 1.4. The method of reflective equilibrium for moral reasoning.

that justifying a moral decision does not rely on some ultimate moral foundation or superior set of principles. Rather, as Rawls (1999, p. 507) has argued, the justification for one's decision "is a matter of the mutual support of many considerations, of everything fitting together into one coherent view."

These schemes for ethical reasoning draw attention to the fact that while learning about research ethics requires instruction and guidance on ethical principles, that type of instruction is insufficient. Based on their empirical study of how to integrate ethics into engineering classes, Davis and Feinerman (2010) identified four goals for education in the responsible conduct of research: ethical sensitivity (being able to recognize ethical issues), ethical knowledge, ethical judgment, and ethical commitment. Learning research ethics also requires understanding how to take the right action, and that decision ought to reflect sound ethical reasoning. That reasoning itself can be put to the test, so to speak. The ethical action one decides to take can be evaluated using the heuristics known as tests of ethicality. They include the following:

- Golden Rule Test—Would I want someone to do this to me? (This test can also be used as a Reversibility Test—If I switched places with the person(s) involved, would I still find the action respectful and just?)
- Universality Test—Would I recommend this action to anyone in the same situation?
- Justice Test—Is the action fair to everyone involved?
- Diversity Test—Is the action fair to the specific person(s) involved in view of considerations of their gender, age, race, cultural orientation, etc.)?
- Reputational/Front Page/Publicity Test—How would I feel if my action was reported on the front page of my local newspaper?

name of society as an expression and reflection of the society's needs, interests, priorities and expected impacts. Like anyone claiming to act in the name or interests of society, there is a largely unwritten, unexpressed contract. While researchers are compensated financially, with intellectual rewards and social status, society expects more than a high-quality product. . . . The social responsibility of scientists requires that they also attend to the foreseeable societal impacts of their work, particularly as these impacts affect the safety, health or welfare of the society. (p. 3)

This macroethical focus on special responsibility may be familiar to researchers aware of the "broader impacts" criterion for evaluation of National Science Foundation grant proposals, the "significance" criterion in National Institutes of Health (NIH) applications, and the inclusion in NIH Responsible Conduct of Research training of the topics "the scientist as a responsible member of society" and the "environmental and societal impacts of scientific research."

The ethical principle of social responsibility of researchers extends further than this concern with the societal impacts of research. Evaluation theorist Ernest House (2020, pp. 32–33) has argued that evaluators examining public programs and policies ought to have an even greater social responsibility, namely, to protect the interests of those less advantaged in society, who often are the beneficiaries of social programs. House claims that evaluators ought to act as moral fiduciaries, giving priority to the perspectives and views of those who most need help. We believe ethics is central to social scientific knowledge production and researcher/evaluator action in at least three fundamental ways: First, as British philosopher Miranda Fricker (2007) explained, epistemic injustice—unfairness related to generating knowledge—arises when the views and perspectives of individuals are ignored or not believed because of prejudice against certain speakers because of their very identity. For example, a woman's statements will not likely be believed because of a prejudice on the part of the hearer regarding her gender. Fricker links ethics directly to knowledge production, arguing that this is an example of being wronged specifically in one's capacity as a knower. Researchers are socially responsible to avoid committing epistemic injustice in the manner in which data are gathered and evidence is analyzed.

Second, as the ethical framework summarized in Box 1.1 reveals, ethical considerations lie at the very heart of decisions about policy choices in the fields of health care, education, and the environment. As political scientist Douglas Amy (1984, p. 573) noted years ago, research and policy analysis that avoids examining the inevitable clashes between competing social values such as equality, efficiency, and justice "runs the risk of being largely irrelevant to contemporary policy choices." Researchers confront ethical dilemmas in these fields because resources are inadequate to meet all reasonable demands and because stakeholders are committed to different values about what it is right to do. Thus, socially responsible research in applied fields is not only a matter of technical competence or skill in developing an evidence base or conducting cost–benefit analysis. Amy observes that "normative assumptions are surreptitiously and arbitrarily introduced into studies (imbedded in the definition of the problem being studied, in the models used in the analysis, in the choice of alternatives to be investigated, etc.) and are [thus] beyond the range of public scrutiny" (p. 574). The ethical principle of socially responsible research requires rational ethical analysis, as, for example, displayed in the framework presented in Box 1.1.

Third, it is an ethical failure when researchers do not take responsibility for the knowledge they produce. Researchers cannot study a situation in its entirety. They must choose what is in and what is out, what is important and what is not. They frame a situation in order to understand it—a frame is a perspective that makes it possible to address a situation in a particular way. Framing involves setting boundaries and thus placing limits on our understanding. Framing is a moral-political and an epistemological choice, not a methodological one—it is about what values and facts are to be considered relevant to an investigation and what values and facts are to be regarded as irrelevant. When we are dealing with the limits of our understanding, we are dealing with ethics (Churchman, 1979; Cilliers, 2005). Thus, ethics is not something that is supplementary to our understanding of the world. Ethics is always already part of what we do. Because boundaries must be set, researchers working in applied settings (indeed, all scientists) as professionals bear responsibility for the consequences of setting boundaries in a particular way. Judgments about boundaries and critical scrutiny on how they are set is a means of engaging this ethical responsibility (Midgley, 2000).

As Werner Ulrich (2017), social scientist, practical philosopher, and originator of critical systems thinking, has explained, researchers cannot justify their claims about framing and boundary setting simply on the basis of their theoretical and methodological expertise. If that were so, we would cede authority to these professionals, for they then must surely know better than ordinary people what is best for everyone. In reaching and offering boundary judgments, researchers have no in-principle advantage over ordinary citizens. What they do have is an ethical obligation as professionals to pursue a "self-reflective, self-correcting, and self-limiting approach to inquiry . . . [one] that question[s] [an] inquiry in respect of all conceivable sources of deception" (p. 9), for example, in its presuppositions, methods and procedures, findings, and the translation of findings into claims.

SUMMARY

Professional ethics is a matter of taking practical action—deciding what is right to do in a given situation. That action is guided by a variety of ethical norms as reflected in professional guidelines, codes, and standards. Those norms reflect particular moral values that are cherished as essential to acting with integrity as a researcher. Danger lies in viewing ethics (and norms) as something that is imposed on the conduct of research rather than something that is part of the very ethos or character of research itself. Ethical norms are debatable and reflect changing historical circumstances as well as cultural beliefs and practices. Hence, acting ethically requires some measure of continual reflection and analysis rather than fairly habitual and routine compliance, as is sometimes the case with efforts to abide by IRB regulations. Instruction in research ethics must be more than a matter of learning ethical principles and codes; it must involve learning the skills and virtues of ethical reasoning. Ethical reasoning can be carried out by using an explicit and careful process of identifying the ethical issue(s) at stake and relevant ethical codes or guidance; questioning assumptions and considering various viewpoints; outlining courses of action; considering potential consequences; and ultimately choosing and justifying what one should do. Danger also lies in assuming that the ethical principle of social responsibility in research is honored by discussing the "broader impact" of one's research. While demonstrating the significance of social research is certainly an important task, the ethical principle is broader, involving issues central to the very production of social scientific knowledge.

IMPORTANT RESOURCES ▪ ▪ ▪ ▪ ▪ ▪ ▪ ▪ ▪ ▪ ▪ ▪ ▪ ▪ ▪ ▪ ▪

▪ National Academies of Sciences, Engineering, and Medicine. (2017b). *Fostering integrity in research.* Washington, DC: National Academies Press. Available as a free pdf download at *www.nap.edu/catalog/21896/fostering-integrity-in-research.*

   Discusses core ethical norms of scientific practice, identifies best practices in research, and recommends practical options for discouraging and addressing research misconduct and detrimental research practices.

▪ *International compilation of human research standards.* (2020). Compiled by the Office for Human Research Protection, U.S. Department of Health and Human Services, Washington, DC. Available at *https://www.hhs.gov/ohrp/sites/default/files/2020-international-compilation-of-human-research-standards.pdf.*

   Lists and provides hot links to over 1,000 laws, regulations, and ethical guidelines that govern the protection of human subjects across the world. The section of the document on "Social-Behavioral Research" is particularly relevant to applied social researchers.

▪ Shamoo, A. E., & Resnick, D. B. (2015). *Responsible conduct of research* (3rd ed.). Oxford, UK: Oxford University Press.

   An extensive and comprehensive guide to ethical issues in biomedical research, but its discussions of matters such as intellectual property, authorship, peer review, conflicts of interest, ethical decision making, and responsible conduct are of value to all researchers.

■ *Research Ethics*
A journal that covers issues in the ethics and regulation of research and the procedures of ethical review on an international scale.

■ Paul, R., & Elder, L. (2013). *The thinker's guide to ethical reasoning: Based on critical thinking concepts and tools* (2nd ed.). Lanham, MD: Rowman & Littlefield.
Discusses the role of/rationale for ethical reasoning as well as the logic and elements of ethical reasoning.

■ Flynn, L. R., & Goldsmith, R. E. (2013). *Case studies for ethics in academic research in the social sciences.* Thousand Oaks, CA: Sage.
Presents 16 brief research ethics cases on topics including research misconduct, peer review, mentoring, collaborative research, and authorship. Each case has clearly defined learning objectives and a list of questions to guide readers through examining the ethical dilemma(s) posed in the case.

■ In the literature there is extensive ethical advice on specific issues, types of studies, and groups of respondents or research participants. Some examples of distinctive ethical guidance include the following:

   • *Specific Issues: Principles and guidelines for ethical research and evaluation in development* (Australian Council for International Development, 2017); *Ethical considerations when using social media for evidence generation* (Berman, Powell, & Garcia Herranz, 2018); *An ethical framework for the development and review of health research proposals involving humanitarian contexts* (Curry, Waldman, & Caplan, 2014); *Wicked problems: Peacebuilding evaluation ethics, determining what is good and right* (Neufeldt, 2016); The ethical tipping points of evaluators in conflict zones, in *American Journal of Evaluation* (Duggan & Bush, 2014).

   • *Types of Studies: International ethical guidelines for epidemiological studies* (Council for International Organizations of Medical Sciences & the World Health Organization, 2009); Ethical challenges in community-based participatory research: A scoping review, in *Quality Health Research* (Wilson, Kenny, & Dickson-Swift, 2018); "The ethics and science of impact evaluation," in *Impact Evaluation in Practice* (Gertler, Martinez, Premand, Rawlings, & Vermeersch, 2016); *The ethics of social research: Surveys and experiments* (Sieber, 1982).

   • *Specific Respondents/Participants: Ethical research involving children* (Graham, Powell, Taylor, Anderson, & Fitzgerald, 2013); *Ethics guidelines for international multicenter research involving people with intellectual disabilities* (Dalton & McVilly, 2004); *Putting women first: Ethical and safety recommendations for research on domestic violence against women* (World Health Organization Department of Gender and Women's Health, 2001); *Ethical principles, dilemmas, and risks in collecting data on violence against children* (Child Protection Monitoring and Evaluation Reference Group, 2012).

BRIDGE TO PRACTICE

The case presented below is slightly modified and used with permission from S. Raghavan, "All in the Interpretation," *Online Ethics Center for Engineering* (available at *www.onlineethics.org/Resources/ Interpretation.aspx*).

Kate is an assistant professor in a psychology research lab just beginning a new line of research on the effects of certain video games on middle school children. Some of the funding for her project comes from a video game manufacturer, but the money does not give the company control over how the research is conducted. Kate believes she has been careful not to let the source of funds influence her project design and data collection.

Discussion Questions

1. Might a researcher's source of funding create a bias or the perception of bias? How might Kate (and the research community in general) deal with potential bias?

2. In what ways might industry funding influence a researcher and affect his/her research?

3. Even if Kate believes the source of funding will not influence her research, should she be concerned with how the presence of industry funding may affect her credibility with colleagues and the public?

4. What should Kate and her institution do to help preserve her scientific integrity in this case?

Kate has collected all of the data, and she has been carefully examining effects of the use of these video games. Looking back, she might have changed some of her data collection methods if she could do it over again; but she knows that is the nature of research and that lessons learned in one project generate new questions to ask in the future. She is excited to see a clear trend in her data that indicates a positive effect of educational video games on mathematics achievement, but the effect washes out after about a year or two, and she is unsure how to interpret that. She creates a rough draft of a paper that carefully outlines all of her analyses and gives it to a senior colleague, Mary, to review. Mary is director of the research lab where Kate does her work. Mary offers the view that the "Results and Conclusions" section of the paper is very weak. She says that Kate does not make a strong case for the importance of her research and that the quality of the journal in which her paper will be published depends largely on her ability to interpret the data. "I'm not saying to leave out data," Mary says, "but the story you tell about the data is at least as, if not more, important than the data themselves.

Kate knows that research papers are rarely airtight. In fact, members of her lab will often spend lab meetings dissecting a research paper in order to stimulate discussion about the author's conclusions and generate ideas for future research. She feels she must choose a black or white stance in her interpretation of the effects of gaming in order to create a strong paper. She also knows that if she emphasizes the positive effects of the games, she could easily write another grant to the video game manufacturer to study the later wash-out period with a high probability of funding.

Discussion Questions

5. What is Kate's responsibility in presenting her research findings? Is her colleague, Mary, correct in stating that her story is as important as the data themselves? Is Kate correct in assuming she must choose one side and stick to it?

6. How might the possibility of future funding influence a researcher's presentation of his/her findings? What should be done to minimize the undue influence of funding on the way a scientist interprets and presents his/her findings?

After thinking about it for a few days, Kate decides that the initial trend in her data is interesting enough that it should be emphasized in her paper. She writes another draft that emphasizes this trend and only briefly mentions the wash-out as a subject for further research. Mary is very excited to see the new draft. She says the results are very compelling and suggests they submit them to a nationally recognized journal. The paper is published, and Kate receives a great deal of recognition and congratulations from others within the university. She also receives a number of requests from news reporters to discuss her findings. The reporters seem not to notice that the numbers wash out and they do not ask about it. Kate knows that all the press attention is good for her career, but she is also not skilled at giving interviews and so she is happy to have Mary speak with many of the reporters for her. Mary is delighted to receive the publicity for her lab, and each time she is interviewed, she is careful to emphasize the value of these games for young children.

Discussion Questions

7. Knowing that most people will not look up the original article when they hear a news report, does Kate's and/or Mary's responsibility to the public change in any way when interacting with the press?

8. How might she approach the situation if Kate feels that the results are not as settled as Mary's interviews seem to imply?

Eventually, Kate's paper is challenged by a competing research group. Their results indicate a deleterious effect of the games over a longer time period. At this point, Kate is working in her own lab on another research topic. She is tired of speaking to reporters, and she is still not comfortable giving interviews. She is also a little worried that the interpretation of her research may have encouraged parents to have their children play games that may ultimately be harmful. Some reporters are even suggesting that her interpretation of the data was motivated by her industry funding, although she doesn't think that is true. She decides to adopt a policy of not communicating with any members of the press.

Discussion Questions

9. Does Kate (or do researchers in general) have a responsibility to communicate with the media?

10. If Kate feels that her research is misrepresented in the press, how might she approach the situation? Is she ultimately responsible for the information that is disseminated to the public?

11. How might the appearance of bias be controlled at this point?

12. This case was inspired by the following articles: Park, A. (2007, August 6). Baby Einsteins: Not so smart after all. *Time. http://content. time.com/time/health/article/0,8599,1650352,00.html?iid=sr-link1*; Augé, K. (2011, June 29). "Baby Einstein" DVD creators find redemption in documents suggesting negative study was flawed. *Denver Post. www.denverpost.com/2011/06/29/baby-einstein-dvd-creators-find-redemption-in-documents-suggesting-negative-study-was-flawed.*

Consider how the controversy is presented in these articles. Is it presented fairly? Why or why not? How do you think it might affect the public perception of science? What do you see as the responsibilities of the researchers and the reporters and editors in this situation? Does the above case present the same or different ethical issues?

CHAPTER 2

From Value Neutrality to Morally Informed Research

Scientific inquiry strives to advance human values,
but for a long time we have been advised to set
those values aside before we undertake it.
—THACHER (2015, p. 317)

INTRODUCTION

Many philosophers of science as well as science practitioners consider science to be valuable to society for its production of robust, empirical knowledge (Douglas, 2014a) and particularly the instrumental value of that knowledge. *Why Social Science?*, a project of the Consortium of Social Science Associations (2019, *www.whysocialscience.com*), promotes the view that "knowledge derived from social and behavioral science research has made our population healthier, our democracy fairer, our nation safer, and our economy stronger." In learning the theories and methods of social science, many of us were taught that to deliver on the promise of that kind of knowledge, science must be objective, value-free, and value-neutral. Paradoxically, although social science is considered highly valuable to society, the authority of social science is thought to rest fundamentally on its being disinterested and distanced from the sociocultural, political world it studies. Most social researchers learn to be concerned only with the facts of the matter, so to speak—that is, descriptions and explanations of phenomena—and neutral with respect to moral-political questions of the way society should be. Threats to the authority of science and the danger of losing objectivity are considered particularly formidable for scientists working in policy domains where decision makers' requests for scientific knowledge and advice are motivated by a mix of personal, social, cultural, and political values and objectives.

This chapter begins with an overview of the doctrine of value-free science. That is followed by a discussion of the multiple criticisms of this idea. A third section of the chapter addresses two roles that social scientists might adopt as alternatives to the role of the value-free scientist. In these roles, social scientists wrestle with issues of objectivity and value-neutrality in practical (and not merely philosophical) ways. The final section of the chapter presents the case for a morally informed social science, one that integrates values and science, the normative and the epistemic, in the production of social scientific knowledge.

VALUE-FREE SCIENCE

Value-free social science is a framework for scientific work based on the separation of facts and values and the principle of value neutrality. Within this framework, only empirical matters are relevant, and concerns about which goals and values to pursue in society are regarded as beyond rational assessment (Fischer, 1980), where rational assessment means based on sound arguments and empirical evidence and not on emotions. Early on in their education university-prepared researchers are introduced by their mentors to the distinction between positive and normative judgments in social science. Positive judgments are the result of the empirical study of *what is*—they are descriptive and explanatory. They are unbiased, objective, and free of the influence of political, moral, and aesthetic values. They deal only with the facts of the matter. Normative judgments, on the other hand, are about *what should be*. They are based on social, political, and moral values and involve evaluating. When this distinction is used to characterize roles adopted by scientists involved in the policy process, the social scientist committed only to positive judgments is often referred to as a dispassionate analyst (Robert & Zeckhauser, 2011), an objective technician (Jenkins-Smith, 1982), or an honest broker of policy alternatives (Pielke, 2007). The normative social scientist is a partisan (Hammersley, 2017), or issue advocate (Jenkins-Smith, 1982; Pielke, 2007), or one who engages in stealth policy advocacy interpreting and presenting scientific information with unstated preferences for a policy choice (Lackey, 2007; Pielke, 2007).

Although among philosophers of social science the doctrine of value-free science and the fact–value dichotomy on which it rests have been extensively criticized in recent decades, it continues to have alluring appeal as a regulative ideal for some (many?) practicing researchers in social science fields (e.g., Gerring & Yesnowitz, 2006; Hammersley, 2014, 2017; Mulkay, 1976). John Pearson, a former program analyst for the federal government, writing for the online news arm of the American Society for Public Administration, offers an especially succinct summary of the case for value neutrality in Box 2.1. While in actual practice scientists may breach the ideal

BOX 2.1. THE CASE FOR VALUE NEUTRALITY

There is no shortage of opinion in the United States regarding advocacy for particular values. We have think tanks, lobbyists, newspapers, cable TV, magazines, and websites literally pouring out opinions. They all make assumptions about values. We don't need an academic field to adopt a "normative" position beyond rule of law and efficiency.

We can study whether less contracting out would save the government money; how procurement rules might be simplified; and how government personnel systems might be improved. It's OK to study the pros and cons of different health insurance systems around the world. It's *not* OK (as part of administrative science) to argue that the United States or any other country *should* have a universal health insurance system. *Should* statements reflect value judgments and are outside the bounds of science.

We can easily observe the wide range of values that people exhibit worldwide. Think about issues that have been recently in the press: police misconduct, sexual slavery, corruption, gay and transgender rights, child pornography, imprisonment without fair trials, separation of church and state, discrimination based on race, ethnicity, or sexual orientation, abortion, mistreatment of immigrants, and denial of religious freedom. Each of us has opinions on these issues in accord with our understanding of the facts but mostly in accord with our internal moral compass. Scholars can study the facts about these issues. Our feelings about these highly charged issues *can* and should be separated from the factual issues. Science cannot tell us what we should value.

Note. From Pearson (2016).

of value-free science, that does not negate the fact that it continues to serve as a normative aspiration for some social scientists (Douglas, 2004, 2011; Resnik & Elliott, 2016).

Central Features

Although some readers may consider it redundant to point out, value-free does not literally mean that the scientific undertaking is entirely free of the influence of all values. The very idea that a scientist should be value-free is a value! The sustained pursuit of scientific knowledge by scientific communities is a value. Ethical values pervade the responsible conduct of scientists. Scientists and their funders pursue research questions and projects that align with their values and interests, and scientists choose methodologies that are ethically acceptable. Defenders of value-free science fully acknowledge that values may play a variety of unproblematic, legitimate roles in scientific inquiry in determining the following kinds of choices (Anderson, 2004; Douglas, 2014b, 2016):

- The direction of research—for example, values acquired in disciplinary training and in association with a community of practice affect selecting the phenomenon to investigate, questions to pursue, and hypotheses to test.

- The choice of methods and procedures—for example, ethical values (e.g., privacy, autonomy, informed consent) impose moral and practical constraints on data gathering.

- The level of certainty required in a theory before accepting it as a guide to action.

- What constitutes sufficient evidence (strength, amount, etc.) to accept or reject a hypothesis.

The core assumption of the value-free claim is that a scientist must analyze evidence and draw inferences about findings and conclusions in a value-neutral way. This assumption is predicated on distinguishing between two types of values, as shown in Figure 2.1: (1) those endogenous to the process of scientific reasoning—cognitive, epistemic, or constitutive values and (2) those exogenous to that process—noncognitive, contextual, or nonepistemic values. The first category includes values such as simplicity, testability, empirical success, explanatory power, and accuracy, whereas the second includes social, political, and moral values held by individual researchers, institutions, and societies.

The value-free or value-neutral ideal for scientific conduct focuses on the endogenous phase of scientific reasoning. As the philosopher of science Heather Douglas explains, that means that "value judgments internal to science involving the evaluation and acceptance of scientific results at the heart of the scientific practice are to be as free as humanly possible of social and ethical values" (Douglas, 2009, p. 45). In other words, ethical, political, and social values may not legitimately influence standards for accepting or rejecting a hypothesis or theory. Sociologist Martyn Hammersley (2017) points out that science can authoritatively validate only factual claims and that scientists—in their capacity as scientists—ought to be neutral with respect to exogenous values about good or bad, right or wrong practices, actions, institutional arrangements, and so forth. Scientists are not to take sides or organize their research to serve particular social or political values. In sum, to be value-free means excluding moral-political knowledge that informs social aims from scientific work, for it will bias, spoil, or otherwise taint efforts to develop genuine knowledge (Proctor, 1991).

The conventional case for value-free science also rests on the conjunction of the constitutive values of impartiality, neutrality, and autonomy, which are characteristic of the scientific community or of science as an institution more generally (Anderson, 2004; Lacey, 2002). All three values

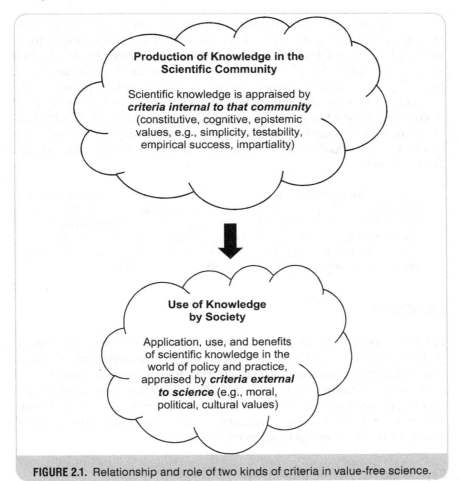

FIGURE 2.1. Relationship and role of two kinds of criteria in value-free science.

are critical even if we can identify cases where one or more of them have been violated. Impartiality presupposes that scientists can distinguish cognitive values from moral, social values so that the latter have no role to play in determining the validity of scientific claims, hypotheses, or theories. In other words, the only grounds for accepting a claim or hypothesis is its relation to the evidence. Neutrality expresses the view that "science does not play moral favorites" (Lacey, 2002, p. 523); it assumes that scientific knowledge is neutral with respect to competing value-outlooks. Autonomy means that research practices and methodologies should not be constrained by moral, political, religious, and other noncognitive interests. In other words, science has a right to self-governance (Resnik, 2008).

Finally, the notion of being value-free assumes that social (contextual, noncognitive) values cannot be allowed in scientific inquiry because to do so would threaten objectivity (Douglas, 2004). As defined in the *Stanford Encyclopedia of Philosophy*, objectivity "expresses the idea that the claims, methods, and results of science are not, or should not be influenced by particular perspectives, value commitments, community bias or personal interests, to name a few relevant factors" (Reiss & Sprenger, 2017). Defenders of the idea of value-free science argue that objectivity in the production of scientific knowledge is the very basis of the authority of that knowledge. To summarize:

> The scientific community presents its members as dispassionate, value-neutral enterprisers dedicated to advancing knowledge and to clearly demarcating where the facts end and speculation begins. . . . Science is portrayed as above the political fray—and scientists as non-partisan truth-seekers who know how to separate their factual judgments from their value judgments—and who are committed to doing so. (Mandel & Tetlock, 2016, p. 452)

CRITICISMS

Practicing social researchers as well as philosophers of science have raised significant criticisms of the value-free doctrine in its entirety and of some of its constituent assumptions. Specifically, they have focused on issues related to (1) the fact–value dichotomy, (2) the value orientations of researchers and funders, (3) the influence of values on scientific reasoning, (4) the distinction between legitimate and illegitimate uses of values in science, and (5) models of the relationship of science to society.

Beyond the Fact–Value Dichotomy

Defenders of value-free science assume that the only kind of objective judgment that scientists can make is one based on facts. They regard value judgments as subjective, like feelings or matters of taste or preferences. Thus, they are unverifiable, and while they may be accepted, they cannot be rationally justified. However, as British social theorist Andrew Sayer (2011) observes, the separation of fact from value and science from ethics is part of a whole family of "flawed conceptual distinctions that obstruct our understanding of the evaluative character of everyday life" (p. 4).

Criticisms of the fact–value dichotomy arise from philosophers of social science (e.g., Anderson, 2004; Gorski, 2013; House & Howe, 1999; Machamer & Osbeck, 2004; Polanyi, 1962; Putnam, 2002) who have demonstrated that a sharp distinction between facts and values cannot be maintained—the two are often entangled and inseparable in both social understandings and social explanations, values are integral to the process of knowing, and values can be reasoned about. Philosopher John Jacobs (2013, p. 567) noted, "Moral considerations are not a matter of two distinct realms—one of facts and one of values. . . . Seeing how to place an action, a reason, a practice, a conflict, a principle (and so on) in a sphere of normativity (however poorly rationalized by those participating in it) is perhaps one of the most basic tasks of social explanation."

This perspective broadly aligns with the observation that many social scientists deal with thick concepts in their analytical frameworks and means of explanation (Gorski, 2013; Thacher, 2015; Williams, 1985). Box 2.2 provides an example of such concepts. It is not possible to neatly disentangle their descriptive and evaluative dimensions or to use them in a morally neutral way. In moral appraisals, these concepts include notions such as cruel, indifferent, dogmatic, generous, and brave. In the social behavioral sciences, thick concepts include citizenship, rational, self-interested, pub-

BOX 2.2. RACISM AND HEALTH

Williams, Lawrence, and Davis (2019) examine the evidence linking structural and cultural racism to mental and physical health outcomes. They identify research priorities for further study of the relationship between racism and health and suggest interventions that can be used to address racism. Notice how the concepts used here (e.g., structural racism, internalized racism, discrimination, and cultural racism) are what philosophers call "thick concepts"—concepts that are simultaneously descriptive and evaluative. Some of the research priorities identified include the following:

- Immigration policy has been identified as a mechanism of structural racism. Systematic attention should be given to understanding how contemporary immigration policies adversely affect population health.

- We need to better understand how internalized racism can affect health. There is limited understanding of the conditions under which internalized racism has adverse consequences for health, of the groups that are most vulnerable, and of the range of health and health-related outcomes that may be affected.

- Future research should aim to understand how and why cultural racism, measured as elevated levels of racial prejudice at the community level, is associated with poorer health for racial minorities and sometimes for all persons who live in that community.

- An enhanced understanding of how discrimination combines with other stressors to shape health and racial/ethnic inequities in health is also needed.

lic health, authentic, crime, open-mindedness, sustainability, and so on. As David Thacher (2015), professor of public policy and urban planning, explains, social science scholarship often involves a "morally freighted conceptual scheme." Writing about the importance of addressing values in social science, Sayer (2011, p. 42) points out, for example, that the statement by a social scientist that "unemployment tends to cause suffering" is at once a claim about what objectively happens (a "positive" description, to use the distinction made at the beginning of this chapter) and implies a normative judgment that the situation is bad and in need of remedying.

Many philosophers have found fault with a strict fact–value separation. Philosopher Hilary Putnam (1981, p. 68), for example, lamented that the idea of facts/values as an absolute dichotomy has assumed the status of a cultural institution despite multiple criticisms demonstrating it is not sustainable. The philosopher and strong critic of logical empiricism, Michael Scriven (1991), explained that objective judgments of value can and are legitimately derived from factual premises and that scientists claiming otherwise suffer from "value-phobia: irrational fear of evaluation" (p. 375). Philosopher Elizabeth Anderson (2004) argued that since considerable applied social science research is devoted to answering evaluative questions, especially those dealing with the relationships between social interventions and well-being, "we need a model of the bidirectional influence of facts and values in which the evaluative presuppositions brought to inquiry do not determine the answer to the evaluative question in advance, but leave this open to determination by the evidence. At the same time, these presuppositions must help us uncover the evidence that bears on our question" (p. 11).

Postmodern critics raise a different set of objections to the idea of a fact–value distinction. Drawing on different intellectual traditions, they reject notions of reasoned argument, objective knowledge, evidential warrants, and the like, arguing that there is no meaningful difference between facts and values because both are primarily ideological commitments (Kuntz, 2012; Patton, 2002). What counts as so-called objective knowledge, in their view, is always relative to a culture or social era. On a generous interpretation of the postmodern position, science is simply one way of knowing that reflects the beliefs, values, and interests of modern Western society. A less generous reading views science as little more than a political game concerned with gaining and exerting power, and value neutrality is but an ideology with which political commitments are disguised (Hammersley, 2000). Either way, for postmodernists, the very idea of value-free science is vacuous.

Maintaining a strict fact–value dichotomy is foundational to the idea of value-free science. Multiple criticisms demonstrating that the idea is not viable have opened the door to consideration of several ways in which valuing perspectives operate in social research. At the very least, members of the social scientific community acknowledge that:

- Ethical values are important in selecting research subjects or participants and in gathering and analyzing data.

- Intellectual values such as curiosity, creativity, efficiency, effectiveness, empirical adequacy, humility with respect to evidence, predictive power, simplicity in explanation, and so on guide decisions across multiple aspects of the research process, including the choice of an epistemological paradigm and research approach (e.g., experimentation, ethnography), problem selection, interpretation of data and findings, the relationship of results to existing knowledge, and the use of scientific findings (Machamer & Osbeck, 2004; Resnick & Elliott, 2016).

- Knowledge acquisition involves costs and hence is based on decisions of what costs to bear and why and that requires decisions about what to value.

But there is much more to understanding how values and valuing shape the production of scientific knowledge. The construction of knowledge that matters to humankind is bound up with values. Philosopher of science and science policy researcher Daniel Hicks (2014) notes that there is widespread agreement among many philosophers of science (if not many practicing scientists) that ethical and political values, and not simply epistemic ones, may play a substantial role in all aspects of scientific inquiry. The agendas and perspectives of researchers as well as those of research funders and sponsors heavily influence knowledge production. A central issue is not *whether* values should be a part of scientific investigation, but *where* in the scientific process values have an influence and *which* values are legitimate. Moreover, the worry is not that value judgments might guide scientific inquiry but that *these judgments might be held dogmatically,* thereby driving inquiry to a predetermined conclusion (Anderson, 2004; Machamer & Osbeck, 2004). Douglas (2014b, p. 171) takes this point of view in claiming that scientific methods must be capable of producing "empirical surprises," methods "which are open to finding out that the world is not the way they thought it was."

Sources of Valuing Perspectives Inherent in Social Research

Applied social science examines issues and problems in education, public health, organizational management and strategy, and social services (e.g., housing for the homeless, vocational training, mental health counseling), all of which are heavily value-laden undertakings. Values held by individuals, groups, and institutions shape perspectives on what is important to study, which outcomes are to be prized above others, and how knowledge is to be used. The sources of some of those perspectives are discussed below.

Social Value Systems

Societies are composed of competing and contested systems of valuation and justification in crime prevention, schooling, social and economic well-being, and so forth. The phenomenon of global health, for example, receives different valuations in evidence-based medicine, economics, security studies, and human rights studies (Hanrieder, 2016); hence, the phenomenon is not an unproblematic object for empirical investigation. Similarly, different moral theories underlie the notions of restorative versus retributive social justice and influence the way programs informed by each theory are evaluated. Moreover, the phenomenon known as normativity—designating some actions or outcomes as good or desirable or permissible and others as bad or undesirable or impermissible—differs depending on how individuals are positioned with respect to an institution or social system. For example, Jonathan Jacobs (2013), Director of the Institute of Criminal Justice Ethics at John Jay College, invites us to consider a maximum-security prison as seen by persons differently situated socially—prisoners, correctional officers, the warden, visitors, journalists, and the local congressional representative: "It is not as though there are the normatively neutral facts and then the diverse valuative perspectives are attached to them" (p. 567).

Theoretical and Conceptual Frameworks

The intellectual and analytical tools employed by researchers entail value perspectives: The late philosopher of medicine and medical ethics, H. Tristram Engelhardt Jr., observed: "What we seek to know and how we structure what we see depends on what we expect to see and want to see. In order to move from poorly structured to well-structured problems, one needs already to know what will generally count as information or noise" (Engelhardt, 1992, p. 1). Incorporating a racial and ethnic equity perspective in the design of social research and evaluation is a rich example of this kind of framing. In their study funded by the Annie E. Casey Foundation of how to go about this, Andrews, Parekh, and Peckoo (2019) advise that researchers critically inspect their own values: "Researchers should examine their own racial, ethnic, and cultural backgrounds, as well as their experiences (or lack of experiences) with racism and/or privilege and consider how they influence the direction of research" (p. 7). The guidance also states that "the most equitable research questions are those that reflect the community's values and perspectives. . . . Research questions should acknowledge and consider cultural assumptions and norms, the community's history and context, and the reality of structural inequities. It is important for researchers to pay keen attention to how race, power, language, and privilege affect the community context, and to determine how to craft research questions that account for these factors" (p. 15).

Moreover, as the political scientist Charles Anderson (1979) explained, in appraising policies "if standards of evaluation are embedded in specific fields of discourse, if they arise from specific paradigms of inquiry and analysis, then our sense for what counts as a good reason and as a mistake depends on the ideological, disciplinary, or cultural context within which we are operating" (p. 714). Thus, for example, the arguments and analyses of environmentalists, engineers, scientists, and lawyers in appraising energy policy as well imperatives for public action will differ. The critical question becomes on what grounds should we choose to regard a policy problem from one of these analytical frameworks rather than another.

Human Ambitions

It is not news that the fields in which social scientists as well as evaluators are trained (e.g., education, economics, geography, sociology, anthropology, public administration) are composed not only of sets of concepts, models, and theories specific to those fields but also normative conventions, including assumptions about the nature of human experience, whether meaning is subject to continual negotiation, whether social problems are in principle solvable, and so forth. In our view, in their educational preparation what is either underemphasized or overlooked, however, is that scientists like everyone else are motivated by interests, desires, and ambitions that affect their work. In other words, the practical-cognitive activity of doing social science is not neatly separable from the moral-practical activity of being a social scientist. Drawing on this insight and employing a functionalist approach to the psychology of human behavior (focusing on the goals that people try to achieve through thinking, feeling, and acting as they do), psychologists David Mandel and Philip Tetlock (2016; see also Tetlock, 2002) "reject idealized representations of scientific behavior that inaccurately portray scientists as value-neutral virgins" (p. 1). They explain that as human beings, scientists often find it difficult to separate the epistemic aspect of their judgments from their social-economic behaviors such as being competitive, maintaining good relations with colleagues, responding to pressures to perform, focusing on career advancement, and promoting moral-political causes that they believe are right. Thus, they argue that scientists ought to be epistemically modest about efforts to be purely objective and value-neutral, given the different mindsets that shape their goals.

Funders' Perspectives and Agendas

Knowledge about human affairs is value-laden inasmuch as research and evaluation commissioned or funded by organizations and agencies (e.g., philanthropic foundations, nongovernmental organizations, policy institutes, government agencies) are directed by the agendas of these entities as well as their preferences for certain forms of knowledge as having greater significance, usefulness, or relevance than others. Grand challenges—ambitious research projects targeted to address complex problems through university, government, or philanthropic funds or some combination thereof—are a contemporary instance of this development. For example, the grand challenges relaunched in 2014 by the Bill and Melinda Gates Foundation specifically target efforts to address the health of infants and mothers, put women and girls at the center of development efforts, and focus on new interventions for global health. Think tanks have long served to broker scientific knowledge in the policymaking process focusing on public policy issues in health care, education, defense, the environment, and so on. They bring to the table both research and political ideology, as well as a focus on different priorities and outcomes. For example, one finds the libertarian perspective of the Cato Institute, the mainstream conservative position of the American Enterprise Institute, conservatism and libertarianism combined in the work of the Federalist Society, and the progressive views of the Center for American Progress. More generally recognized for their nonpartisan views are, for example, the Urban Institute and the Kaiser Family Foundation. Likewise, think tanks of diverse political persuasions support different ways of studying social and educational phenomena, promote values in their respective bailiwicks, and often come to different conclusions about the same issue (e.g., charter schools, environmental degradation, climate change, poverty).

Political influences on the production and acceptance of scientific knowledge, often referred to as the politics of scientific knowledge (Suhay, 2015), involve not only these intentional (as well as unintentional) actions of research sponsors but also the very fact that scientific knowledge is power (resting in its epistemic authority) and power is political. At the extreme, we can also observe the politicalization of science—the manipulation, censoring, or suppression of scientific knowledge for political gain or to serve a political ideology. In some circumstances, the politicalization of science means that scientific knowledge that does not align with, or contradicts, a certain political agenda is ignored or suppressed. For example, the National Task Force on Rule of Law and Democracy of the Brennan Center for Justice at New York University School of Law released a report in 2019 in which it presented the following argument:

> Recent administrations have manipulated the findings of government scientists and researchers, retaliated against career researchers for political reasons, invited outside special interests to shape research priorities, undermined and sidelined advisory committees staffed by scientists, and suppressed research and analysis from public view—often material that had previously been made available. . . . This trend has culminated in the efforts of the current administration not only to politicize scientific and technical research on a range of

topics, but also, at times, to undermine the value of objective facts themselves. Now, we are at a crisis point, with almost weekly violations of previously respected safeguards. (Mehrbani, Kinsella, & Weiser, 2019, p. 1)

The converse of the politicalization of science is the scientization of public policy. That is the belief that political disputes about social direction can be resolved through the application of scientific expertise. There are echoes of this view in the evidence-based approach to policy and practice (EBPP). EBPP is a political and not simply a methodological and epistemological perspective. Evidence-based approaches to practice promote the use of protocols, practice guidelines, and in some cases rules according to which practitioners ought to behave (e.g., rules regarding nursing care for patients with dementia or rules regarding what tests a physician in a health maintenance organization may order) and, in some circumstances, the development of performance measures for practitioners based on those protocols. In these situations, EBPP is an instrument of politics because it is used to control professional work by reducing the discretion and autonomy of professionals. In the policy arena, strict adherence to the idea of evidence-*based*, versus, evidence-*informed*, decision making (Prewitt, Schwandt, & Straf, 2012) fails to recognize that the real world of political decision making is characterized by bargaining, entrenched commitments, and the interplay of diverse stakeholder values and interests. EBPP typically relies on a rigorous examination of the strength of causal inferences to determine "what works." In so doing, it often makes the unwarranted assertion that methodological rigor is an indication of policy relevance and mistakenly equates the idea of evidence of effect with evidence of social desirability (Parkhurst, 2017). Policy decisions often involve choices between competing sets of interests and values as well as competing bodies of evidence.

Values Influencing Scientific Reasoning

Philosophers and ethicists Kevin Elliott (2011, 2013) and David Resnik (Elliott & Resnik, 2014) argue that a sharp distinction between science and human values or policy is untenable because personal, ethical, political, and cultural values influence scientific reasoning. They point to studies revealing the ways financial relationships reflect scientific judgment and how risk perception differs between those employed in industry and those working in academic settings. Support for this notion also comes from scholars in the field of science and technology studies (e.g., Jasanoff, 1990, 2004) who argue that while claiming to be above the political fray in its pursuit of knowledge, the scientific community often ignores or takes for granted values and social preferences embedded in its own community, thus putting methodological choices and research priorities beyond the reach of critical scrutiny.

Resnick and Elliott (2016) emphasize that values may operate at both conscious and unconscious levels:

> At conscious level, a value would impact science by playing a role in deliberate choices that affect research. Some deliberate choices might include designing a study to minimize harm to human subjects, falsifying data in order to maintain grant funding. . . . At a subconscious level, values might impact science by influencing judgment and reasoning in ways that scientists are not aware of. Value influences might go unnoticed because they are inherent in the institutional, social, and economic context of research. For example, a scientist whose research is sponsored by a pharmaceutical company might make choices pertaining to data analysis or interpretation that are favorable to the company. (p. 34)

Given the unavoidable conscious and subconscious influence of values, they conclude that the best way for scientists to do policy-relevant research is for them to be as transparent as possible about the ways in which interests and values may influence their work (Elliott, 2017a; Elliott & Resnick, 2014, p. 649). Transparency can mean consistently publishing results regardless of whether findings confirm or disconfirm a hypothesis or theory, using open-access journals; making data publicly available; providing data analysis plans before studies begin; making materials and methods available to other researchers; and disclosing conflicts of interest. In his blog, Elliott has further claimed that

> [b]oth citizens and scientists also need to scrutinize and discuss the influences of values as effectively as possible, using many different venues: Journals can promote thoughtful peer-review processes, government agencies can maintain effective science advisory boards, scientific societies can create reports on debated topics, citizens can get involved in research projects and the scientific community can encourage new perspectives by promoting greater diversity in its membership. By taking these steps, scientists and stakeholders can decide how best to handle important judgments, and they can distinguish scientific conclusions that are well supported from those that are more tenuous. (Elliott, 2017a)

Legitimate and Illegitimate Roles for Values

According to philosopher of science Heather Douglas (2009, 2014b), it is relatively noncontroversial that social, moral, and political values influence the direction of research and methodological choices. The contentious matter is the role of such values in scientific inference—the drawing of a conclusion or claim from data. Here she points out that values can play two roles: an illegitimate direct role and a legitimate indirect role.

An illegitimate, *direct* use of values occurs when values serve as "reasons in themselves to accept a claim" (Douglas, 2009, p. 96). This occurs in scientific reasoning when scientists' social, moral, or political values lead them to employ a methodology that ensures a particular result or when scientists' values distort how they view available evidence or allow their values to trump evidence, thereby either ignoring it or fabricating evidence more in line with their values. Douglas states that this use is deeply worrying for

> [i]f, at the moment when we interpret a complex set of evidence, our values are determining what we see in that evidence, or even what comes to be seen as evidence, then we are merely reproducing our own wishful thinking rather than investigating the world. It is because of such worries that many scientists and philosophers of science have argued that the internal reasoning of science should be "value-free," in the sense that ethical, social, and personal values should not influence such reasoning. (p. 173)

However, Douglas (2014b) contends that values may influence scientific reasoning in a more subtle way; she calls this an *indirect* role that operates through the uncertainty in a claim a scientist makes. In deciding what to make of evidence, she argues, there is always some uncertainty, unless of course there is a clear and strong deductive argument in which the claim follows logically from the evidentiary premises. More often, a scientist must decide what to do in the face of uncertainty, that is, to judge whether the evidence is sufficient to support the claim the scientist wishes to make. "It is the making of this judgment," Douglas writes, "that values play an invaluable role, the indirect role" (p. 174). The classic example of this (raised first by Churchman, 1948, and Rudner, 1953) is that the acceptance of any claim (hypothesis) is underdetermined by evidence. That is, evidence available at any given time is insufficient to guarantee a claim, and a scientist can always find a way to deal with evidence so as to maintain the claim she or he favors. For example, in evaluating the results of an experiment, a scientist must consider both Type I (false positive) and Type II (false negative) errors in deciding whether to accept a hypothesis. That decision rests on appraising the risks associated with each type of error, and that appraisal is a matter of both moral and political judgment. The critical observation here is that the amount and strength of evidence to accept a hypothesis depend on the consequences of accepting it (Rudner, 1953). So, for example, the evidentiary standard needed to assess the efficacy of a drug designed to treat Alzheimer's disease will be quite different than the evidence needed to assess a hypothesis that has few dire social implications.

For Douglas (2014b), because social, moral, and political values are involved in deciding what constitutes sufficient evidence for a claim, scientists should be forthcoming about the values shaping their decisions about whether evidence is sufficient in any given study. That means: "scientists must culturally abandon the value-free ideal. . . . Different scientists will have different values and thus see different inferences as warranted. But with the value-free ideal set aside, this source of rational disagreement can be brought out into the open and become a source for robust discussion both within and beyond the scientific community" (p. 178). Douglas (2009) bases her argument for the indirect role played by nonepistemic values in scientific reasoning on the claim that scientists have an ethical responsibility to society. Specifically, they are responsible for avoiding being either reckless or negligent in the claims they make that might cause societal harms. Hence, "scientists should be clear about why they make the judgments they do, why they find evidence sufficiently convincing or not, and whether the reasons are based on perceived flaws in the evidence or concerns about the consequences of error" (Douglas, 2009, p. 155).

Rethinking the Science–Society Relationship

The stance of value neutrality is antithetical to scientists taking an active role in policy debates and policy decision making as well as to an active role for knowledge users (i.e., citizens) in scientific knowledge production. In Figure 2.2, we portray how the idea of value-free science links to a transfer model of knowledge production in which those stakeholders known as knowledge users have no direct role in generating scientific knowledge. Knowledge is a product transferred from scientists to stakeholders in a one-way communication, with the transfer facilitated by knowledge brokers or translational science. Knowledge brokers may be individuals or institutions that build relations and linkages between knowledge producers and knowledge users. Well-known examples include the work of the National Research Council of the National Academies of Science and at least part of the mission of the Regional Educational Laboratory Program of the Institute of Educational Sciences in the United States. Translational science is the effort to move basic research from "bench to the bedside" as is often expressed in medical research—applying the knowledge of basic science to tools and procedures useful in clinical medicine. Translational science also embraces efforts to improve the implementation of the knowledge base of evidence-based practices in professional fields of nursing, social work, and counseling.

Scholars in philosophy and in the natural and social sciences criticize this model as an inaccurate depiction of the production and use of scientific knowledge. It is also noteworthy that the Pew Research Center's surveys of issues in the science–society relationship (*www.pewresearch.org/science/2019/08/02/partisanship-influences-views-on-the-role-and-value-of-scientific-experts-in-policy-debates*) reveal that a majority of U.S. adults support the participation of scientific experts in policy debates, clearly challenging the idea of a distinct separation between producers and users of scientific knowledge.

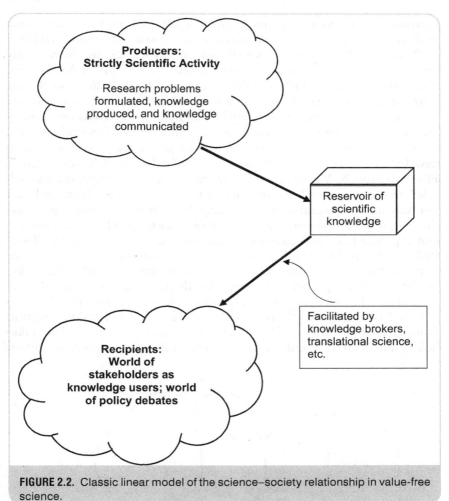

FIGURE 2.2. Classic linear model of the science–society relationship in value-free science.

Science is embedded in economic, social, and cultural contexts, reflecting shifts in society's views, values, and understandings of science (both social and natural) as one among many social enterprises and evident in the ways in which science is supported, how it is evaluated as meeting society's needs, and how society shapes scientists, their interests and the problems that are to be addressed. As Daniel Sarewitz (2016, p. 8), at Arizona State University's School for the Future of Innovation and Society, has argued, "science will be made more reliable and more valuable for society today not by being protected from societal influences but instead by being brought, carefully and appropriately, into a direct, open, and intimate relationship with those influences." In recent years, research on wicked problems (Rittel & Webber, 1973) in both the social and natural sciences has increasingly turned to concepts of co-production (Jasanoff, 2004; Miller & Wyborn, 2020) and transdisciplinarity (Jahn, Bergmann, & Keil, 2012) to characterize interactive models of the relationship of science to society as depicted in Figure 2.3. Co-production in public administration signals the involvement of citizens in producing public policies and services. In social research, co-production is an exploratory space and a generative process leading to new forms of knowledge, values, and social relations (Chambers, 2017; Filipe, Renedo, & Marston, 2017). Transdisciplinary or integrated research refers to types of knowledge production for social change which are based not only on the integration of knowledge from different disciplines (interdisciplinary), but also on the inclusion of values, knowledge, know-how, and expertise from nonacademic sources (Klein, 2010; Polk, 2014). Roger Pielke (2007, p. 14), who has written extensively about the role of science in policymaking, describes the alternative to the linear model as the stakeholder model that presumes not only that the values and interests of users of scientific knowledge should have some role in its production but also that understanding the effectiveness of science in decision making requires knowledge of how it is used by policymakers and practitioners. The stakeholder model broadly understood as purposeful engagements between sci-

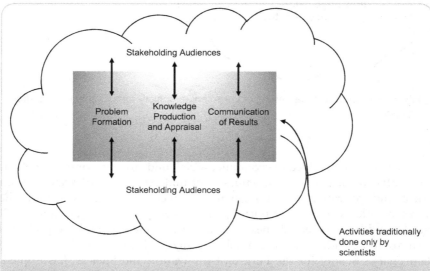

FIGURE 2.3. Interactive model of knowledge production involving science and society.

entists and citizens has received extensive attention both in the field of science and technology studies and in development studies (Leach, Scoones, & Wynne, 2005). The model encompasses a variety of concerns, including the role of lay knowledge, citizen's rights, orchestration of deliberative and participatory processes, and reframing of dominant expertise.

ALTERNATIVE STANCES TO THE VALUE-FREE IDEAL: NEUTRALITY AND PARTISANSHIP

Criticisms of value-free science yield insights into how scientists might legitimately address the presence of moral, political, and social values in their work. Yet, these criticisms often do not directly speak to the roles or stances that the professional social scientist can adopt as an alternative to the role of value-free scientist. Two such roles widely discussed in the social science literature are those of the neutral broker and the partisan social scientist.

Neutrality in Research

As a researcher stance, neutrality goes a step further than acting with transparency. It refers to whether a scientist takes a stand. For example, in social research concerned with policy, the neutral scientist seeks to facilitate decision making on complex policy issues by being impartial (or nonaligned) with respect to any specific value bases of policy alternatives. Pielke (2007) describes this idealized role of scientists as that of honest brokers of policy alternatives. In this role, the scientist clarifies and sometimes expands the scope of choice available to decision makers by "placing scientific understandings in the context of a smorgasbord of policy options" (p. 17). In other words, as a broker, the scientist might indicate that there are several policy options, each with a range of possible consequences. In this role, the scientist invites the user of scientific results to consider what evidence might be necessary to change a policy position, and, given that a range of policy positions is consistent with scientific results, within such a range, what factors other than science might be used to settle on one policy option over others (pp. 141–142). In the role of honest broker, the scientist aims to expand or clarify the scope of choice for decision makers as opposed to the scientist acting in the role of issue advocate who narrows the decision maker's range of choice by making a case for one alternative versus others. Honest brokers are not partisan. That is, they express no stake or stated interest in a policy choice or outcome.

Resnik and Elliott (2016; see also Resnik, 2008) argue that scientists ought to strive for value neutrality, which they make clear does not mean being literally value-free but "only that research outcomes should not be deliberately biased toward any particular set of competing values in a dispute, especially without making the influences of values transparent" (p. 35). Value-neutrality for them means being objective and minimizing bias in making scientific claims. Like Douglas, they declare that scientists ought to address the nonepistemic values inherent in their work. However, they emphasize that this does not mean that scientists ought to be partisan in promoting particular social and political values or normative commitments. In sum, scientists should clearly distinguish between the scientific evidence relating to an issue and endorsing a particular value position on an issue; for example, some parents and policymakers demand voucher programs for school choice as an option for public education as opposed to those parents and policymakers who believe public money should not be used for private or parochial education. Resnik and Elliott (2016) find an important justification for this position in the claim that the public relies on scientists to provide evidence and expert advice in public policy debates. Furthermore, they argue that scientists have social responsibility and that to ignore the value implications of one's work would be to act irresponsibly.

Resnick and Elliott's position differs from that of the honest broker role, and yet it still emphasizes the ideal of neutrality. Political scientist David Weimer (2005) defines neutral competence as using appropriate methods to identify policy alternatives and their consequences and "neutrality in choosing and arguing for the social values that provide a basis for comparison of [policy] alternatives. . . . [N]eutral competence does not mean 'value-free,' if indeed such analysis were possible. Rather, it means identifying policy impacts that affect values held by any members of society" (p. 132). Weimer adds that this means giving standing to all values and how they are affected by policy alternatives, those of both organized and unorganized interests. Yet, this stance can amount to a scientist saying something to the effect "that if you value X this is likely to be the case, but if you value Y then this is likely to be the case." Douglas (2004) refers to this stance as being reflectively centrist: "One needs to be aware of the range of possible values at play in the situation, aware of the arguments for various sides, and to take a reflectively balanced position" (p. 460). In the field of evaluation research, this neutral stance is equivalent to a descriptivist approach to evaluating wherein evaluators limit their role to describing the values held by different stakeholders (Hall, Ahn, & Greene, 2012; House & Howe, 1999).

It may well be that social scientists, especially those more intimately connected to the political process (e.g., researchers at the Congressional Research Office, the Government Accountability Office), are forced to take refuge in a stance of neutral competence. Although these applied social scientists are working as experts in settings where they are called upon to reach conclusions and offer recommendations, this can be a challenging task in environments characterized by claims of fake news, alternative facts, and hyper-political partisanship.

Partisan Social Research

Viewing the relationship between values commitments and scientific inquiry as a matter of maintaining value neutrality contrasts sharply with the notion of the social researcher as partisan. At the outset, it is important to distinguish carefully the idea of social science partisanship from the widely recognized notion of political partisanship (see Box 2.3). The latter often signifies prejudice (in a negative sense, compared to a preference), selective reliance on anecdotal evidence, lack of genuine curiosity about views other than one's own, and an unwillingness to work across differences in values and perspectives. In this sense, being partisan means lacking respect for evidence and objectivity. This is not the way the notion of being partisan has been understood in the social science literature in which a commitment to objectivity remains a guiding ideal.

Nonetheless, scholars interpret the idea of partisanship in social science in multiple ways. One of the most widely discussed expressions of the partisan position in social science appeared in sociologist Howard Becker's (1967) essay "Whose Side Are We On?," where he claimed that sociologists

---

BOX 2.3. POLITICAL PARTISANSHIP AND NEUTRALITY

Political partisanship is a commonly recognized view of what it means to be partisan. For example, the Milbank Memorial Fund recognizes that on any issues surrounding Medicaid expansion or Medicare reform "voices are shrill, slogans are wielded like swords, and opinions are ossified." The Fund accepts that political bipartisanship around health policy issues is elusive. Yet, it seeks to bring policymakers together in respectful, nonpartisan settings to learn from one another and examine evidence (Koller, 2015). The Fund clearly has the goal of improved population health and thus is not neutral because it recognizes that as a collective priority improved public health is in conflict with other social values and goals (e.g., limiting personal choices that would negatively affect one's health or the health of others—smoking indoors, not getting vaccinations for children, eating a lot of trans fats). In this sense, the Fund is partisan using Lindblom's understanding of the term. The Fund also recognizes that evidence alone will not decide how to reach the goal of improved public health because addressing the problem is fundamentally a matter of political compromise and each policymaker will likely gauge success in different ways.

Note. From Koller (2015).

appeared to face the horns of a dilemma between calls for a sociology that does not take sides, is neutral, technically correct and value-free, and arguments that sociologists ought to clearly express a value position. However, he claimed:

> This dilemma, which seems so painful to so many, actually does not exist, for one of its horns is imaginary. For it to exist, one would have to assume, as some apparently do, that it is indeed possible to do research that is uncontaminated by personal and political sympathies. I propose . . . that it is not possible and, therefore, that the question is not whether we should take sides, since we inevitably will, but rather whose side we are on. (p. 239)

A radical reading of Becker's position would be that, given that all research is biased, there can be no such thing as valid, objective, empirically grounded claims emanating from scientific research (Hammersley, 2001). However, this would be a mistake. In a clarification of his position, Becker (1971) distinguished two senses of bias. In one use of the term, the charge to the effect that scientists are biased may mean that they are presenting statements of fact that are demonstrably false and that claims arise solely from the preferred values, opinions, or stance of the researcher. This is similar to Douglas's claim of the illegitimate use of direct values in scientific reasoning. On a second use of the term, the charge of bias may refer to the situation when research results dealing with matters of public concern (e.g., health, education, the environment) appear to favor one side or another in a controversy. For example, imagine research studies comparing student achievement in charter schools to student achievement in traditional public schools showing greater gains for charter school students. Advocates of public schooling may well level claims that the research was biased. If the results of the studies were just the opposite, advocates of charter schools might claim bias in the research.

The charge of bias can arise when a researcher does not defer to an established order and perspectives, much as Becker did in studying deviant behavior and claiming that deviance does not inhere in an act but in the labeling of minorities by majorities as deviant from cultural norms. In other words, this type of charge of bias against researchers arises when research results do not agree with the prejudices of those who have certain stakes in those results. Becker argues that in this sense, researchers are always taking sides because their research will either confirm or challenge the conventional views of different stakeholding audiences (see Box 2.4). He also claims that more studies are biased in favor of the established status order in society than the other way around. In this sense, researchers cannot avoid being seen as biased. However, being seen as biased in this second sense does not mean that the scientists do not aim to being unbiased and objective in the first sense.

> ## BOX 2.4. TAKING SIDES?
>
> Becker (1967) asked, "Whose side are we on?" and pointed out that if a researcher's well-supported claims do not coincide with established perspectives, the researcher will likely be accused of being biased or partisan. Here are two examples:
>
> 1. In 2012, Tom Hungerford, an economist with the Congressional Research Service (CRS), published a paper that concluded, "Analysis of . . . data suggests the reduction in the top tax rates have had little association with saving, investment, or productivity growth. However, the top tax rate reductions appear to be associated with the increasing concentration of income at the top of the income distribution." Republicans called the report flawed; Democrats cheered it.
>
> 2. At the end of 2012, another CRS analyst's report about pending legislation related to coal ash raised concerns about its environmental effects. The report was praised by environmentalists and trashed by industry supporters. When the Senate held off acting on the legislation, its supporters blamed the CRS for a biased analysis.
>
> *Note.* From Kosar (2015).

While agreeing that "taking sides" does not compromise objectivity, the late professor of political science and economics, Charles Lindblom (1986), argued for a somewhat different notion he called "thoughtful partisanship" in social research linked to policymaking. To Lindblom, being partisan did not mean being narrow-minded or bigoted; rather, for him, being partisan meant advancing certain values, interests, or preferences over others. The partisan scientist, he said, is

> [o]ne who acknowledges that his [sic] work is guided by a selection of some among other possible interests and values; who so far as feasible, reveals his selection; who makes no claims that his values or interests are good for everyone. . . . I do not mean someone who lies, conceals evidence, or violates conventional standards of scientific integrity. (p. 350)

Lindblom (1986) maintained that everyone, scientists included, aim to advance some values over others and thus the interests and preferences of some people over those of others. The danger comes not in being partisan, as he has defined it, but in believing that one's view is somehow generalizable as nonpartisan, is impartial, and speaks on behalf of the good for all. Because in his view democratic discussion is "overwhelmingly partisan discussion," for social scientists to be of use they must enter into that partisan discussion rather than "obscure it with a pretense of neutrality" (p. 352). Lindblom was a strong believer in value pluralism and the competition of ideas and feared that nonpartisan pursuit of the public interest "puts the influence of social science and research at the service of central, conventional, established interests and values" (p. 353). He believed that partisan social science should develop and use knowledge that leveled the playing field among competing social interests. Thus, the kind of partisanship that Lindblom had in mind was not some general advocacy of the importance of democracy, democratic pluralism, or redressing the plight of the underprivileged, but rather a particular perspective or stance on addressing a controversial issue such as voting rights, climate change, welfare reform, or poverty reduction.

Lindblom developed this perspective in the framework of incrementalism (often referred to as "muddling through") as an alternative to a highly rational, comprehensive model of policymaking. He argued that almost always one finds disagreement over policy objectives and an inadequate knowledge base. There are always conflicting partisan versions of the public good, and policy alternatives to achieve it represent different trade-offs among contending values and interests. In such a framework of incrementalism or muddling through, the best society can do is to work out politically some resolution to a social problem in an actual context and at a particular time. In that act of social problem solving, social science research and analysis is at best just part of the effort. Finally, Lindblom (1986, 1990) argued that instead of serving the needs of leaders and officials alone, social scientists should focus on the information needs of citizens. Citizens, he argued, form volitions (commitments decided by choice and influenced by principles, judgment, motives), and for those choices they need empirical, moral, and practical analyses that social science can provide.

Thoughtful partisanship is similar to Pielke's (2007) idealized scientist role of issue advocate. In this role, the scientist openly promotes an interest, value, or outcome. This role might be apparent in a think tank or an environmental or social activist group (e.g., Earth Watch, Save the Children, Oxfam) where researchers assemble scientific evidence and arguments in support of a vision, mission, or perspective. In the field of evaluation, Hall and colleagues (2012) defend this stance of issue advocacy. They explain:

> [A] primary value promoted in our approach is that of inclusion. We aspire to inclusively describe and engage the perspectives, concerns, and values of all legitimate stakeholders in the evaluation, with particular attention to ensuring inclusion of the interests, perspectives, and values of those traditionally unheard, underrepresented, or least well served in that context. . . . More prescriptively and more importantly, we privilege and therefore seek to engage and advance the democratic ideal of equity. We define equity as being concerned with the treatment of program stakeholders, specifically, how well the evaluand [the program, policy, project being evaluated] affords program access, meaningful participation, and accomplishment for all relevant stakeholders. (p. 33)

Straightforwardly and openly advocating a value stance (in this case, inclusion and equity) contrasts with what Pielke (2007) describes as stealth advocacy, a form of covert promotion through which a researcher smuggles in assumptions that point to preferred polices or programs while pretending to offer purely scientific advice. Human rights lawyer and public health scholar Gorick Ooms (2015) argues that it is difficult to imagine meaningful social research—in his case that of global health—that is *not* supporting a cause or proposal. Thus, he advocates being transparent about the fact that global health research is a normative undertaking. Ooms consequently objects to stealth advocacy (or perhaps we might call it stealth partisanship), finding it problematic for five reasons: (1) It is misleading because it buries a normative premise somewhere under empirical evidence, (2) because the normative premise is buried, it makes debate with others who hold different normative premises (partisan views) impossible, (3) it may lead to unrealistic policy proposals or actions because the policymaker's normative premise may not agree with that of the researcher, (4) by pretending that it is only the evidence that matters, it covers up the role of politics and power in social research, and (5) that coverup leads to a failure to challenge the influence of powerful actors in a given social problem area because the true scope of their influence is either ignored or downplayed.

DECOUPLING OBJECTIVITY AND THE VALUE-FREE IDEAL

Thoughtful partisanship need not conflict with scholarly rigor. Acceptance of this claim depends on how researchers understand the concept of scholarly rigor and importantly, on what the notion of objectivity means. Many social scientists and philosophers of science argue that "immersion in values need not compromise science's objectivity" (Smith, 2004, p. 143). Philosopher Tara Smith (2004), for one, makes a case for a cognitive-oriented, epistemological objectivity as

> [a] person's manner of using his or her mind. . . . It consists in thinking and drawing conclusions based on strict logical adherence to the relevant facts. By this I mean that a person's inferences from his or her observations are disciplined by a rational understanding of the relationships among facts. The objective person does not leap to sweeping or unwarranted conclusions on the basis of paltry evidence, for instance. (pp. 152–153)

Sociologist Joseph Davis (2013) argues that objectivity does not require being value-free but rather having an "openness to critical scrutiny, including value considerations in research decisions, description, and explanation. Such openness will improve analysis and set the terms for a proper and delimited role for the social sciences in our ethical reflection and public life" (pp. 554–555),

Douglas (2007) agrees with Davis that there is no necessary connection between objectivity and value-free inquiry. Like Smith, Douglas criticizes interpretations of objectivity that regard it as aperspectival—a "view from nowhere"—or somehow signifying the grasp of a reality "out there" independent of human thought. She argues that these understandings of objectivity, along with equating it to the notion of being value-free, are "functionally unhelpful" in determining whether a given claim is in fact objective. She claims that the notion of objectivity is composed of an irreducibly complex set of meanings, all of which are needed to make sense of any claim to be objective. Box 2.5 displays Douglas's understanding of two different senses of the term, only one of which has to do with the idea of value neutrality.

Philosopher Ian Hacking (2015) argues in favor of doing away with the term *objectivity* because it is ambiguous, and it is usually better to discuss specific "ground level questions." He invites readers to consider the following two questions that fall under the heading of objectivity: "Can we

---

BOX 2.5. SOME SENSES OF OBJECTIVITY OTHER THAN "VALUE-FREE"

Objectivity Understood in Terms of Reasoning Processes

- *Detached objectivity:* The prohibition against using values in place of evidence. Simply because one wants something to be true does not make it so, and one's values should not blind one to the existence of unpleasant evidence.

- *Value-neutral objectivity:* A value position that is neutral on the spectrum of debate, a midrange position that takes no strong stance.

Objectivity Focused on Social Processes That Structure Procedures and Ways to Reach Agreement through Those Processes

- *Procedural objectivity:* Involves setting up a process such that regardless of who is performing that process, the same outcome is always produced.

- *Concordant objectivity:* Occurs when a group of people all agree on an outcome, be it a description of an observation or a judgment.

- *Interactive objectivity:* Occurs when an appropriately constituted group of people meet and discuss what the outcome should be. The difficulty with interactive objectivity lies with the details of this process: What is an appropriately constituted group? How diverse and with what expertise? How are the discussions to be framed? And what counts as agreement reached among the members of the group?

Note. From Douglas (2007, pp. 132–135).

trust medical research when it is funded by pharmaceutical companies?" and "Whose research in climate science meets the standards of scientific objectivity?" He then observes:

> The first question is an excellent one. It does not mention objectivity. It is a ground-level question. The second question is a second-story question . . . couched in terms of "standards of scientific objectivity." In *The Social Construction of What?* I spoke of "elevator words" (Hacking, 1999). They are words . . . used for what Quine called semantic assent such as "true" and "real." Instead of saying that the cat is on the mat, we move up a story and say that it is true that the cat is on the mat. That is a statement about a statement. "Objective" is an elevator word. . . . Let us stick to ground-level questions. Ascending to the second story and posing a question in terms of scientific objectivity does nothing to help us with a ground-level question, such as one about research in climate science. (p. 20)

The point here is that the term *objectivity* is no longer about some specific object in the world (e.g., medical research) but about an expression that we assign to the object ("standards of scientific objectivity"). What this does, in effect, is shift the conversation from a question of substance to a question of meaning.

Finally, neutrality and objectivity are not the same thing (Proctor, 1991). As noted above, neutrality refers to whether a scientist takes a stand; whereas objectivity refers to whether scientific claims are dependable, valid, trustworthy, or warranted. As is apparent in the discussion of partisanship above, social scientific claims may be completely objective and yet intended to serve particular interests.

TOWARD A MORALLY INFORMED SOCIAL SCIENCE

Arguments about the relationship between value commitments and social scientific inquiry often focus on how values might negatively influence the world of facts. However, we advocate for a type of inquiry that is less oriented to the place of values in a world of fact than to the place of fact in a world of values (Rein, 1983). The emphasis on the potential biasing influences of scientists' interests, values, or perspectives on scientific reasoning is a consequence of trying to maintain a fundamental distinction between facts and values. That distinction has also served to keep scientific study separate from moral inquiry, or, to put it differently, to prevent the exploration of how social science might serve moral purposes. The common view is that social scientific work is solely descriptive and explanatory. It can clarify the nature of social problems and describe the value perspectives of the public. The Pew Research Center's studies of social values are a classic example of the latter. Social science may also explore the cause-and-effect relationships between value perspectives and behaviors, as, for example, in explaining voting preferences. Yet, David Thacher (2016), a professor of public policy and urban planning, notes:

> By contrast, the claim that close observation of social life can contribute *directly* to moral enlightenment—that we gain clarity about what our values should be, not just about the most effective instruments for achieving them . . . is foreign to the dominant tradition of contemporary social research, and it seems to violate . . . its underlying philosophy, such as the supposed dichotomy separating facts from values and the prohibition against deriving 'ought' from 'is.' (pp. 94–95, emphasis added)

In a recent memo to the faculty of Columbia University, President Lee Bollinger called for research universities to adopt a "Fourth Purpose" (beyond the three of research, teaching, and service) focused on the merger of research and action—long a characteristic of many of the professional schools—and serving humanity on a larger scale. Taking his cue from Bollinger, Ken Prewitt (2019) at Columbia argues that this notion institutionalizes the ideal of social science being in the broadest sense practical and moral and that, in turn, may well require thoughtful partisanship on the part of social scientists as well as moral reasoning about the aims and purposes of the social sciences. Of course, it may be that neither Bollinger nor Prewitt is wedded to the idea of uniting social scientific inquiry with moral inquiry, but their reflections are in keeping with a variety of scholars who have been concerned with such an undertaking (e.g., Anderson, 1998; Fischer, 1999; Flyvbjerg, 2001; Gorski, 2013; Haan, Bellah, Rabinow, & Sullivan, 1983; O'Conner, 2007; Schwandt, 2002; Selznick, 2008; Thacher, 2006, 2016). Social scientists are not without guidance on how to engage the practical, the normative, and the empirical simultaneously, and that is the subject of Chapter 5. Here, we argue that the task of uniting these three rests on several assumptions about: (1) the purpose of the human (i.e., social and behavioral) sciences, (2) the researcher as a moral agent, and (3) a concern with morality versus that of moralism.

The Purpose of the Social Sciences

The commonly discussed legitimate goals of all social scientific inquiry include description; theory construction, testing and refinement; and identification and explanation of patterns and relationships. Social scientific studies in applied fields have an additional aim of serving, in an instrumentally rational way, as a consulting practice informing planning and practitioner as well as policymaker decision making by answering the questions "Are interventions working as planned?" and "Are we doing things right?" (Flyvbjerg, 2001; Ragin & Amoroso, 2011). However, the effort to foster traffic between facts and values and between empirical social science and moral judgment (Fox & Westbrook, 1998) is more concerned with the normative questions "Are we doing the right thing" and "What makes this the right thing to do?" (Schwandt & Gates, 2016). As sociologist Joseph Davis (2013, p. 558) explains, social inquiry of this kind is "conceived as a form of critique—in the tradition of an older political philosophy—exploring and accessing social life in a deliberative rather than manipulative or legislative mode." It is an attempt to position social inquiry as a contributor to society's deliberation and action around the value-rational questions, "Where are we going?" "Is this development desirable?" "Who gains and who loses, and by which mechanisms of power?" "What should we do now?" (Flyvbjerg, 2001, 2004; Schwandt, 2002).

Social scientific inquiry organized to address value-rational (and not just instrumental) questions is closely allied with the idea of civic science that, in a democratic context of inquiry, explores the question, "What should we do in the face of complex problems?" By a democratic context we mean

> [a]n ethos that conditions and affects *how* discussion, debate, and argumentation are *practiced*. Such a democratic substantive ethos does not by itself determine specific norms, values, and decisions. . . . [It involves] a *willingness* to listen to and *evaluate* the opinions of one's opponents, *respecting* the views of [others, particularly] minorities, advancing arguments *in good faith* to support one's convictions and having the *courage* to change one's mind when confronted with new evidence or better arguments. (Bernstein, 1998, p. 290, original emphasis)

Civic science is part of a larger movement to cultivate a robust civic politics in which human beings are regarded as co-creators and designers of their actions and of the power structures within which they act (see the Framing Statement for the first Institute of Civic Studies at *https:// tischcollege.tufts.edu/civic-studies/summer-institute/framing-statement*). This is a multidisciplinary social science examining what is good and just in order to both envision and debate ways of relating and living as civic agents (Levine, 2019).

The Social Scientist as Moral Agent

The enterprise of science is a normative endeavor with discernible moral purposes such as improving the human condition, relieving suffering, enhancing health, and enriching life (Levin, 2006). To claim that individual scientists are moral agents is minimally to argue that they (1) present themselves as moral actors with these ethical aims to do good, (2) are capable of judgments about what is right and wrong, and (3) can be held accountable for their actions. However, a thicker interpretation of the idea of social scientists as moral actors views the very process of knowledge production as a form of moral inquiry. Writing from his perspective as a professor of urban planning and policy development, Robert Lake (2014) argues that John Dewey's pragmatism provides a framework for this way of thinking based on three notions. First, knowledge of social life should be viewed less as a representation of reality and more as a guide to navigating that reality. The idea that knowledge is a guide to action is a moral interest because it is concerned with what we would have social life to be (hence, social science addresses the four value rational questions noted above). Second, Dewey invites us to look to social inquiry as less a form of demonstration than a form of discovery. Lake (2014) writes, "Representation mirrors a world as it already is and has been, while action forms a world in the process of its becoming. . . . Dewey advocated a move from 'contemplative' to 'operative' forms of knowledge production advanced through a 'method of discovery' rather than a 'method of demonstration'" (p. 662). The third notion on which Dewey's idea of knowledge production as moral inquiry rests is that knowledge claims are proposals for what actions to try out next. They are warranted assertions (i.e., claims and conclusions with enough support in argument and evidence to be acted upon with confidence).

As the historian of science Robert Proctor (1991) has pointed out, scientific knowledge production is typically focused on the purely epistemological question, "How do we know" and the concomitant concern that bias will compromise objective knowing. He claims that more interesting and fruitful questions are moral-political ones, for example, "How is science involved in patterns of dominance and/or exclusion?" "Why do we this and not that?" "Why are our interests here and not there?" "Who gains from knowledge of this and not of that?" "What is to be done—or undone?" (p. 11)

A Concern with Morality versus Moralism and Moralizing

Finally, from our perspective, reuniting social scientific knowledge production with moral inquiry need not mean restricting us to moralism or the activity of moralizing. Moralism is "a kind of vice involved in certain ways of practicing morality or exercising moral judgment, or thinking you are doing so" (Coady, 2008, p. 15). It is evident when we equate the term *morality* with *moralizing*, that is, with being judgmental (Sayer, 2011). Moralists assume that their moral views are the most legitimate. Individuals who are overly judgmental, intolerant of other points of view, and unforgiving are often accused of being "moralists." Moralism is closely allied to dogmatism sometimes found among social scientists who embrace a methodological, epistemological, or political perspective (or a combination thereof) with utter certainty and hold it to be incontrovertibly true.

However, as the economist Albert Hirschman (1983) noted in his critique that normative judgments go unmentioned in economic research, the union of moral and social inquiry does not mean foregoing probing for preaching. Social scientists engage the values and standards that communities have developed to cope with complex problems, and they do so following a set of principles similar to those found in civic studies (Levine, 2014):

1. Use deliberative methods to decide what should be done and structure comments in those deliberations to facilitate interaction and mutual learning.
2. Be conscious of the limitations of human cognition; be humble.
3. Criticize from within, resisting the temptation to import the "correct" view from outside.
4. Avoid the assumption that there is a root cause and hence a single solution to the problem—the reality of situations, the stakes people hold in those situations, the issues at hand, and yet to arise are all intertwined and full of feedback loops.
5. In addressing the value rational questions, keep the ship together, rebuild, repair, modify as we sail.

SYNOPSIS OF THE STANCES

Figure 2.4 displays social researchers' stances on value-neutrality, reaching from that of value-neutral scientist to morally engaged researcher. Several assumptions underlie the portrayal of these standpoints: (1) that social researchers and evaluators working in applied fields are almost always dealing with situations where values conflict and knowledge is uncertain; (2) that these researchers and evaluators are typically conducting their

Value-free	Neutral with respect to competing social/ political/moral values	Thoughtful partisanship/ Issue advocacy	Morally engaged social science and Research as social criticism
Technical/instrumental focus	- -		Value-rational focus
Positive judgments	- -		Normative judgments
Above the political fray	- - - - - - - - - - - - - - - - - -	Involvement in the political fray	

FIGURE 2.4. Possible stances of the social researcher.

inquiries in circumstances where the decisions about social policies and programs are informed by scientific knowledge but are largely political (i.e., decision makers engage in bargaining, negotiating, and compromise); (3) that all researchers consider objectivity—understood as the effort to warrant claims through sufficient argument and evidence—an important characteristic of their work, except those who hold their moral and political values dogmatically, thereby driving their inquiries to a predetermined conclusion (or in the language of Douglas employ "direct" values), and (4) that the continuum of conditions portrayed in Figure 2.2 is viable only to the extent that the fact–value dichotomy is justifiable.

SUMMARY

The aims of this chapter are modest: to help readers recognize the myth of value-free science; to portray the production of social scientific knowledge as a value-laden affair in multiple respects; to advocate for transparency, particularly with respect to where, as a social scientist, one stands on aspirations to neutrality, partisanship, and objectivity; and to invite consideration of a type of social scientific work that simultaneously deals with matters of evidence, value, interests, and perspectives.

We might grant that the production of social scientific knowledge is always situated within the perspectives of the researcher. Yet, there can be little doubt that wishing for a particular outcome or scientific conclusion to conform to the values and interests of the scientist or research sponsors and allowing that to influence in a direct way the choice and interpretation of evidence is egregious and unethical behavior. Beyond that obvious alert, raising the topic of moral inquiry in the context of social science is bound to startle because it conjures all kinds of negative connotations, including moralizing and fears that social scientists are treading into moral questions best left to colleagues who study faith, religion, and powerful ideologies. Yet, it is possible, from a pragmatic point of view, to recognize that facts and value judgments are not always neatly distinguishable, that noncognitive values can play a nonbiasing role in the activity of scientific knowledge production, and that social science can serve as a nondogmatic partner in society's efforts to appraise and improve the social condition.

IMPORTANT RESOURCES ■ ■ ■ ■ ■ ■ ■ ■ ■ ■ ■ ■ ■ ■ ■ ■ ■

■ Elliott, K. (2017b). *A tapestry of values: An introduction to values in science.* Oxford, UK: Oxford University Press.
    Describes roles for values in scientific inquiry and examines when their use is legitimate. Draws on case studies from climate science, anthropology,

chemical risk assessment, ecology, neurobiology, biomedical research, and agriculture; although these examples are from the natural and physical sciences, the issues they raise about value commitments are relevant to the social sciences as well. Highlights multiple strategies for fostering engagement between stakeholders so that value influences can be subjected to careful and critical scrutiny.

■ Hammersley, M. (2000). *Taking sides in social research: Essays on partisanship and bias.* New York: Routledge.

Although the text is a bit dated, covers the classic texts on partisanship in sociological research (C. Wright Mills, Becker, Gouldner) and makes a strong case for why partisan social research is unconvincing and untenable and why objectivity and value neutrality must remain regulative ideals.

■ Douglas, H. (2009). *Science, policy and the value-free ideal.* Pittsburgh, PA: University of Pittsburgh Press.

Argues that the moral responsibilities of scientists require consideration of values that are at the heart of the scientific enterprise. She explores the history of the value-free science ideal and argues her case for the direct (illegitimate) and indirect (legitimate) roles of values in scientific reasoning.

■ Douglas, H. (2004). "The irreducible complexity of objectivity." *Synthese,* *138*(3), 453–473. Discusses the seven senses of objectivity that are an alternative to equating objectivity with being value-free.

■ Longino, H. E. (1990). *Science as social knowledge: Values and objectivity in scientific inquiry.* Princeton, NJ: Princeton University Press.

A widely cited work in which Longino develops the argument for the important role that social values play in scientific reasoning, and she develops and defends the view of objectivity as a characteristic of the community of scientists and not the attitude of individual scientists.

■ Proctor, R. N. (1991). *Value-free science? Purity and power in modern knowledge.* Cambridge, MA: Harvard University Press.

A work that readers with interests in the history of the notion of value-free science will find invaluable. Proctor offers an empirical-historical analysis of the notion and explains how it has been used to accomplish different political purposes in different historical periods.

BRIDGE TO PRACTICE

The following brief scenarios are intended to foster discussion of the issues surrounding the role of values in the production of social science knowledge. In the following scenarios, discuss with colleagues whether you agree or disagree with the stance taken and explain why:

• Terry Eagleton in his book *After Theory* (London: Penguin Books, 2004) points to the necessity of value-laden language in enabling us to describe and make sense of the world we experience and observe (pp. 149–150): "To see a situation as abusive or exploitative is inevitably to offer an interpretation of it. We will only see it as such within a certain context of assumptions. Oppression is not there before our eyes in the sense that a patch of purple is." Does this mean that oppression is just a matter of opinion?

- A colleague claims, "Assigning moral values to social phenomena is an inescapable result of being part of society, rendering truly value-free research inconceivable. Despite this fact, sociologists should still strive for value neutrality."

- Value-neutrality does not mean having no opinions, however. It just means that scientists must strive to overcome personal biases, particularly subconscious biases, when analyzing data. It also means that scientists must avoid skewing data in order to match a predetermined outcome that aligns with a particular agenda, such as a political or moral point of view.

- Martyn Hammersley, a strong defender of value-neutrality, argues that the capacity for rational public debate about the values a society should pursue is undermined when researchers and evaluators produce recommendations about social issues and public policies, that is, when they go beyond reporting the facts of the matter, so to speak. He argues that there is no warrant for such action and that presenting value conclusions as if they derived from research amounts to an abuse of scientific authority.

CHAPTER 3

The Conventional Frame
for Evaluating Social Interventions

When one examines and judges accomplishments and effectiveness,
one is engaged in evaluation. When the examination of effectiveness is
conducted systematically and empirically through careful data collection
and thoughtful analysis, one is engaged in evaluation research.
—PATTON (1990, p. 11)

INTRODUCTION

Evaluating conducted in education, social welfare, public health, urban
planning, housing, economic and organizational development, and public
administration is the process of asking and answering questions about the
activities and effectiveness of policies, programs, and projects. The terms
evaluating or evaluation typically cover a broad array of related empirical
investigations, including evaluation research, impact evaluation, performance monitoring, policy evaluation, comparative effectiveness research,
program evaluation, implementation or process evaluation, cost–benefit
and cost–effectiveness analysis, and program auditing. The examples in
Box 3.1 show that evaluating programs and policies is a staple of the work
of federal and state agencies, foundations, and nongovernmental organizations concerned about the effectiveness, efficiency, and impact of the
policies and programs they fund. Eleanor Chelimsky (2006), who served
for many years as the Director of the Institute for Program Evaluation at
the U.S. General Accounting Office (now the Government Accountability
Office, GAO) and later as the Assistant Comptroller General and Director
of the GAO Program Evaluation and Methodology Division, argues that
evaluating in democratic societies ought to serve three purposes: (1) gain
new knowledge useful in program or policy areas, (2) improve agency capa-

BOX 3.1. EXAMPLES OF THE CENTRALITY OF EVALUATION TO PROGRAMMING AND POLICYMAKING

- *Organisation for Economic Co-operation and Development* (OECD Development Assistance Committee, 1991): An evaluation is an assessment, as systematic and objective as possible, of an on-going or completed project, programme, or policy, its design, implementation, and results. The aim is to determine the relevance and fulfilment of objectives, developmental efficiency, effectiveness, impact, and sustainability. An evaluation should provide information that is credible and useful, enabling the incorporation of lessons learned into the decision-making process of both recipients and donors.

- *U.S. Agency for International Development* (USAID, 2016): Evaluation is the systematic collection and analysis of information about the characteristics and outcomes of strategies, projects, and activities as a basis for judgments to improve effectiveness and timed to inform decisions about current and future programming.

- *U.S. Department of Health and Human Services* (HHS): Evaluation and analysis provide essential evidence for HHS to understand how its programs work, for whom, and under what circumstances. HHS builds evidence through evaluation and analysis in order to inform decisions in budget, legislative, regulatory, strategic planning, program, and policy arenas. *https://aspe.hhs.gov/evaluation-evidence*

- *William and Flora Hewlett Foundation:* Evaluation is the independent, systematic investigation of how, why, and to what extent its objectives and goals are being achieved. It is considered a critical part of outcome-focused philanthropy. *https://hewlett.org/value-evaluations-assessing-spending-quality.*

bility in problem solving, and (3) contribute to the determination of agency accountability by examining program effectiveness and efficiency. These purposes remain relevant to and reflective of the aims for evaluating in social science research.

Researchers conduct evaluating in a variety of ways, and there is a rich literature on issues in the methodology, politics, ethics, and use of evaluation (e.g., Alkin, 2013; Mathison, 2005; Schwandt, 2015; Shaw, Greene, & Mark, 2006). Professional evaluation practitioners are familiar with multiple approaches to evaluating, including utilization-focused, evidence-based, culturally responsive, participatory or collaborative, transformative, realist, and developmental, to name a few (see also Fitzpatrick, Worthen, & Sanders, 2011). The practice is growing both nationally and internationally (EvalPartners, n.d.; Nielsen, Lemire, & Christie, 2018) with about 160 national, regional, and international associations and societies of evaluation professionals in 110 countries numbering about 34,000 members collectively.

Across the global practice and the variety of ways of conducting evaluations, a conventional framing for evaluating is discernible. In the language of Martin Rein (1983):

> A frame is a way to understand the things we say and see and act on in the world. It consists of a structure of thought, of evidence, of action, and hence of interests and of values. In brief, a frame integrates theory, facts, interests, and action. . . . A frame . . . deals with the perspective by which we see reality and act on it. . . . (p. 96)

As used here, a frame is a way of representing evaluation knowledge as well as a guide to thought and action with respect to positioning evaluating in policy and program planning and decision making. In the discussion that follows, we use the terms *conventional* and *mainstream* interchangeably to refer to the frame in question, which is a largely taken-for-granted way of thinking about the purpose and function of program and policy evaluation in society.

FEATURES OF THE CONVENTIONAL FRAME

The major characteristics of the mainstream framing of evaluating are discernible in how the frame addresses the following issues: (1) the motivation and rationale for evaluating; (2) the specific questions to be asked about planned interventions; (3) the way in which the scope of and audience for an evaluation is circumscribed; (4) how the activity of evaluating is linked to learning; (5) how interventions are treated as solutions to solvable problems; (6) how evaluation is used to reduce uncertainty via evidence generation; (7) how evaluation researchers adopt a technical and expert-driven role; (8) how stakeholders are treated in evaluation; and (9) how evaluative judgments are understood as determinations of the value of interventions. We discuss each of these features, and we highlight where evaluation theorists and practitioners have challenged these features leading to creative tensions within the field of evaluation. In Chapter 4, we discuss an expansion of the conventional frame that addresses some of these challenges and raises new ones. Then, in Chapter 5, we explore an alternative to this conventional frame.

The Impetus for Evaluating

In its mainstream framing, evaluating is undeniably a modernist undertaking (Schwandt, 2002; Schwandt & Dahler-Larsen, 2006). Contemporary societies embrace the Enlightenment, modernist belief in the power of reason and evidence to "fix things." Evaluation transports, or carries in its ambition as a social undertaking, the idea that no social, political, or economic problem, no set of beliefs, values, or practices is beyond the reach of evaluation—beyond the capacity of critique based on reason and evidence. This redemptive idea is central to the rationale for evaluating in the conventional frame. Improving society by using objective knowledge and providing rational feedback to policymakers and practitioners is a modernist mandate. Evaluation researchers serve as experts providing a special kind of knowledge distinct from the unsystematic and supposedly prejudicial, partisan, and unreflective viewpoints of evaluating that occurs in everyday life.

Social theorists, philosophers, sociologists, and many other scholars have, of course, challenged this idea of achieving social progress through objective knowledge. Scholars in the field of evaluation are no exception. One could read the history of the field over the past 50 years as a history of criticisms of the modernist ideal of evaluating and the subsequent emergence of alternative framings of the undertaking. Evaluation theorist Peter Dahler-Larsen (2012) has undertaken an extensive sociological analysis of the effects of reflexive modernity on evaluation's motivation and self-understanding. Our purpose here is not to retrace that history but to indicate the kinds of challenges that have arisen to specific aspects of what remains a rather durable primary framing of evaluating.

Focus on Empirical Investigations of the Effects of Planned Interventions

In the mainstream framing, evaluating uses the tools of social research (experimental methods, observation, interviewing, statistical analyses, etc.) to conduct "systematic assessment of the operation and/or outcomes of a program or policy, compared to a set of explicit or implicit standards as a means of contributing to the improvement of the program or policy" (Weiss, 1998, p. 4; see also Rossi et al., 2019, p. 1). Programs are the administrative umbrellas of policies through which funds are distributed and regulated, and projects are the local implementation of programs (Shadish, Cook, & Leviton, 1991). Social researchers also refer to policies and programs as interventions. An intervention is an intentionally planned, organized, and implemented activity or set of activities, supported by a set of resources, aimed at ameliorating some social problem or condition by achieving specific and intended objectives and results.

Evaluation in the conventional frame is intervention focused: "The overarching goal of the program evaluation enterprise is to contribute to the improvement of social conditions by providing scientifically credible information and balanced judgment to legitimate social agents about the effectiveness of interventions intended to produce social benefits" (Lipsey

& Cordray, 2000, p. 345). Interventions can be simple or complex and range widely in scope of coverage and targeted audience. Examples of the types of interventions that might be evaluated in the field of public health, for example, are shown in Box 3.2. Similar lists could be developed in the arenas of education, employment, housing, criminal justice, and international development.

Evaluation researchers examine interventions using evidence of implementation, impact, and efficiency based primarily on experimental and quasi-experimental methods and cost–benefit analyses. Also referred to as process evaluation (Leithwood & Montgomery, 1980), the study of implementation examines whether an intervention is operating as designed and planned. Evaluation researchers often refer to implementation as a matter of intervention fidelity and examine it using a detailed multi-step process beginning with the identification of a change model—a model composed of the constructs the intervention designer believes will be involved in the causal process, in the causal relationships the designer envisions. They

---

BOX 3.2. EXAMPLES OF SOCIAL INTERVENTIONS IN THE PUBLIC HEALTH FIELD

- Direct service interventions (e.g., a program that offers free breakfast to improve nutrition for grade school children)
- Community mobilization efforts (e.g., organizing a boycott of California grapes to improve the economic well-being of farm workers)
- Research initiatives (e.g., an effort to find out whether inequities in health outcomes based on race can be reduced)
- Surveillance systems (e.g., whether early detection of school readiness improves educational outcomes)
- Advocacy work (e.g., a campaign to influence the state legislature to pass legislation regarding tobacco control)
- Social marketing campaigns (e.g., a campaign in the Third World encouraging mothers to breast-feed their babies to reduce infant mortality)
- Infrastructure building projects (e.g., a program to build the capacity of state agencies to support community development initiatives)
- Training programs (e.g., a job training program to reduce unemployment in urban neighborhoods)
- Administrative systems (e.g., an incentive program to improve the efficiency of health services)

Note. From U.S. Department of Health and Human Services, Centers for Disease Control and Prevention (2011).

translate that model into a logic model that serves as a road map for implementation, developing appropriate indices of fidelity, and so on (Nelson, Cordray, Hulleman, Darrow, & Sommer, 2012). Implementation evaluation is supported by monitoring—the routine tracking of program inputs, activities, outputs, outcomes, and impacts. Around the globe, it is common to hear governments and nongovernmental agencies refer to their systems of monitoring and evaluation.

Questions about program effectiveness or impact focus on causality, that is, on whether observed effects are attributable to the program in question. What evidence best supports a causal link between program and observed outcomes is an ongoing, contested issue in the field of evaluation. Some evaluators subscribe to the view that when impact evaluations are required of interventions with high stakes and extensive investments, the best and only trustworthy evidence for a causal inference comes from experimental or quasi-experimental designs. Social policy analyst Lisbeth Schorr (2012; Schorr & Farrow, 2011) argues that these evaluators, whom she calls "fundamentalists," are opposed by another group she labels "inclusionists." The latter group recognizes that there are circumstances when evidence from experimental designs in evaluation can be important but relying on these designs exclusively is too narrow to be useful. Schorr (Schorr & Farrow, 2011) argues that a much richer array of evidence coming from practice as well as other types of designs and sources of information is necessary to address complex, multifaceted, evolving problems, including racial disparities in health, high rates of academic failure and school dropout, teen births, substance abuse, family and neighborhood violence, and concentrated poverty. These are problems that cannot be "fixed" by applying a narrowly circumscribed experimental treatment (intervention) but require solutions involving collective impact—broad cross-sector collaboration (Kania & Kramer, 2011)—that, in turn, involves using methods of data gathering that have the following characteristics: (1) allow interventions to be adapted to refine strategy and improve implementation over time, (2) avoid the large costs of randomized trials, (3) obtain measurable results promptly enough to be relevant, and (4) enable stakeholders to learn.

Other researchers focus less on the matter of whether observed outcomes are directly *attributable* to the intervention in question (Rogers, 2014) and more on the issue of whether and how the intervention *contributes* to observed outcomes (Mayne, 2001, 2011). Outcome mapping (Earl, Carden, & Smutylo, 2001) and outcome harvesting (Wilson-Grau & Britt, 2012) are methods useful in this regard. Gates and Dyson (2017) discuss how the conversation about causality in the evaluation field has broadened to include a wider array of causal questions and means of addressing them. These may include process tracing techniques, narrative accounts of an intervention's influence in beneficiaries' lives, evidence of multiple interventions working together to produce outcomes/impacts, or causal loop diagramming of data-based and hypothetical variables. Similarly, in a study commissioned by the UK Department for International Development, Stern and colleagues (2012) explored multiple means other than experimental designs of demonstrating the impact of development interventions. Among those evaluators focused especially on generating evidence of causal impact (e.g., Boruch, 1997; Mark & Henry, 2006), an emphasis on causal attribution, the use of experimental designs, and counterfactual thinking (what would have happened without the intervention) remains strong. However, a broader consensus exists around using an array of methods that provide multiple kinds of evidence to address questions of implementation and impact. That is, rather than claiming that any given method is always the best one to use, the choice of research methods should be matched to specific research questions (Breckon, 2016; Petticrew & Roberts, 2003).

A focus on intervention effectiveness may also include examination of *how* a program achieves its effects. Thus, the concern is not simply whether program goals and objectives were attained but how (i.e., through what processes) effects of all kinds, including intended and unintended results, consequences, and changes, came about. Many evaluators who practice theory-driven evaluation (Chen, 1990; Coryn, Noakes, Westine, & Schröter, 2011; Donaldson, 2007) favor developing this kind of explanation. They aim to explicate and test the theory of an intervention by identifying postulated relationships among inputs, activities, mediating process, outputs, and short- and long-term outcomes, and they gather and analyze data on these relationships to determine whether they in fact occurred.

When researchers examine an intervention for return on investment or value for money (VfM)—that is, "how well are we using resources, and are we using them well enough to justify their use?" (King, 2016, p. 7; King & OPM Vfm Working Group, 2018)—several economic methods for generating evidence are employed. These methods utilize financial and resource data combined with quantitative outcome data, which may be supported by qualitative data capturing stakeholder conceptions of outcomes and their value. Methods include cost–effectiveness analysis that measures costs in monetary terms and consequences in natural or physical units, usually a single quantifiable outcome measure (e.g., years of life saved by a health intervention) and cost–benefit analysis that values all costs and consequences in the same (usually) monetary units (Cordes, 2017; Fleming, 2013; King, 2017, 2019; King & OPM, 2018). In recent years, social return on investment (SROI; Gargani, 2017) has gained in popularity as a means of economic evaluation. SROI takes the financial notion of return on investment and applies it to social and environmental impact, placing a monetary value on the social and/or environmental outcomes of an intervention or service.

Circumscribed Scope and Audience

The reach and influence of evaluation (i.e., the systematic investigation of planned interventions) in the conventional frame is evident in four key features: purpose, users, use, and effect. First, it is "purposive" evaluation, which means that purpose is intrinsic (built in) to the intervention as well as to the evaluation (Reynolds, 2007). The policy, program, or project has predefined goals and intended results, and evaluation employs technical or instrumental reason to assess the means of reaching those goals. Action researcher and evaluator Yoland Wadsworth (2011) explains that mainstream evaluating "starts and ends with existing goals, objectives, and aims and their logically derived indicators, activities and outcomes. Its purpose is 'to check,' that is to answer the questions: Have we done what we set out to do? Is this service, activity, etc., meeting its objectives? What did we set out to achieve? What are the signs we have done this?" (pp. 71–72). Purposive evaluation produces practical, matter-of-fact causal statements of what worked. Purposive evaluation is primarily a methodological matter, that is, a task of applying social science research methods to the study of interventions. It is also measurement focused. The extent to which an intervention was faithfully implemented and intended results or outcomes were achieved is a measurement question, not a valuing question.

Second, the primary intended users for the knowledge generated through evaluating are individuals in positions of authority and influence in government and nongovernmental agencies and philanthropies. These are the individuals who have the responsibility to make policy and programming decisions, develop and change strategies, make expenditures, and change policies. Primary users may also be individuals engaged in some professional practice (e.g., teachers, social workers, mental health counselors). The purpose of providing them with information from evaluating is to inform and improve the decisions they make in their respective practices. For example, knowledge forthcoming from evaluating different ways of teaching reading to elementary students is to provide the teacher with the best way of doing so. Similarly, best ways of practicing social work, mental health counseling, nursing, and so forth are informed through evaluations of the effectiveness of different treatments and services provided by these practitioners.

Third, conventional evaluations limit themselves to consideration of programs and projects that fit within the prevailing social order. Evaluation funders often want a planned intervention studied in such a way that it precludes unconventional and radical conclusions. As Charles Lindblom (1986, p. 362) noted many years ago in his appraisal of the relationship between social research and policymaking, "one of the blindnesses of contemporary research is its assumption that all problems have solutions within the existing institutional order." Consider, for example, the ongoing efforts to engage in and evaluate education reform (including experiments with class size, curriculum, leadership change, voucher programs, charter schools, etc.). These reform efforts unfold largely within a rarely questioned existing social order of institutional and structural racism and white privilege (Feagin, 2013). In contrast, operating outside of the conventional frame, some evaluators see evaluation as a form of criticism and a means of putting social institutions and practices on trial by specifically examining how planned interventions attend to the involvement of poor and marginalized peoples and how they incorporate attention to gender equity, human rights, and social justice in their design and operation (e.g., Segone, 2012).

Fourth, consistent with the literature on path dependence in political science (Howlett & Geist, 2015; Pierson, 2000), evaluating planned interventions unfolds in a context of policy and program continuity rather than wholesale policy and program transformation and change. Path dependence in policymaking means adhering to initial policy and program directions. Because these first choices involve making institutional arrangements (staffing responsibilities, budgets, agreements among agencies, data gathering mechanisms, etc.) reversal of direction from the established path is not easily done. Thus, rather than supporting wholesale program change involving transformation and replacement, conventional evaluating tends to primarily serve incremental program improvement (Shadish et al., 1991). The central function of the conventional framing of evaluation is to support the improvement of the performance of social interventions. It is not primarily to encourage visioning new possibilities, innovation, redefinition of goals, changes in power structures and authority (e.g., from centralized to decentralized decision making), and so on. Several evaluation scholars and practitioners challenge this conventional framing by arguing for the transformation of evaluation itself to address the complexity of social changes and challenges reflected, for example, in the 17 Sustainable Development Goals (SDG). The Evaluation Working Group of the SDG Transformations Forum (2018) claims that

> [e]valuative processes are largely incremental and tend to focus on isolated interventions or portfolios of interventions, rather than on large or global systems change. . . . This means that our evaluative practice itself, and the systems that shape and direct its theories and practices, need to be transformed to reflect the complex challenges posed by issues of inequality, unsustainable consumption patterns, weak governance and more. (p. 2)

Betterment and Learning

Evaluating serves the public interest, broadly envisaged. By informing the decisions of policymakers and practitioners, it contributes to the betterment of society, understood generally as improvement of the human condition, reduction of social problems, and increased meeting of human needs. Mark, Henry, and Julnes (2000) claim that "without the possibility of social betterment, evaluation would be at worst an empty exercise, at best a fulfillment of curiosity," and "that the possibility of social betterment exists is both a personal motivation for evaluators and a critical part of the rationale for the field" (p. 24). However, the mainstream view is quite silent on just what constitutes improvement, except in a rather general way of endorsing stately goals such as serving the public interest, reducing poverty, increasing literacy, combating malnutrition, and improving access to health and education (Schwandt, 2017; Shadish et al., 1991). This high-level commitment is evident, for example, in one of the five Guiding Principles of the American Evaluation Society (*www. eval.org/p/cm/ld/fid=51*) that states, "Evaluators strive to contribute to the common good and advancement of an equitable and just society."

However, betterment or improvement, like serving the public interest or common good, is a normative concept reflecting some conception of desirable social direction and aims and how they are to be realized. For example, is improvement understood as the will of the majority, reflective of some ideally "true" interests of the public, or is it the result of bargaining and negotiating among interest groups? In the conventional evaluation frame of evaluating, policymakers, not evaluators, address these kinds of questions and issues.

The conventional frame for evaluation is instrumental and technical (Marsden & Oakley, 1991) and is primarily a means of determining goal attainment. It is concerned mainly with what is known as single-loop learning in the organization responsible for the program or project being evaluated. In single-loop learning, goals and objectives are considered sound and unquestioned, and evaluating makes use of the best scientific methodologies to assess the relationship between given goals (ends) and the means used (or proposed) to reach those goals. Evaluating contributes to single-loop learning by identifying shortcomings in realizing the desired outcomes of policies and programs and making it possible to correct them by, for example, altering the design of the program, improving its implementation, redefining its target audience, and improving measures of outcomes. Evaluating contributes to this kind of learning while staying largely within the existing framework of stated goals and intended program processes (Rogers & Williams, 2006). In other words, evaluators take program or project goals and objectives for granted. Learning is thus a matter of focusing on adherence to prescribed implementation procedures (referred to as program monitoring); on success in meeting stated goals (outcome evaluation); and, in some situations (where there is a robust theory of how the program is supposed to work) on how programming processes led to meeting stated goals. Overall, however, conventional evaluation addresses the core learning question: "Are we doing things right?"

The mainstream approach may also contribute to what is known as double-loop learning. The learning question then becomes, "Are we doing the right things?" as evaluators question the definition of goals and targets, investigate whether expectations for meeting targets or achieving goals were realistic, and reach beyond assumed principles for program implementation (Hummelbrunner, 2015). Double-loop learning, however, is not common in conventional evaluation. It requires stepping out of the mental model of the conventional frame, including its emphasis on instrumental reasoning and taken-for-granted understandings of the merits of program goals. It also demands more than expertise in social scientific methodologies. It requires skilled facilitation in questioning goals and assumptions with stakeholders. Figure 3.1 displays both learning models.

Critics of the conventional frame offer two challenges to its view of betterment and learning. On the one hand, some evaluators challenge the goal attainment approach as insufficient and claim that a theory-of-change approach (focusing not simply on goal attainment but on the means by which goals are reached) should be used to facilitate double-loop learning. In this alternative framing of evaluating, a theory-of-change approach is more than a road map of how a project or program moves from inputs to activities to outcomes (often referred to as a program theory [Funnel & Rogers, 2011]). Rather, it functions as a tool for reflection among parties to an evaluation (the stakeholders) to uncover and critically investigate assumptions about how change happens, how context and program rationales integrate (or not), and so on (Valters, 2015; Valters, Cummings, & Nixon, 2016). On the other hand, other evaluators deeply committed to the political nature of both program development and program evaluation resist the technical, instrumental approach to determining improvement, question the claims to legitimacy and authority made by experts in policy-making, and address issues of power and culture in the politics of program design, resource distribution, and project management (Hood, Hopson, & Kirkhart, 2015; Marsden & Oakley, 1991).

Social Problem-Solving and Solution-Driven Approach

Theorists and practitioners of the conventional frame value it because it is, ideally at least, straightforwardly connected to policy and program decision making, both of which aim to solve social problems through the design of social interventions. As an essential, scientifically sound tool for informing decision making, evaluating provides evidence useful in policy and program development, implementation, and assessment of consequences, including impact, efficiency, and sustainability (Vedung, 1997; Weiss, 1999).

The conventional orientation to evaluating connects directly to a closed-loop program/project management cycle, as depicted in Figure 3.2. The approach links, in a relationship of interdependence, evaluation researchers and policymakers. As Shadish and colleagues (1991) explain, from a policymaker's point of view "evaluation is part of a problem-solving sequence

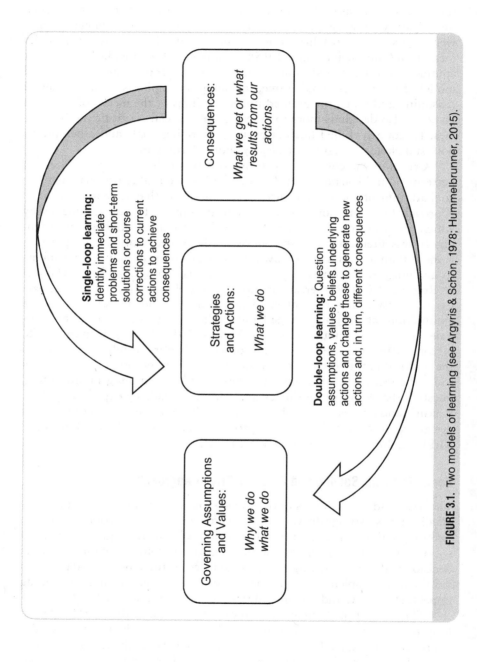

FIGURE 3.1. Two models of learning (see Argyris & Schön, 1978; Hummelbrunner, 2015).

that includes problem definition, solution generation, solution implementation, solution evaluation and solution dissemination" (p. 264). In this framework, a program or project—a closed, controllable entity formulated with a clear purpose and objectives—leads to a problem's solution (Picciotto, 2020). For example, a nurse visitation program that teaches positive health-related behaviors, competent care of children, and family planning for low-income, first-time mothers during pregnancy and children's infancy seeks to solve the problem of teenage pregnancy, insufficient postnatal care, as well as inadequate cognitive development of infants. Monitoring data helps to guide implementation, and evaluation examines whether the program *qua* solution achieved intended results (and in some cases whether unintended effects were observed as well).

The conventional frame of evaluating is also wedded to a policymaking perspective that treats the major issues confronting society as matters of social ill-health. Social problems such as racial discrimination, the achievement gap in education, poverty, public health, immigration, criminal justice reform, and well-being of children and families are social ills requiring remedies in the form of solutions. In the view of critics, this problems-and-their-remedies way of thinking ignores the notion that so-called problems "amount to contests between various groups over the control of desirable resources, including wealth, privilege and, above all, the application of political power" (Rule, 1971, p. 47). Critics argue that major social issues are essentially political in nature and cannot be resolved apolitically through the use of expert-designed-and-evaluated interventions.

Evaluating in the conventional frame involves several additional assumptions about social problem solving, including: (1) social problems function independently such that policymakers/practitioners can address

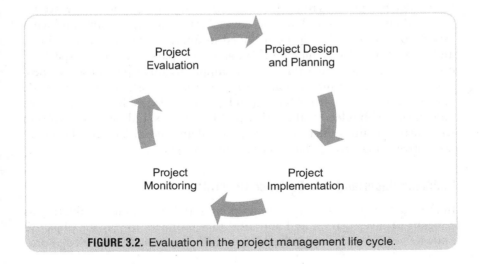

FIGURE 3.2. Evaluation in the project management life cycle.

them and evaluators can evaluate their solutions independently of other problems (and their alleged solutions); (2) a problem remains relatively stable over time and across levels of analysis (e.g., location, size, scale); (3) the "right" solution will reduce or eliminate the problem altogether; and (4) evaluation activity primarily appraises solutions to already defined problems.

This union of evaluation with a problem-solving, solution-driven approach to project planning and management does not mean that social researchers concerned with social problem solving might not first attempt to understand the problem at hand, assess its extent, define and identify the targets (e.g., individuals, families, communities) that an intervention aims to address, and examine and describe the service needs of these target populations (Rossi et al., 2019). Evaluators may devote efforts to context and problem clarification (Newcomer, Hatry, & Wholey, 2015; Rog, 2012). Some evaluation scholars urge greater attention to problem definition for political reasons—that is, understanding the cultural context in which a problem is considered to be a problem, by whom, and why, and so forth (e.g., Archibald, 2020; Kirkhart, 2010; SenGupta, Hopson, & Thompson-Robinson, 2004). Yet, few of these efforts involve the use of problem-structuring methods as discussed in the literatures on participatory methods in social science (e.g., Chambers, 2017), deliberative planning and policymaking processes (e.g., Hajer & Wagenaar, 2003), and operations research. Problem structuring refers to techniques and processes for moving from a situation characterized by differing perspectives, multiple and changing evidence, and some degree of uncertainty to consensus or a negotiated decision about how to bound and frame the situation into a problem that lends itself to inquiry and action. Some operational researchers, action researchers, and urban planners, for example, use these methods to broaden perspectives to facilitate new framings of a problem, new strategies, and new actions, and include asking "(1) Whose viewpoints and what aspects of the issue should be included in analysis and decision making, and what should be excluded; (2) What are people's different perspectives on the issue, and what values and assumptions underpin those perspectives; and (3) What interactions within and across organisational, social and environmental phenomena could produce desirable or undesirable outcomes?" (Midgley et al., 2013, p. 144). This standpoint on problem structuring signifies the profoundly political and moral (i.e., conflicts over normative perspectives) character of problem solving.

Reducing Uncertainty via Evidence Generation

In the mainstream orientation, practitioners and funders use evaluating as a means of investigation and appraisal that promises to provide objective knowledge and rational feedback to decision makers. As knowledge producers, evaluators create and supply scientifically sound information that aims to meet decision makers' (consumers') demand for that information, as depicted in Figure 3.3. The purposive evaluation of planned interventions acquires social significance in a market model of giving scientific advice. In addition to a near-exclusive focus on cognitive matters—generating knowledge of the effectiveness and efficiency of policies, programs, and projects—evaluation researchers are concerned with the utilization of their work and its downstream impact on decision making in policy and practice. Larry Orr, the author of the widely known text *Social Experiments: Evaluating Public Programs with Experimental Methods,* explains that evaluators do not traffic in the kinds of value-rational questions characteristic of problem-structuring activities, but rather keep their eyes on the prize of obtaining evidence:

> Faced with a proposal for a new program or policy, decision-makers must ask crucial questions. What is its objective? Is that objective desirable? And if so, will this program or policy achieve that objective? The first two questions call for value judgments, and I have little to say about them. But the third calls for evidence. Only by examining evidence can we hope to learn whether an intervention achieves its objectives. The role of evaluation is to provide and interpret that evidence. (2018, p. 31)

Evaluators in the conventional frame focus on eliminating uncertainty in decision making by providing evidence on whether the proposed solution to a social problem "worked"—that is, whether the intervention achieved its intended outcomes. Former co-chair of the U.S. Commission on Evidence-

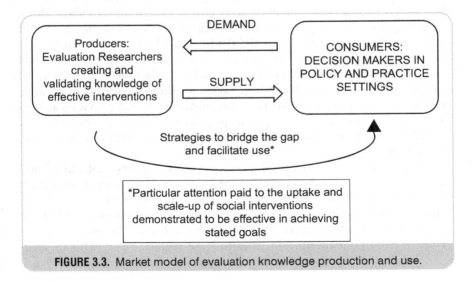

FIGURE 3.3. Market model of evaluation knowledge production and use.

Based Policymaking, Ron Haskins (2018, p. 9), explains, "We have a set of scientific methods, the most important and useful of which is the random assignment experiment, which allow the field to determine in a reliable way whether our social programs are effective. Without this capacity, it would be nearly impossible to fix social problems—and to know when we are doing so." Paul Cairney (2019), a professor of politics and public policy who studies policymaking processes, further clarifies this focus on producing an evidence base by noting that "reducing uncertainty can be thought of as a technical process through which to address an already well-defined policy problem: supplying the best evidence and delivering it to the right people at the right time" (p. 1).

The most valued evaluation evidence in the conventional frame is evidence of what worked (broadly understood to encompass matters of goal achievement, impact, outcomes, and efficiency) to make better decisions in both practice and policymaking. Ideally, evaluating interventions yields best practices that can become the foundation of practitioner and policymaker action. Such is the logic behind the establishment of evaluation registries such as the U.S. Department of Labor's Clearinghouse for Labor Evaluation and Research (CLEAR), a repository of evaluations of studies on labor practices; the California Evidence-Based Clearinghouse for Child Welfare; the What Works Clearinghouse of the U.S. Department of Education's Institute of Education Sciences; and the Campbell Collaboration, the international social science research network that produces policy-relevant evidence syntheses in the fields of education, crime and justice, disability, and social welfare.

Typically, the methodology of "what works" is a matter of determining whether observed effects are attributable to a given intervention. Given this focus on testing causal hypotheses, many evaluators, particularly those evaluating programs in international development—for example, the Abdul Latif Jameel Poverty Action Lab and the International Initiative for Impact Assessment (3ie)—advocate the use of randomized controlled field trials (RCFTs) and econometric methods (Abadie & Cattaneo, 2018; Lance, Guilkey, Hattori, & Angeles, 2014). Likewise, there is significant reliance on evidence–synthesis methods that may involve systematic reviews as well as the construction of evidence-gap maps (Saran & White, 2018; Snilstveit, Bhatia, Ranking, & Leach, 2017; Snilstveit, Vojtkoa, Bhavsar, Stevenson, & Gaarder, 2016).

In examining the effects of interventions in the fields of public and behavioral health as well as clinical medicine, evaluators working within the conventional frame often appeal to the notion of a hierarchy of evidence (as used in clinical medicine) to decide what constitutes good or the best evidence. Evidence from RCTFs sits at the top of the hierarchy, and evidence from nonexperimental studies (case studies, observational studies, etc.) places far lower down in importance. Specific evidence hierarchies have been developed for use in a variety of organizations including GRADE (Grading of Recommendations Assessment, Development and Evaluation) and GRADE-CERQual (Confidence in the Evidence from Reviews of Qualitative Research), a recently developed companion framework to GRADE to examine findings from a body of qualitative studies, and the Evidence to Decision Framework (EtD; Alonso-Coello et al., 2016; Guyatt et al., 2008a, 2008b; National Academies of Sciences, Engineering, and Medicine, 2019).

This focus on building an evaluation evidence base through near-exclusive reliance on experimental methods and meta-analyses is not an uncontroversial issue, as is evident from decades of literature examining the meaning, merits and shortcomings of using such methods in education, social work, nursing, clinical medicine, international development, and behavioral health. The central issues appear to be these:

1. Given what are often the practical and ethical difficulties of implementing experimental designs with random assignment, some authors advise evaluation researchers to consider ways of examining causal hypotheses using means other than experimental studies, for example, process tracing and case-based approaches such as qualitative comparative analysis (e.g., Gates & Dyson, 2017; Rihoux & Ragin, 2008; Stern et al., 2012).

2. The focus on evidence from experimental studies alone is too narrow to be useful given the multifaceted, complex problems addressed in social welfare (e.g., poverty, homelessness, access to public health services, child and family welfare). Evidence from multiple types of studies is needed as, for example, is found in the review of the effectiveness of after-school programs, scout groups, and other community-service activities on youth development (National Research Council & Institute of Medicine, 2002). The evaluation researcher operates at a disadvantage by not accepting and practicing methodological and methods pluralism (Midgley, 2000) because the causality underlying the real problems that policymakers and public organizations face is often much too complex to be captured by one type of methodology (Gilad, 2019; Lawrenz & Huffman, 2006; Schorr & Farrow, 2011).

3. A strict focus on assembling an evidence base for policymaking and professional practice and assuming decisions in both arenas will become more rational as a result reflects a rather naïve, narrow notion of rational behavior. In the world of realpolitik, a direct, linear, highly rational relationship between evidence and decision making does not comport with the fact that policymaking involves an array of nonscientific considerations, including political considerations and value preferences (DuMont, 2015;

Gamoran, 2018). Evidence of intervention effectiveness is but one input to a complex process of forming a policy argument (Prewitt, Schwandt, & Straf, 2012). Policy decisions involve competing sets of concerns such as social desirability and acceptability, impact on individual liberties, human rights, and equity and not just evidence of what works (Parkhurst & Abeysinghe, 2016). In professional practices, this concern is manifest in calls for practice-based evidence as a complement to evidence-based practice (Ammerman, Smith, & Calancie, 2014; Green, 2006). A report from the National Research Council (Prewitt et al., 2012, p. 14) examining the use of scientific evidence in policymaking argued for a switch from the language of evidence-based policy to evidence-influenced politics. The change in terminology better describes what happens when scientific evidence enters political deliberations about policy options. The term also signals the obligation of scientists to legitimately advocate that policymakers attend to warranted scientific knowledge related to social problems and their solutions.

4. While evidence itself requires appraisal, this occurs too rarely (Parkhurst, 2017, is a notable exception). For example, considering specifically the use of evidence in health policymaking, Hawkins and Parkhurst (2016) argue that the following four components are required for the "good governance" of evidence: (a) Consider appropriate evidence, that is, evidence addressing the multiple political considerations relevant to a policy decision; (b) attend to accountability in evidence use to ensure use reaches back to citizens; (c) foster transparency in order to open evidence use to scrutiny; and (d) be open to contestability, that is, appeals processes and opportunities for public debate.

Finally, in the mainstream frame, evaluators and other applied researchers are also concerned with making sure there are no major gaps between the supply of and demand for evidence. Thus, they pay considerable attention to the means of successfully bridging the demand–supply gap through translation science, the use of knowledge brokers, communication strategies, and other processes to improve the relationship between evaluators/researchers and policymakers so as to lead to improved use of evidence. The National Academies of Science, Engineering, and Medicine (2017a), for example, has a standing committee on the Science of Science Communication. The extensive social science literature in knowledge utilization (e.g., Boswell & Smith, 2017; Green, Ottoson, Garcia, & Hiatt, 2009; Nutley, Walter, & Davies, 2007) addressing these concerns is complemented by an equally extensive literature specifically addressed to evaluation use (Alkin & King, 2017; Contandriopoulos & Brousselle, 2012; Cullen & Coryn, 2011; King & Alkin, 2018).

Technical, Expert-Driven Approach

Social scientist Donald Campbell (1971, p. 133; see also Campbell, 1969) argued for an experimental approach to social problem solving "in which we try out new programs designed to cure specific social problems . . . in which we retain, imitate, modify, or discard them on the basis of apparent effectiveness on the multiple imperfect criteria available." Although in an experimenting society not all intervention-focused evaluation relies exclusively on experimental methods, the general idea of experimenting as rigorous testing of interventions to validate them as potential remedies for social problems persists. The kind of "testing" that yields evaluative judgments in intervention-focused evaluation rests on both explicit and implicit appeals to professional expertise. Technically trained knowledge elites employed in universities, think tanks, private-sector firms, government agencies, and research firms conduct evaluations making use of instrumental rationality to calculate the effectiveness and efficiency of means to achieve given ends (Dryzek, 1993). Broadly speaking, these experts present their technical training and evaluation knowledge as an alternative to politics, supporting a view of decision making as technical rather than marked by clashing interests, conflict, and compromise. Evaluators cite their theoretical and methodological expertise as justification for the claims they make about the objective necessity of their evaluative judgments as well as about their personal objectivity and impartiality. The authority of the expert evaluator takes precedence over ordinary, lay knowledge.

The buying and selling of expertise in evaluating also rests on a traditional conception of the professional–client relationship. Fischer (1993) explains that this relationship is

> a set of superior-subordinate interactions founded upon the professional's scientific and technical expertise. Conferring authority, status, and legitimacy on the professional, the relationship functions as a two-sided agreement or understanding, formal or informal. On the professional side of this understanding, experts agree to deliver their services to the limits of their competence, to respect the confidences of their clients, and not to misuse for their own benefit the special powers accorded to them by the relationship. In return, the clients agree to accept the professional's authority in specific areas of expertise, to submit to the professional's ministrations, and, of course, to pay for services rendered. (p. 168)

Stakeholder Participation

In the evaluation literature, stakeholders are individuals or groups that have an interest in or are affected by an evaluation and include policymakers, funders, program developers, administrators and managers, intended beneficiaries of a program, and the general public. Their involvement, to one degree or another, in an evaluation is standard practice (Gregory, 2000; Rebien, 1996; Reineke, 1991). Evaluators in the conventional frame consider stakeholder involvement in evaluation—beyond the rather passive role of providing information—beneficial because of its instrumental value in achieving other important evaluation objectives including open communication, learning, and enhanced potential for evaluation use. Thus, stakeholders may be involved in developing evaluation questions, selecting appropriate and acceptable evaluation methods, reviewing evaluation findings, and making recommendations. Practical and pragmatic reasons for involvement include reducing stakeholders' distrust and fear of evaluation, increasing stakeholders' awareness of and commitment to the evaluation process, gaining commitments from stakeholders on what they perceive as relevant and credible data and evidence, enhancing the acceptance of evaluation judgments, and increasing the chances that evaluation findings will be used (Cousins & Whitmore, 1998; see also Shulha, Whitmore, Cousins, Gilbert, & al Hudib, 2016).

This conventional view of stakeholder participation contrasts with that of other evaluators who regard the involvement of stakeholders as an intrinsic good and consider any effort to evaluate as fundamentally flawed if it is not, for the most part, driven by key stakeholders. Often, the stakeholding groups of greatest interest are those most directly affected by the program evaluated (Hood et al., 2015; Mertens, 2009). Stakeholder involvement is defended not simply on the grounds of local "buy-in" to an evaluation but also especially in terms of empowering stakeholders through participation as found, for example, in the tradition of participatory action research (PAR) (Fals-Borda & Anisur Rahman, 1991; Freire, 1970). Compared to PAR, the mainstream frame pays little attention to how the production of evaluation knowledge (judgments) and power are intertwined and how wider cultural, political, and economic systems shape the development and implementation of planned interventions (e.g., Taylor & Balloch, 2005).

Evaluating as Determining Performance

In the conventional framing of evaluation, the value of a planned intervention is a matter of documenting the intervention's performance. Performance is defined as effectiveness. Effectiveness means that the program solves (or adequately addresses) a social problem. Thus, social problem solving is the primary criterion of interest. Effectiveness is determined by some means of comparison, either comparing outcomes for a group that receives a planned intervention to outcomes for a group that does not receive it (e.g., a placebo group) or comparing groups that receive two different interventions, each with the same intended outcomes. In either circumstance, an effective program is judged as performing better than its alternative(s).

An evaluator is responsible for resolving the question of the performance of an intervention. Following the *Oxford English Dictionary,* the term *resolving* signifies a conviction and connotes certainty and the removal of doubt. Resolving an intervention's value is necessary, for if one cannot determine clearly and definitively what worked, then such an intervention cannot serve as a useful means of social problem solving and be included in a registry of evidence-based practices. Thus, in the conventional frame, there is little or no room to be hesitant or indecisive or to have misgivings about the assessment of value. Nor are judgments of the value of interventions regarded as matters that are inherently contestable, contested, or open-ended. The level of confidence and certainty in evaluative claims is attributable to scientific procedures employed by the evaluation researcher, including the study design, instruments, and statistical analyses used. Resolving an intervention's value is thus primarily an empirical matter. The roles and responsibilities of evaluation researchers working in the conventional frame do not include making normative judgments on whether the intervention evaluated should be something undertaken by society or appraisals of the ethical and political values embedded in the intervention.

SUMMARY

A half-century ago, surveying the state of the art of evaluation at the time, social scientists Carol Weiss and Martin Rein (1970, p. 97) observed that "there is an approach to the evaluation of social programs which seems so sensible that it has been accepted without question. The underlying assumption is that action programs are designed to achieve specific ends and that their success can be established by demonstrating cause–effect relationships between the programs and their aims." Weiss and Rein would go on to criticize this approach on methodological grounds, and as noted in this chapter, subsequent years revealed additional criticisms and challenges. Yet, 50 years later the conventional frame for evaluating, writ large, endures in some fields of study and in some institutions. For example, criminal justice evaluation (Tilley & Clarke, 2006) tends to focus on systematic, rigorous studies of the association between an intervention (e.g., policy change, policing practice, victim services) and the reduction of crime by potential and known offenders and other trends in crime. The Crime and Justice Coordinating Group of the Campbell Collaboration (*https://campbellcollaboration.org/contact/coordinating-groups/crime-and-justice.html*) prepares systematic reviews of interventions aimed at the prevention, treatment, or control of crime or delinquency. Similarly, the What Works Clearinghouse of the U.S. Institute of Education Sciences (*https://ies.ed.gov/ncee/wwc*) supports evaluations that answer the question of "What works in education?" and is a leading federal source of evidence-based information about education programs, policies, and interventions that show promise for improving student outcomes. In the field of public health, as illustrated in the online learning program evaluation module for Boston University's Master in Public Health degree (*https://sphweb.bumc. bu.edu/otlt/mphmodules/ProgramEvaluation/ProgramEvaluation2.html*), a common understanding is that evaluations answer several basic questions: "Is the program meeting its intended objectives?" "Through the originally intended process?" "Why or why not?" As a nongovernmental organization, the International Initiative for Impact Evaluation (3ie) both funds and produces rigorous evaluations of development effectiveness, specifically what works, for whom, why, and at what cost.

The conventional frame endures largely because of a belief that social problems are amenable to technical problem solving and scientific expertise. As noted by political scientist Frank Fischer (2007, p. 224), the conventional frame treats difficult economic and social problems "as issues in need of improvement management and better program design; their solutions are to be found in better collection of data and the application of technical decision approaches." The strength of that belief in professional practices was described in a different way by the organizational theorist Donald Schön (1992) who noted, "In the varied topography of professional practice, there is a high, hard ground which overlooks a swamp. On the high ground, manageable problems lend themselves to solution through the use of research-based theory and technique. In the swampy lowlands, problems are messy and confusing and incapable of technical solution" (p. 54).

The conventional frame in the field of evaluation has more in common with the high, hard ground of technical problem solving than the swampy lowlands. It is wedded to an analytical approach linked to a program/project management cycle, and its principal aim is to determine whether a program/project was implemented as planned and whether objectives were met. If evaluating reveals that an intervention was successful, ideally it can become designated as a best practice and can be recommended for use in circumstances other than the one in which the original evaluation took place. In the mainstream frame, the knowledge that evaluating generates can be highly technical to the nonexpert. Hence, evaluation researchers pay special attention to ensuring that such knowledge is well communicated, understood, and usable by policymakers and practitioners.

IMPORTANT RESOURCES ▪ ▪ ▪ ▪ ▪ ▪ ▪ ▪ ▪ ▪ ▪ ▪ ▪ ▪ ▪ ▪ ▪

▪ Rossi, R. H., Lipsey, M. W., and Henry, G. T. (2019). *Evaluation: A systematic approach* (8th ed.). Thousand Oaks, CA: Sage.

A comprehensive text on evaluation research. Chapters are dedicated to explaining the rationale for program evaluation, addressing social problems targeted by a program, developing program theory, and evaluating implementation, outcomes, impact, and efficiency. It illustrates the mainstream frame for evaluating.

- *Annals of the American Academy of Political and Social Science*, July 2018.

  Presents 17 papers prepared by leading experts and policymakers committed to evidence-based policy approaches. The papers explore the history of the movement, its key assumptions and empirical bases, and the role played by evaluation research.

- Julnes, G., and Rog, D. (Eds.). (2007). Informing federal policies on evaluation methodology: Building the evidence base for method choice in government sponsored evaluation. *New Directions for Evaluation, 113*.

  Seven papers that examine the issue of the choice of evaluation methods to generate evidence to inform decision making, with a specific focus on the merits and limitations of using randomized experiments.

BRIDGE TO PRACTICE: Making the Case for or against the Mainstream Frame of Evaluating

Select a guide in your field of research that describes the relationship between program evaluations and evidence-based decision making in ways useful not simply to evaluation researchers but to policymakers and practitioners as well. Here are some possibilities:

1. Pew–MacArthur Results First Initiative "Targeted evaluations can help policymakers set priorities," available at *www.pewtrusts.org/en/research-and-analysis/issue-briefs/2018/03/targeted-evaluations-can-help-policymakers-set-priorities.*

2. Australian Government, Australian Institute of Family Studies, "Evidence-based practice and service-based evaluation," available at *https://aifs.gov.au/cfca/publications/evidence-based-practice-and-service-based-evaluation.*

3. Urban Institute, "Principles of evidence-based policymaking," September 2016 available at *www.urban.org/sites/default/files/publication/99739/principles_of_evidence-based_policymaking.pdf.*

Then review the following article that discusses some of the problems and limitations of the evidence-based policymaking movement: Brian W. Head (2010), Reconsidering evidence-based policy: Key issues and challenges, *Policy and Society, 29*(2), 77–94.

Reflect on your own views of the evidence-based policymaking movement and the conventional frame for evaluating as discussed in this chapter. What do you see as the advantages of this way of thinking about evaluating social policies, programs, and other change initiatives? What are some of the disadvantages and criticisms? Then, consider and carry out one of the following options:

- Prepare a two-page research brief directed at convincing a commissioner of evaluation (or other users) of the merits of the conventional frame for evaluating or of the rationale for *not* using this conventional approach and conducting evaluation in some other way.

- Reflect on a situation you were involved in or heard about in which a social intervention was being evaluated. Consider whether and how aspects of the conventional frame were at play (or not) in the way the evaluation was scoped, designed, and carried out. Why do you think the conventional frame was (or was not) at play?

- Discuss with others your views on the conventional frame for evaluating. Clearly articulate your position or perspective and back it up with reasonable arguments. Hear others out and together develop an understanding of the merits and drawbacks of this frame.

CHAPTER 4

Expanding the Conventional Frame for Evaluating

Evaluation . . . is much more than applied social science research.
E-*valu*-ation . . . involves not only collecting descriptive information
about a program, product, or other entity but also using . . . values
to (a) determine what information should be collected and (b) draw
explicitly evaluative inferences from the data, that is, inferences that
say something about the quality, value, or importance of something.
                                    —DAVIDSON (2005, p. xi, original emphasis)

INTRODUCTION

The features of the conventional frame for evaluating are no doubt familiar to researchers in sociology, psychology, education, public health, criminal justice, and political science who are well prepared in social science
research methodology. They are likely to see themselves applying the tools
of their trade in service of determining the value of planned interventions.
The primary value of interest in this research is the instrumental value of an
intervention. The intervention is a means to some desired end or result, and
its value (worth, significance) is usually determined in terms of its effectiveness and efficiency in reaching that end. Evaluations informed by the conventional frame share a focus on answering positive questions about social
interventions—descriptive and causal questions about what has happened
and why. These evaluations may also address questions like those asked in
performance auditing. These are questions that invite comparison of performance to some standard, for example, "Is the program operating as
intended" (or "Have the right things been done")? and "Have things been
done in the right way?" In the conventional frame for evaluating, value
judgments other than instrumental ones are considered arbitrary, subjective, and unscientific and thus violate the stance of value-neutrality. In

other words, an evaluation might ask the positive question, "Does a higher minimum wage cause higher youth unemployment?" but not the normative question, "Are higher minimum wages better for young workers?"

There is nothing inherently misguided about assessing instrumental value through evaluation. To take a simple example, we want to know if our washing machines get our clothes clean at a reasonable price and with limited use of energy. Regarding much more complicated policy issues, we want to know if the United States Welfare to Work legislation introduced in the mid-1990s helped people move from relying on government assistance to gainful employment, and, more recently, if cash payments made to individuals under the CARES Act in the United States during the COVID-19 crisis actually kept individuals from descending into poverty.

However, both the concept and practice of evaluating interventions have expanded considerably beyond this way of thinking of evaluation as applied social science. A variety of evaluation theorists and practitioners have endeavored to develop evaluation as a distinct kind of professional practice. Specifically, a practice that, while employing the traditional methods of the social sciences, attends carefully to several additional considerations having to do with matters of criteria, politics, use, and stakeholder involvement. In this chapter, we introduce these kinds of expansions of the conventional frame, beginning with a singular effort to distinguish professional evaluation from social research. We then use that effort as a cornerstone of sorts from which to explore other developments in what we refer to as the science of evaluating. These developments include (1) aligning evaluation with critical thinking and bias control; (2) expanding criteria for evaluating beyond achieving intended results and stated goals; (3) increasing stakeholder involvement in evaluation practice and expanding the audience for evaluation findings and use; (4) developing standards as the basis for making evaluative judgments; and (5) questioning who bears the responsibility for rendering evaluation judgments.

DISTINGUISHING EVALUATING FROM SOCIAL RESEARCH

Philosopher Michael Scriven (1959, 1991, 1994a, 2007, 2012, 2016a) is a primary pioneer, developer, and apologist for the science of evaluation across all fields of human endeavor. According to Scriven, evaluators are (or ought to be) in the business of appraising essential or real-value claims— claims that are not matters of mere preference but tangible and robust— about everything from arguments to personnel, to products, to programs, to policies. That kind of appraisal should not be arbitrary but should be done conscientiously, objectively, and accurately (Scriven, 1994a). To distinguish evaluating from social research, Scriven (2003) argued that it is not simply a matter of determining facts about states of affairs, that is, "What's so?", or their effects "Why so?"; rather, "an evaluation must, by definition, lead to *a particular type* of conclusion—one about merit, worth, or significance—usually expressed in the language of good/bad, better/worse, well/ill, elegantly/poorly, etc." (p. 16, original emphasis). These evaluative conclusions require combining value-based evidence with performance data. Value-based evidence consists in the preference claims of individuals and groups commonly examined in anthropological and sociological studies; these claims take the form of "I (we) value, prefer, endorse, want X." For example, we value safety in children's toys; we want to better serve the homeless population in our community; and so on.

Scriven (1972) uses the example of evaluating the merits of a life insurance policy to illustrate that value-based evidence would include the purchaser's expressed needs, economic abilities, and expectations (e.g., tax treatment of the policy, payout options). Performance data would involve examining alternative policies that might be purchased for their features relative to the value preferences of the purchaser. The two would be combined to reach a nonarbitrary evaluative conclusion to the effect that "policy ABC is the best for you." Scriven's central argument is that "value claims can be based on reason, properly understood, and that they can be objective in a straightforward sense of that word" (House & Howe, 1999, p. 5).

The key issue in defining evaluating is that of making an evaluative judgment, that is, an inference about merit, worth, importance, or significance based on factual premises. Scriven (1994b) defines this type of inference as follows:

> If the performance of X on criteria A, B, C, etc. is high (these being all the leading criteria), and there is no evidence of Q, R, or S (these being all of the serious threats to the inference, that is, most of the possibilities excluded by the ceteris paribus consideration), then one may conclude that the evaluand is a prima facie good (better, best, competent, etc.) X, i.e., the object being evaluated. (p. 373)

To explain how such an inference is justified, Scriven proposed the logic of evaluation (Fournier, 1995; Scriven, 2005) depicted in Figure 4.1. This is a probative (vs. deductive) logic, meaning it is the kind of practical reasoning we use in everyday pursuits in law, teaching, and so on (Scriven, 1994b). Douglas Walton (2008), who has written extensively about informal logic, refers to this kind of reasoning as what takes place "in the real marketplace of persuasion on controversial issues in politics, law, science, and all aspects of daily life" (p. xi). As a probative inference, an evaluative judgment lacks the kind of support that we would say entitles it to the status of being "provable" beyond a reasonable doubt. Probative inferences demonstrate or tend to substantiate a conclusion (Scriven, 2005, 2009) but not guarantee or irrefutably prove a conclusion. Nonetheless, they have more

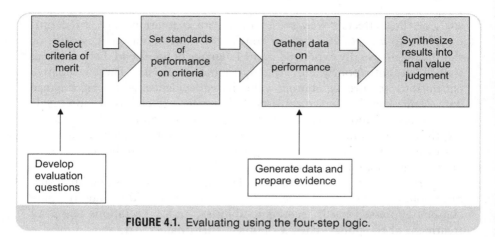

FIGURE 4.1. Evaluating using the four-step logic.

than enough support to justify the contention that they are as well supported (Scriven, 2005). It is enough for the inference drawn that the data
and evidence point in a certain direction and that no significant evidence is
pointing in an opposite direction (Scriven, 2000). Evaluative judgments are
similar in kind to the claims resulting from a Toulmin (2003/1958) model
of practical argument—that is, they make a *prima facie* case for a conclusion; they are presumptive (plausible, reasonable) given available evidence,
consideration of context and qualifiers, and anticipating rebuttals. Jane
Davidson (2005, p. xv) adds that evaluative judgments are " 'demonstrably'
true when a solid mix of evidence supports a conclusion at or above the
level of certainty required in [a given] decision-making context."

Following Scriven's lead, Jane Davidson (2005, 2014a, 2014b) emphasizes that absent efforts to follow this logic and to use evaluation-specific
methodologies (discussed below), one is not actually doing evaluation.
Use of the logic separates genuine evaluation from mere data collection or
information gathering. In Scriven's (1994b) view, this logic, particularly
given its emphasis on empirically based reasoning, is an antidote to the
potential overreliance of evaluators on professional judgment, intuition,
connoisseurship, and impressionism.

THE RELEVANCE OF CRITICAL THINKING AND BIAS CONTROL

Scriven's way of defining evaluation shifts the focus of that professional
practice from what are principally methodological concerns in the conventional frame to logical and rational concerns. This shift also aligns the
activity of evaluating with critical thinking and careful attention to bias
control.

Although there is no single agreed-upon definition of critical thinking, Scriven has contributed to its definition in multiple ways. In a statement he coauthored with Richard Paul (former Director of Research and Professional Development at the Center for Critical Thinking), presented in 1987 at the 8th Annual International Conference on Critical Thinking, critical thinking was defined as

> the intellectually disciplined process of actively and skillfully conceptualizing, applying, analyzing, synthesizing, and/or evaluating information gathered from, or generated by, observation, experience, reflection, reasoning, or communication, as a guide to belief and action. In its exemplary form, it is based on universal intellectual values that transcend subject matter divisions: clarity, accuracy, precision, consistency, relevance, sound evidence, good reasons, depth, breadth, and fairness. (*www.criticalthinking.org/pages/defining-critical-thinking/766*)

Fisher and Scriven (1997, p. 20) defined critical thinking as "the skilled, active interpretation and evaluation of observations, communications, information and argumentation." The term *skilled* signifies that standards of quality must be met before something qualifies as critical thinking. The logic of evaluative reasoning discussed in this chapter is an example of what standards of quality (an "intellectually disciplined process") would look like in using critical thinking in evaluation. Scriven emphasizes the normative character of critical thinking. That means it is a form of "good" thinking that requires skills, abilities, and dispositions (e.g., valuing good reasoning, open- and fair-mindedness). The emphasis on critical thinking as a type of thinking that meets certain criteria of acceptability is different than the more commonly discussed psychological account that is largely a descriptive rendering of psychological process and procedures regarded as central to critical thinking (Bailin & Siegel, 2003). Recent scholarship on evaluation practice joins critical thinking directly with evaluative reasoning as a cognitive process:

> Evaluative thinking is critical thinking applied in the context of evaluation, motivated by an attitude of inquisitiveness and a belief in the value of evidence, that involves identifying assumptions, posing thoughtful questions, pursuing deeper understanding through reflection and perspective taking, and informing decisions in preparation for action. (Buckley, Archibald, Hargreaves, & Trochim, 2015, p. 378)

Evaluative thinking and learning to think evaluatively are about evaluators developing and exercising higher-order thinking skills, relying on intellectual habits (open-mindedness, confidence in reason, respect for evidence, probing ideas, curiosity, imagination, etc.), and employing the logic of evaluating to arrive at or account for judgments of value. In the literature in evaluation, evaluative thinking, reasoning, and making sense of claims (as well as data, evidence, assumptions, and arguments) are portrayed mainly as individual or solo cognitive affairs. Of course, evaluators encourage the development and refinement of these skills in stakeholders, and many are keen to help organizations establish the conditions where these skills and dispositions are incorporated into organizational norms and routines. Yet, the primary focus is on critical thinking as a cognitive skill set and collection of intellectual virtues practiced by the professional evaluator (Scriven, 2016a).

Critical thinking in evaluation plays important roles, not least of which is to help form judgments about the magnitude and direction of potential sources of bias that unaddressed could lead to faulty evaluative judgments (House, 2015, 2020; Scriven, 1976, 2016b). Cognitive biases (Kahneman, 2011) particularly relevant when making evaluative judgments include anchoring bias (the tendency to rely too heavily on the first piece of information offered in forming an evaluative judgment or reaching a conclusion); confirmation bias (attending only to perspectives and data that confirm preexisting views while ignoring or dismissing perspectives and data that threaten those views); and cultural bias (e.g., ethnocentrism—interpreting practices, values, and standards in light of one's own cultural norms).

FROM GOALS- AND OBJECTIVE-FOCUSED TO QUESTION- AND CRITERIA-DRIVEN EVALUATING

Criteria are expressions of what parties to an evaluation value when examining the thing to be evaluated; they are, in effect, dimensions of merit. As the Davidson quote at the beginning of this chapter showed, these values *qua* criteria determine what data an evaluator should collect. For example, *Consumer Reports* evaluates automobiles on multiple criteria including fuel economy, acceleration, braking, and handling; and it uses the criterion of reliability based on users' ratings. Most readers are likely to be familiar with the idea of evaluating a scientific theory on the basis of criteria that scientists generally agree are important such as parsimony, testability, internal coherence, pragmatic adequacy, and empirical adequacy. The conventional frame for evaluating is largely content to use achievement of an intervention's stated goals and objectives as the basis (criterion) for evaluating. Goals and objectives may reflect how program designers and policymakers assume an intervention addresses the needs or gaps in services, benefits, or outcomes for the target population(s) (Rossi, Lipsey, & Henry, 2019). The science of evaluating expanded the question of criteria and introduced the idea of organizing evaluations around evaluative questions.

Criteria Expanded

The choice of criteria commits the evaluator to look for certain kinds of evidence and to appeal to certain kinds of warrants in order to justify resulting evaluative claims (Fournier, 1995, p. 22). Teasdale (2019) identifies two domains of criteria as shown in Box 4.1: criteria that address the conceptualization and implementation of an intervention and criteria related to an intervention's results.

In many evaluations conducted in international development, the criteria recommended by the Development Assistance Committee of the Organisation for Economic Co-operation and Development (OECD/DAC) and shown in Box 4.2 function as a de facto normative guide. Agencies (e.g., United Nations Development Programme, the former United Kingdom Department of International Development, USAID) that employ them in evaluations emphasize some over others, sometimes neglect one or more, sometimes add more criteria, and so forth. In the past few years, evaluators working in international development have questioned the relevance and applicability of these criteria to all international development evaluations. See, for example, the 11-part series of posts on this issue in the blog "Evaluation for Development" (*http://zendaofir.com*) written by Zenda Ofir, an international consultant in evaluation and change management, as well as the blog posts from the former Director of the Independent Evaluation Group at the World Bank, Caroline Heider, at "Rethinking Evaluation" at (*https://ieg.worldbankgroup.org/blogseries/20326*). Ofir (2017) argues that the OECD/DAC criteria are inadequate because, among other shortcomings, they fail to incorporate the importance of cultural norms and the co-evolution of culture and contexts and they ignore the pressing need for transformative change in international development.

In 2018–2019, OECD/DAC considered these and other criticisms and solicited advice from users of the criteria. As a result, updated definitions provided two principles to guide their use and another criterion—namely, coherence—was added. The two principles state that these criteria (1) should be "applied thoughtfully" and "contextualized"—that is, examined for relevance in a given evaluation focused on a particular type of intervention and considering the stakeholders involved and (2) should not be applied mechanistically—that is, data availability, resource constraints, timing, and methodological considerations may influence how (and whether) a particular criterion is covered.

Evaluators may also choose criteria to align with or reflect a specific intention of a policy or program. For example, in evaluating humanitarian assistance programs, UNICEF suggests that the following criteria be used: *coverage* (extent of reaching major populations facing life-threatening suffering), *coordination* (of multiple actors involved in emergency response), protection (extent and effectiveness of provision of security and protec-

BOX 4.1. DOMAINS OF CRITERIA

Domain	Description
I. Criteria addressing the conceptualization and implementation of an intervention	
Relevance	Aims and activities are consistent with the needs, requirements, culture, interests, or circumstances of the intended beneficiaries.
Design	Activities and implementation are consistent with relevant theoretical principles, best practices, standards, and laws; implementation is timely.
Alignment	Intervention is consistent and coordinated with larger initiatives, related interventions, funder aims, and/or interconnected problems.
Replicability	Components, activities, or the underlying model or principles can be duplicated or adapted to another context.
Experience	Activities are delivered in a way that is respectful (ethical), legal, rewarding, consistent with cultural principles values and norms, etc.
Efficiency	This criterion refers to the extent to which monetary costs, time, and effort are well used.
II. Criteria addressing intervention results	
Efficacy	Intervention achieves desired results, outcomes, or objectives in optimal conditions.
Effectiveness	Intervention achieves desired results, outcomes, or objectives in real-world conditions.
Effects/ consequences	Intervention yields significant benefits to intended beneficiaries and other relevant populations and/or reaches a significant number of people or locations.
Side effects/ unintended consequences	Intervention is associated with unintended positive consequences and/or the absence of negative consequences.
Equity	Opportunities, experiences, benefits, and results are fair and just, with particular consideration to prioritizing marginalized populations.
Resource use	Funding, personnel, and materials are used economically; funding, personnel, and materials are sufficient to implement the intervention; and/or intervention yields an appropriate level of benefit in relation to the funds, personnel, and materials required.
Sustainability	Intervention has long-term benefits and/or activities and can continue beyond the initial start-up period.
Social impact	Social, public, and/or civic values are created by some intervention(s).

Note. From Teasdale (2019). Adapted with permission from author.

tion of the target population), and *policy coherence* (ensuring consistency across security, development, trade, and military policies and humanitarian policies; Peersman, 2014). The World Health Organization (2013) advises consideration of the following criteria in addition to those of OECD/DAC: *additionality*—the extent to which something happens as a result of an intervention that would not have occurred in the absence of the intervention; *deadweight*—change observed among direct beneficiaries following an intervention that would have occurred even without the intervention, underscoring the fact that resources have funded activities that would have taken place even without public support; and *displacement*—the effect obtained in an area at the expense of another area, or by a group of beneficiaries at the expense of another group within the same territory. The choice and justification of relevant criteria may also rest on evaluators' preferences based on their experience with evaluating similar programs and policies.

Given that in most every situation more than one criterion for rendering an evaluative judgment is potentially applicable, some means of weighing the importance or priority of criteria must be employed. Davidson (2005, pp. 105ff.) points to six evaluation-specific methodologies for determining importance: (1) having all stakeholders "vote" (rank or rate importance), equivalent to "whatever most people think is important"; (2) relying on the

---

BOX 4.2. OECD/DAC CRITERIA FOR EVALUATING INTERVENTIONS IN INTERNATIONAL DEVELOPMENT (REVISED DECEMBER 2019)

- *Relevance:* The extent to which the intervention objectives and design respond to beneficiaries (the individuals, groups, or organisations, whether targeted or not, that benefit directly or indirectly, from the development intervention).

- *Coherence:* The compatibility of the intervention with other interventions in a country, sector, or institution.

- *Effectiveness:* The extent to which the intervention achieved, or is expected to achieve, its objectives and its results, including any differential results across groups.

- *Efficiency:* The extent to which the intervention delivers, or is likely to deliver, results in an economic and timely way.

- *Impact:* The extent to which the intervention has generated or is expected to generate significant positive or negative, intended or unintended, higher-level effects.

- *Sustainability:* The extent to which the net benefits of the intervention continue or are likely to continue.

Note. Available at *www.oecd.org/dac/evaluation/revised-evaluation-criteria-dec-2019.pdf.*

views of well-informed stakeholders; (3) using evidence from the empiri-cal literature that documents key predictors of success or failure of the kind of program or policy under consideration; (4) relying on specialist judgment, the views of expert evaluators or researchers with considerable experience with what constitutes success and failure; (5) using the results from a performance needs assessment that underlies the policy or program (a performance need is the level of performance or state of affairs necessary for satisfactory functioning); and (6) using program theory and evidence of causal linkages. Of course, each of these methods has both advantages and disadvantages.

Question-Based Approaches

Evaluators may also organize their studies around key evaluation questions that reflect or divulge criteria. It is not unusual that those who have com-missioned or funded the evaluation define evaluation questions (and crite-ria) in advance and specify them in terms of reference. Some examples of evaluation questions and the criteria they reflect include the following:

- Is the program delivering outcomes as planned? (effectiveness)
- Is the wider public aware of this program? What range of outcomes (intended and unintended) has the project contributed to taking into account social, economic, environmental, and cultural consider-ations? (relevance and impact)
- Was the intervention delivered on budget? (efficiency)
- How do stakeholders (managers, beneficiaries) rate the relevance of the program activities? (appropriateness)
- Were program participants treated with dignity and respect on intake and in the assessment of their needs? (ethical responsibility)

While evaluation questions and criteria are for the most part aimed at determining the performance (e.g., implementation, results) of programs or projects ex-post, this is not always the case. For example, evaluators and policy analysts may judge public policy proposals ex-ante on criteria of social, political, administrative, and technical feasibility.

EXPANDING STAKEHOLDERS FROM COMMISSIONERS TO THOSE INVOLVED AND AFFECTED

Criteria can originate from multiple sources including, as already noted, the objectives of the intervention; program staff; program beneficiaries; evalu-ation commissioners; previous studies; expert opinion; legal requirements or standards; and the general public. Shifting beyond a near-exclusive focus on an intervention's stated goals and intended effects opens the question of who or what should shape the questions and criteria used in an evaluation. Numerous evaluation scholars have broadened the class of relevant stakeholders well beyond commissioners to multiple groups (and their interests) involved in and affected by an intervention and its evaluation. Consideration of stakeholders necessitates attending to the value preferences and perspectives brought to bear by these groups. Evaluation scholars and practitioners raise questions not only about which groups and value perspectives to consider in an evaluation but also about how to prioritize across these. We offer the following sampling of different views on stakeholder involvement.

In Scriven's view, evaluation should not be directed to serving the interests of any specific stakeholder group, but rather should serve the public interest generally. The function of evaluation is to inform the public on whether a program meets important needs, for without such decisive information a society has no reliable and systematic means of allocating resources and detecting fraud and incompetence (Shadish et al., 1991). Scriven assumed that policymakers would be responsive to the kind of rational information that evaluating provides. While placing a premium on logical and rational considerations in evaluating, Scriven tended to ignore the idea that stakeholders might have an important role to play in evaluative judgments. He also paid little attention to features of the policymaking milieu in which evaluative judgments are used.

Unlike Scriven, Robert Stake (1986) is less interested in evaluation serving the broad public interest and more focused on incremental change in local programs managed and implemented by local stakeholders. Stake (1975) argued that there is no single true value of a program. For example, teachers, administrators, students, and parents will value an educational program differently. An evaluation, in Stake's view, should respond to stakeholders' value perspectives, issues, and requirements for information. As an educational evaluator, Stake was particularly keen on using evaluation to support the educational practitioner and the improvement of instructional practice. He was a strong advocate for preparing evaluations as case studies, arguing that they were effective means to elicit vicarious experiences in readers whom they readily identified with, thereby increasing the use of evaluations as a means of understanding (Stake, 1995). In this way, he was critical of the idea that evaluation use is primarily instrumental (i.e., a specific decision is made about program changes based directly on the results of an evaluation).

Like Stake, Carol Weiss stressed that evaluation should be useful to stakeholders. But unlike Stake, she had a different audience in mind and a different idea of what it meant to be useful. Weiss emphasized that evaluators needed to pay greater attention to the role evaluation played in political decision making. Weiss's work (1972, 1980; Weiss & Bucuvalas, 1980) reveals that she was extremely skeptical of the notion of instrumental use of evaluation. She argued that policymakers rarely made decisions based on a rational, linear problem-solving model (define the problem→ generate alternative solutions→ evaluate the merits of each solution→ make a decision). Thus, she held that the assumption made by Scriven and others that decision makers would be directly responsive to rational information was unwarranted. Weiss (1973) also maintained that evaluators needed a much better understanding of the relationship of evaluation to the political environment in which evaluation takes place; that the programs being evaluated were creatures of political decisions; that evaluations enter the political arena where evaluative judgments compete with other influences on the political decision-making process; and that evaluation itself makes implicit political statements about programs such as the problematic nature of some programs, the legitimacy of program goals, and so on. Weiss (1978) brought her ideas about the relationship of evaluation to political decision making to bear in her enlightenment versus social engineering model of evaluation research:

> Researchers as social engineers are expected to answer specific requests for information and knowledge in a straightforward manner. They are expected to take the government's ends as given and to devise means to achieve them. . . . The enlightenment model, on the other hand, assumes that social science research does not so much solve problems as provide an intellectual setting of concepts, propositions, orientations, and empirical generalizations. No one study has much effect, but, over time, concepts become accepted. (p. 77)

Lee J. Cronbach also weighed in on the matter of the proper stake-holding audience for evaluation and, like Weiss, argued that the field of evaluation should pay greater attention to how policy decisions are made. Cronbach (Cronbach et al., 1980) regarded evaluation as a critical aspect of policy research, thus needing an understanding of the political world of social programming. Like Weiss's findings, his empirical research revealed that a rational model of political decision making was flawed: Decisions are rarely made by a single decision maker; data are often trumped by political considerations; and rarely are evaluation findings used in an instrumental way to modify programs. According to Cronbach and colleagues, instead of operating in a political context of command and control with a single, clearly defined, responsible decision maker, evaluation unfolds in a process of political accommodation; in a milieu characterized by a policy-shaping community. That community of stakeholders includes three groups of public servants (responsible officials at the policy level, the program level, and the local level) and two groups of members of the public (program constituents or beneficiaries and illuminators-scholars, journalists, and others who disseminate information about social programs). At best, in this milieu, evaluation contributes to enlightened discussions of alternative paths to social problem solving.

Eleanor Chelimsky (2014) identified public-interest values central in U.S. democracy, including "liberty from foreign control; public safety vis-à-vis natural catastrophes, crime, public health and the environment; equality of citizens before the law; openness and accountability of the government to the people; and protection of minority rights" (p. 533). She urged evaluators to consider public-interest values as criteria in evaluations of government-sponsored interventions: "All changes in public-interest values matter to evaluators not only because they can help in assessing the eventual fate of an intervention, but also because they shed light on the fairness, balance, and comprehensiveness with which the program's formulation has considered opposing sides of the public-interest ledger" (p. 530).

Finally, concerns about social justice, human rights, gender equality, and racial equity have led some evaluators to privilege the perspectives of stakeholders historically or currently most marginalized or least well served (Hall, Ahn, & Greene, 2012; Hood, Hopson, & Frierson, 2015; Mertens, 2009). In societies and circumstances that are inequitable—that is, when resources, power, decision making, and other assets are distributed unevenly across groups—not questioning which stakeholders' perspectives and values are at issue risks reinforcing inequities. Moreover, approaching stakeholders neutrally and attempting to include all interests fairly also risk perpetuating imbalances as some groups are advantaged and others disadvantaged going into an evaluation.

While the views of Scriven, Stake, Weiss, Cronbach, and Chelimsky differ on the involvement of stakeholders in evaluation, they nonetheless share two major characteristics. First, they shift the focus of evaluation away from privileging the viewpoints of policymakers, program designers, and those commissioning evaluations. Second, they reveal more careful attention to the relationship between evaluation, politics, and decision making, expanding the science of evaluating beyond a focus on logical matters of evaluative judgment to both political and ethical concerns.

At the present time, the consensus in the field of evaluation is that stakeholders, along with a variety of contextual considerations, influence (or ought to influence) the choice and justification of criteria. Many evaluators recognize the necessity of including stakeholders' perspectives on the importance, magnitude, and significance of the problem being addressed by a given intervention as well as stakeholders' vested interests in and perspectives on what constitutes an adequate solution to the problem in question. In addition, these evaluators endeavor to take into account the norms and values of the organizational and political system(s) in which a program or policy is developed, situated, and administered; concerns about social desirability, cultural relevance, and responsiveness in policy and program design, implementation, and determination of value; and their own perspectives on relevant criteria based on their prior practical experience.

USING PERFORMANCE STANDARDS AS THE BASIS FOR MAKING EVALUATIVE JUDGMENTS

Criteria are the characteristics by which the quality of something is judged. While criteria identify what qualities are valued or of interest, they do not specify anything about the attainment of actual quality. To make that determination, one needs standards of performance that define levels of achievement or performance. The conventional frame for evaluating uses comparative standards. The effectiveness and efficiency of an intervention are compared to some alternative (and that could be another similar intervention or some form of a control or comparison group). In the science of evaluating, absolute standards are also used. These standards link performance to specified levels as found in the use of key performance indicators, benchmarking, and rubrics.

Key Performance Indicators

Also called outcome indicators, key performance indicators (KPIs) are usually quantifiable measures used to determine whether goals and outcomes are being achieved. Historically, private-sector management has used this tool to track progress toward organizational goals. Since the 1970s, public-sector evaluators have used them to evaluate public-sector performance (Hatry, 2014). In the nonprofit sector, the Urban Institute's Outcome Indicators Project (see *www.urban.org/policy-centers/ cross-center-initiatives/performance-management-measurement/proj-ects/nonprofit-organizations/projects-focused-nonprofit-organizations/ outcome-indicators-project*) produced sets of indicators for 14 specific program areas from adult education and family literacy to transitional housing and youth mentoring. The 2030 Agenda for Sustainable Development includes 17 Sustainable Development Goals and associated targets. Measures of achievement of the goals are tied to a global framework of 232 indicators (*https://unstats.un.org/sdgs/indicators/indicators-list*). Indicators can be developed through a process of discussion and negotiation among experts, as was the case with the global indicator framework developed by the 27-member Inter-Agency and Expert Group on Sustainable Development Goal Indicators (IAEG-SDGs) created in 2015 by the United Nations Statistical Commission. Indicators may also be developed based on program logic models. The activities, outputs, and outcomes displayed in the logic model are quantified into measurable units as shown in the example of the use of performance indicators for emergency shelter programs for the homeless in Figure 4.2.

Performance on key indicators is a way of monitoring outputs and outcomes in a timely fashion. However, monitoring by means of indicator data does not directly lead to answering evaluative questions. Consider, for example, two kinds of monitoring data collected on intermediate and end outcomes as shown in Figure 4.2: "Number and percent of clients who complete service plan/shelter program," "Number and percent of clients who report their immediate shelter needs were met." Neither kind of data answers the evaluative questions of whether the number and percent were *adequate* and whether the *right* people were being reached. To develop answers to those questions, some standards for performance or targets would have to be set either by the consensus of program developers and managers or based on standards for performance used in similar emergency shelter program evaluations.

Benchmarking

Setting a benchmark or point of reference involves a process of comparing the performance of one program to the same or very similar program in a different locale or setting or to an accepted set of standards for performance. Benchmarks may be established through empirical study. Coffman, Beer, Patrizi, and Thompson (2013) benchmark best practices in the positioning, resourcing, and function of evaluation units in foundations. The consensus of experts in a particular policy or program may also be the basis for developing benchmarks. For example, the Sphere Project created in 1997 by a group of humanitarian nongovernmental organizations (NGOs) and the Red Cross and Red Crescent movements aim to improve the quality of NGOs' humanitarian responses and to hold them accountable for their actions. The Sphere Handbook (Sphere Association, 2018) lists a Core Humanitarian Principle with nine specific commitments that spell out what communities and people affected by crisis can expect from organizations and individuals delivering humanitarian assistance. It also lists four ethical Protection Principles that apply to all humanitarian action and humanitarian actors: (1) Enhance the safety, dignity, and rights of people, and avoid exposing them to harm; (2) ensure people's access to assistance according to need and without discrimination; (3) assist people to recover from the physical and psychological effects of threatened or actual violence, coercion, or deliberate deprivation; and (4) help people claim their rights. The Protection Principles underlie Minimum Standards that humanitarian programs must meet in the following four areas: water sup-

104

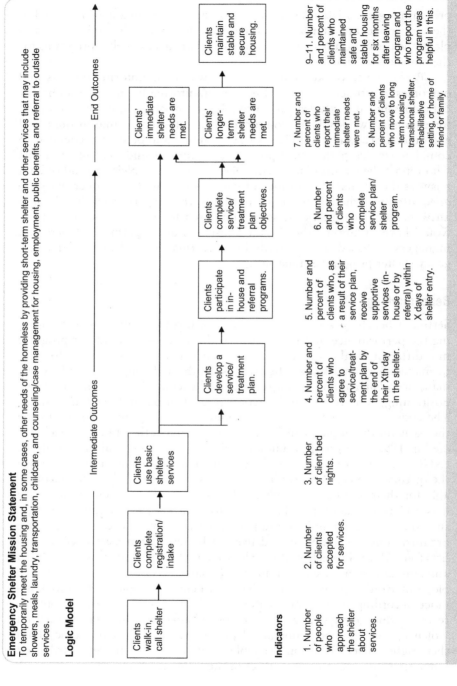

Emergency Shelter Mission Statement
To temporarily meet the housing and, in some cases, other needs of the homeless by providing short-term shelter and other services that may include showers, meals, laundry, transportation, childcare, and counseling/case management for housing, employment, public benefits, and referral to outside services.

Logic Model

Intermediate Outcomes ─────── End Outcomes

| Clients walk-in, call shelter | Clients complete registration/ intake | Clients use basic shelter services | | Clients develop a service/ treatment plan. | Clients participate in in-house and referral programs. | Clients complete service/ treatment plan objectives. | Clients' immediate shelter needs are met. | Clients maintain stable and secure housing. |

Clients' longer-term shelter needs are met.

Indicators

1. Number of people who approach the shelter about services.

2. Number of clients accepted for services.

3. Number of client bed nights.

4. Number and percent of clients who agree to service/treat-ment plan by the end of their Xth day in the shelter.

5. Number and percent of clients who, as a result of their service plan, receive supportive services (in-house or by referral) within X days of shelter entry.

6. Number and percent of clients who complete service plan/ shelter program.

7. Number and percent of clients who report their immediate shelter needs were met.

8. Number and percent of clients who move to long –term housing, transitional shelter, rehabilitative setting, or home of friend or family.

9–11. Number and percent of clients who maintained safe and stable housing for six months after leaving program and who report the program was helpful in this.

FIGURE 4.2. Indicators derived from a logic model.

ply, sanitation, and hygiene promotion; food security and nutrition; shelter and settlement; and health.

Rubrics

Rubrics are a means to provide an evaluative description of what quality looks like at each of two or more defined levels of performance. Evidence of program or project quality typically looks different at different levels of performance, and the evidence may be a combination of both qualitative and quantitative data. Dickinson and Adams (2017) explain that the two basic elements of a rubric are the evaluation criteria and performance standards. The criteria to identify the dimensions of interest will be used as the basis for judging how well a program has performed on particular outcomes.

RQ+ (*Research Quality Plus*) (Ofir, Schwandt, Duggan, & McLean, 2016) was developed to evaluate the quality of the research funded by the International Development Research Centre (IDRC). *RQ+* provides an example of an analytical or component-based evaluation. That is, the phenomenon to be evaluated—the quality of research funded by IDRC—was explicitly analyzed in terms of multiple criteria or dimensions (as opposed to a single criterion or dimension without consideration of separate dimensions or subdimensions). Based on extensive consultation with IDRC management and staff, representatives of agencies funded by IDRC, and careful review of the literature on appraising the quality of scientific research, the evaluation team identified four dimensions (research integrity, research legitimacy, research importance, and positioning for use) and associated subdimensions of research quality as displayed in Box 4.3. These were the evaluative criteria. For example, research integrity was defined as

> consideration of the technical quality, appropriateness and rigor of the design and execution of the research as judged in terms of commonly accepted standards for such work and specific methods, and as reflected in research project documents and in selected research outputs. Specific points of emphasis include the research design, methodological rigor, literature review, systematic work, and the relationship between evidence gathered and conclusions reached and/or claims made. (Ofir et al., p. 10)

Rubrics were then developed for rating performance on each of the dimensions and subdimensions. King, McKegg, Oakden, and Wehipeihana (2013) have found rubrics useful in bringing "stakeholders to the table to surface the range of values and reconcile these (possibly diverse) perspectives together with more formally documented expectations" (p. 14), and in enhancing the transparency of the value and evidentiary bases of evaluative claims

BOX 4.3. IDRC DIMENSIONS OF RESEARCH QUALITY AND ILLUSTRATION OF A SAMPLE RUBRIC

Dimensions of Research Quality

1. Research Integrity
2. Research Legitimacy
   2.1 Addressing potentially negative consequences
   2.2 Gender-responsiveness
   2.3 Inclusiveness
   2.4 Engagement with local knowledge
3. Research Importance
   3.1 Originality
   3.2 Relevance
4. Positioning for Use
   4.1 Knowledge accessibility and sharing
   4.2 Timeliness and actionability

Sample Rubric from the IDRC RQ+ Evaluation

Dimension 4: Positioning for Use; Subdimension 4.2: Timeliness and Actionability

UNACCEPTABLE 1–2	LESS THAN ACCEPTABLE 3–4	ACCEPTABLE TO GOOD 5–6	VERY GOOD 7–8
There is little or no evidence that any analysis of relevant user(s) environment(s) was undertaken and that institutional, political, social, or economic contingencies were considered.	There is evidence that some analysis of the user setting was undertaken; however, consideration is incomplete and, furthermore, the analysis is not accompanied by discussion of actual strategies or plans to move the knowledge to policy or practice.	There is evidence that the user environment and major contingencies have been examined and reflected upon and connected to strategies and plans for moving the research into policy or practice in a timely manner.	The analysis of the user environment and contingencies is exceptionally thorough and well documented or articulated. There is evidence of careful prospective appraisal of the likelihood of success of strategies designed to address contingencies.

ROLES OF THE EVALUATOR, STAKEHOLDERS, AND PUBLIC IN EVALUATING

In the science of evaluating, there are two related, unresolved issues surrounding the making of evaluative judgments. One issue is whether and how to make a single, composite judgment of quality based on synthesizing results across multiple criteria. The other issue is who should have the responsibility for making an evaluative judgment.

Health care providers commonly employ synthesis judgments in arriving at a diagnosis. Clinical judgment or clinical reasoning takes into account objective and subjective information about a patient, including the results of medical tests, physical examination, patient history, patient perceptions/feelings/experiences, and so on. Both automatic, intuitive reasoning as well as reflective, analytic reasoning are involved (widely referred to in psychology as System 1 and System 2 thinking, respectively; see Kahneman, 2011). In Scriven's (1994b) view, the final step in evaluative reasoning is a synthesis judgment as well, but it ought to rely solely on analytic reasoning, a "rule-governed synthesis," that, while not quite algorithmic (i.e., a set of rules for solving a problem in a finite series of steps), must nonetheless provide clear guidance on how to proceed.

However, little or no synthesis is attempted (Coryn et al., 2017) in many evaluation circumstances (perhaps too many in the view of some evaluators). Instead, evaluators use an approach that is often referred to as "interest group depiction" (House & Howe, 1999), which involves documenting program performance on several criteria without reaching an overall judgment across those criteria. It involves making summaries of performance matched to the preferred criteria (values) of different interest groups. In the complex process of political decision making where ideology, interest group pressure, and political concerns can often weigh more heavily in policy decisions than empirical evidence from evaluations (Stone, 2002), evaluators and program analysts may avoid making synthesis judgments. For example, some policymakers may argue that the government has an obligation to foster the healthy development of young children even in the absence of significant evidence revealing that an investment in preschool programs is yielding expected outcomes. Or decisions over the value of programs of school choice may be made not on the basis of evidence of whether charter schools yield positive effects but on the basis of ideological stances pitting those in favor of market solutions to education against those who support the government's responsibility for public education. In such circumstances, the evaluator, like the policy analyst, may be content to simply make plain the empirical and normative (value) arguments involved in the debate over the merits of a program or policy in order to facilitate assessment, comparison, and debate among policymakers. The former Assistant Director of the Center for Evaluation Methods and Issues at the U.S. Government Accountability Office (GAO) has argued that GAO does not make aggregate judgments of a program's value. She explains that the GAO takes this position because a synthesis requires a political decision to prioritize some criteria of performance over others and most program evaluations are designed for a particular policy purpose and thus the choice of criteria applies to the specific situation: "The weighing or prioritization of criteria or values is in essence a political decision, assigning priority to some values over others. GAO, as an audit agency, is charged with providing objective, nonpartisan, nonideological analyses, which precludes it from making these political choices" (Shipman, 2012, p. 60).

Although Scriven is keen to emphasize that the evaluator has a professional responsibility to render an evaluative judgment, not all evaluators agree. Alkin, Vo, and Christie (2012) discuss three primary roles evaluators might take. Evaluators might provide the empirical evidence for program stakeholders (e.g., funders, administrators, program managers) while leaving the rendering of evaluative judgments to those stakeholders; they might serve as facilitators, setting up processes to guide stakeholders in reasoning their way to evaluative judgments; or the evaluator(s) could take the sole role of valuing and rendering evaluative judgments.

Additional considerations beyond those of working with the most immediate stakeholders factor into this decision about responsibility as well. Because the work of evaluators serves the public interest (i.e., it contributes to social betterment, as explained in Chapter 3), evaluators may be obliged to consider what, if any, role the interests and concerns of the public ought to play in reaching evaluative judgments as well as how the process of making evaluative judgments might be designed so as to attend to those members of the public who potentially might be negatively affected by evaluative conclusions. Incorporating public input could be carried out when identifying criteria, for example, by using crowdsourcing (Harman & Azzam, 2018) or incorporating public interest values (Chelimsky, 2014). Gates (2018) draws on critical systems heuristics as a way to incorporate a witness role for groups, interests, and worldviews potentially affected by an evaluation: "Witnessing means identifying and calling attention to who or what may be negatively affected and fostering responsibility in an evaluation for mitigating further exclusion and marginalization" (p. 15). Beyond who is involved and how, evaluators may also consider potential imbalances in power and legitimacy (Mark & Shotland, 1985). Davidson (2014a, p. 8) identifies five considerations when determining who should be involved in the making of evaluative judgments: (1) validity (i.e., whose expertise is needed to get it right), (2) credibility (i.e., whose involvement will ensure that evaluative conclusions are believable to various groups), (3) utility (i.e., who will use the evaluative conclusions and, therefore, who should be involved in producing them), (4) voice (i.e., whose perspectives and experiences need to be considered, especially considering who or what have historically been excluded or marginalized), and (5) cost (i.e., are the time and resources of involving various people worthwhile).

SUMMARY

The conventional frame for evaluating effectively narrows the scope of evaluation to a technical undertaking involving the instrumental assessment of whether interventions achieve goals and desired results. Expanding this frame opens professional evaluation practice and responsibility to essentially nontechnical, political, and ethical issues, including careful consideration and justification of values that ultimately influence the kinds of evaluation that will be done; selecting and justifying the choice of criteria from multiple possible domains and from a range of sources; and explaining and justifying the respective roles for researchers/evaluators, stakeholders, and the public in evaluation. Expansions to the conventional frame are all improvements on realizing the promise that evaluation can deliver determinable assessments of quality ("How did we do?"). Assessment will be useful—perhaps instrumentally, but more likely enlightening—to decision makers. However, such assessments offer no guidance on questions such as "Where are we going?" "What should be done?" and "Is this desirable?" The contribution of professional evaluation practice to these concerns is the subject of the chapters that follow.

IMPORTANT RESOURCES

■ Scriven, M. (2015). Key evaluation checklist. Available as a free Word download from *https://wmich.edu/evaluation/checklists*
   Outlines Scriven's view of the key components of an evaluation. Includes a section on values that discusses the potential sources of criteria for an evaluation and a section on synthesis that discusses the traps and possibilities in rendering overarching evaluative conclusions.

■ King, J., and Oxford Policy Management. (2018). Approach to assessing value for money. Available as a free PDF download at *www.julianking.co.nz/wp-content/uploads/2018/02/OPM-approach-to-assessing-value-for-money.pdf*.
   An approach to determining value for money (VfM) in evaluation that incorporates explicit evaluative reasoning by integrating a theory of change for the intervention with VfM criteria and standards, followed by data collection and analysis and, ultimately analysis, synthesis, and judgment.

■ Peersman, G. (2014). *Methodological brief for impact evaluation No. 3. Evaluative Criteria.* Florence: UNICEF Office of Research. Available as a free PDF download at *www.unicef-irc.org/publications/748-evaluative-criteria-methodological-briefs-impact-evaluation-no-3.html*.

Defines evaluative criteria as the values on which the merit of an intervention can be determined and discusses the use of various criteria in evaluations of the impacts of interventions in international aid and development. Includes the standard OECD/DAC criteria; criteria about equity, gender equality, and a human-rights-based approach to programming; and criteria for humanitarian assistance.

- Davidson, J. (2014a). *Methodological brief for impact evaluation, No. 4 Evaluative reasoning.* New York: UNICEF. Available as a free PDF download at *www.unicef-irc.org/publications/pdf/brief_4_evaluativereasoning_eng.pdf.*

  Builds on the brief No. 3 (above) by explaining how evaluative reasoning can be used to develop and use standards of performance on each criterion to inform ratings of value or quality, such as poor, adequate, very good, or excellent. Defines evaluative reasoning as putting evidence and definitions of quality or value together to answer the evaluation question(s).

- Stufflebeam, D. (2001b). Evaluation values and criteria checklist. Available as a free PDF download at *https://wmich.edu/sites/default/files/attachments/u350/2014/values_criteria.pdf.*

  Part of the Evaluation Checklist Project of the Evaluation Center at Western Michigan University (see *https://wmich.edu/evaluation/checklists*), this is a four-page summary of values and criteria often used in evaluation including societal values; criteria in the CIPP (context, input, process, product) evaluation model; and institutional values, among others. Also includes a category called idiosyncratic criteria that cannot be specified in advance and are negotiated in specific contexts.

BRIDGE TO PRACTICE

Institutions of higher education are increasingly offering online graduate programs in applied fields for students who are attracted to flexible education that could advance career opportunities. These programs are generally competency-based in that the curriculum focuses more on skill-building than on acquiring abstract and conceptual knowledge. With the expansion of accredited online advanced degree programs, the need to evaluate such programs has increased. Evaluation of online advanced degree programs provides an opportunity for collaboration among major external stakeholders, such as accrediting bodies and institutional partners, along with internal stakeholders, including program administrators, faculty, and students. Evaluations are also used to provide internal feedback and evidence of program quality.

At a large public university in the Midwest, the dean of an interdisciplinary college of advanced studies and program director for an online master's degree program came together to commission an external evaluation of the online program. They were motivated to evaluate the program in order to identify any major issues with the program as currently designed and implemented in view of plans to pursue accreditation in the near future. After discussion with the evaluation team, the dean and program director agreed on two overarching questions to guide the evaluation:

1. How well do the courses provide high-quality learning opportunities that allow students to gain knowledge, competencies, and communication skills identified by the program as important for academic and professional success?
2. According to students and faculty, how well has the program provided support, in terms of technical, instructional, and professional support?

The evaluation team developed a set of criteria and benchmarks based on a review of scholarly literature on online, competency-based professional programs and prior evaluations of similar programs. The full list of criteria and benchmarks as shown below were reviewed by the evaluation team and program director, who collaboratively prioritized those of highest relevance to the program being evaluated.

Evaluation Rubric: Criteria and Benchmarks Used in the Evaluation	
Criterion	**Benchmark**
Technology Infrastructure	• The technology delivery system is reliable. • The technology system is centralized for infrastructure.
Course Development	• Courses reflect student competencies and program outcome at an appropriate level and rigor, with guidelines providing a dependable pathway to completion of the degree. • Instructional materials and resources are accessible. • The relationship between objectives or competencies and learning activities is clearly stated.
Teaching and Learning Practices	• There is faculty–student, student–student, and team-based interaction. • Faculty provides constructive and timely feedback. • Teaching methods are driven by adult learning principles.
Student and Faculty Support	• There is access to technical assistance. • Students receive transparent and open program information and promotion. • Students receive advising, career, and instructional support.

Having considered this scenario, reflect on or discuss the following questions:

- On what value bases do you think these criteria were developed? Are there missing criteria from your perspective?
- Do the benchmarks as described here provide sufficient detail to serve as standards of performance? How so or not so?
- In what ways might these criteria and benchmarks be used to inform the data collection methods and sources?
- How could the evaluator(s) use this rubric to explicitly guide evaluative reasoning?
- What challenges might they run into if they are trying to use this rubric and the data collected to render an overall evaluative judgment of the quality of this program? How might they address these challenges?

CHAPTER 5

An Emerging Alternative Frame for Evaluating

The world has changed significantly in the past decade: rising inequality, conflict and insecurity, mass migration, terrorism, and climate change all present major global challenges. . . . Responding to global challenges requires more than just methodological improvement and innovation. There is a need for a bolder evaluation agenda, recognizing the evaluators' role in contributing to change: acting not just as providers of evidence, but to proactively engage in an ethical obligation to society, stimulating deliberation and re-examination of evidence by a broader range of citizens—citizens who can be emboldened to use such evidence to improve their situations and hold others to account.
—BARNETT AND EAGER (2017, p. 294)

INTRODUCTION

There is growing interest in the fields of social, health, and environmental program and policy planning, international development, and philanthropic funding in rethinking the mainstream framing of evaluating. As portrayed in Chapters 3 and 4, both scholars and practitioners have typically regarded the professional practice of evaluating as a reliable scientific means of providing objective appraisal of the value of planned social interventions. However, that practice continues to evolve as it responds to developments in the technical, social, and political environments in which it unfolds, while simultaneously influencing how those contexts are understood and assessed. Evolving has increasingly been a matter of addressing a variety of uncertainties and risks not simply in the conventional manner of appraising interventions but in the design and management of interventions as well. New ways of thinking and forms of evaluation practice linked to models of adaptive planning and decision making are emerging. Unpredictability as well as incompleteness, instability, and a plurality of perspectives in value determination are coming to be taken as a normal state of affairs rather than an exception.

Evaluating in the conventional frame endeavors to distinguish itself from related professional activities, such as strategy and design, project planning and management, and organizational development. It does so by claiming professional authority for determining judgments of the value of planned interventions. However, efforts to rethink evaluation are blurring the lines between what is and what is not considered evaluation as well as challenging that authority. Evaluators are acting less like external judges or appraisers and more as engaged, thoughtful partners working with a variety of groups to continuously make sense of pervasive social issues and inequalities and to steer a path of action through these difficult situations. To researchers and evaluators classically trained in social research methodology, such engagements may look more like action research and collaborative forms of planning and analysis.

As suggested in Chapters 3 and 4, some of this "new" thinking has always been present, at least to some degree, in challenges to the conventional framing of evaluation or to what Schwandt (2019a) elsewhere has called "normal evaluation." Recall that this frame is wedded to notions of scientific rationality, social progress, effectiveness and efficiency in social programming, and the broad ideology of modernization. It is also linked to what Michael Patton (2019) refers to as the "project mentality," a mental model underlying planning and evaluating and a generally accepted and unquestioned practice:

> The dominant focus of evaluation (unit of analysis) has been and remains a project or program model. What is called in evaluation jargon the "evaluand," *the thing evaluated*, determines the focus and methods of an evaluation. Evaluators have been socialized to design interventions using project thinking, indoctrinated in how to make meaning of what we see by reducing complex dynamic systems to linear logic models. (p. 310)

In Patton's view, this mentality "limits our effectiveness in dealing with global problems like climate change, worldwide poverty, the international refugee challenge, and the other global issues at the center of planetary sustainability" (p. 310).

A growing number of social scientists who identify as evaluators, including Patton, are criticizing the current state of the practice. For example, Kim Forss (2019), who conducts evaluation through his private Swedish firm, argues that evaluation is a "systems-preserving activity, an intellectual effort which is inherently conservative and that assists in defending rather than challenging the powers that be, the established wisdoms, the current technologies and administrative practices" (p. 190). Osvaldo Feinstein (2019), former manager and advisor at the World Bank Independent Evaluation Office and senior evaluator at the United Nations International Fund for Agricultural Development (IFAD), observes that standard evaluation criteria (relevance, effectiveness, efficiency, sustainability, and impact) do not cover the possibility of assessing the kind of transformative change called for in the 2030 Agenda for Sustainable Development. Transformational development requires changes in social structures and relations, including addressing the growing economic and political power of elites and patterns of stratification related to class, gender, ethnicity, religion, or location that can lock people (including future generations) into disadvantage and constrain their choices and agency. It also means changing norms and institutions, both formal and informal, that shape the behavior of people and organizations in the social, economic, environmental, and political spheres (UN Research Institute for Social Development, 2016).

Other evaluators and researchers are exploring the implications of contemporary social and environmental issues and developments in technology, governance, climate change, political polarization, migration, and the like for the task of evaluating (Deloitte Consulting GmbH, 2017; Guijt & Artuso, 2020). For example, USAID (Menocal et al., 2018) advocates integrating evaluation into applied political economy analysis—an approach to thinking and working politically (*https://twpcommunity.org*) that examines power dynamics and economic and social forces that influence development. Borrowing from the literature in postnormal science (Funtowicz & Ravetz, 1993), Schwandt (2019a) characterized the exploration of new ways of thinking about evaluating as the emergence of postnormal evaluation defined in part by circumstances where facts are uncertain, complexity is the norm, values are in dispute and unstable, stakes are high, processes of contestation and bargaining between interest groups are common, and decisions are urgent.

In this chapter, we explore this emerging alternative frame by discussing an amalgam of interdisciplinary influences, as displayed in Figure 5.1, and the ways each influence gives rise to alternative thinking and practices. We draw on learning theory, planning and policymaking literature, and literatures in practical philosophy, deliberative decision making, and systems thinking and complexity science. By the very fact that the emerging alternative frame draws on multiple intellectual and practical resources for its composition, it exhibits a defining feature, namely, its character as a flexible, multiperspectival, multimethodological bricolage.

Recall that "a frame is a way to understand the things we say and see and act on in the world" (Rein, 1983, pp. 96–97). It does not prescribe exactly how to think, what to do, or how to do it. It acts as an organizing lens and orientation for evaluation practice within which there may be multiple theories, approaches, and methods (Alkin, 2013). Some aspects of the alternative frame discussed below may intersect with the conventional frame at times. Others stand in stark contrast, leading to altogether alternative ways of thinking. To depict this emerging frame, we discuss the fol-

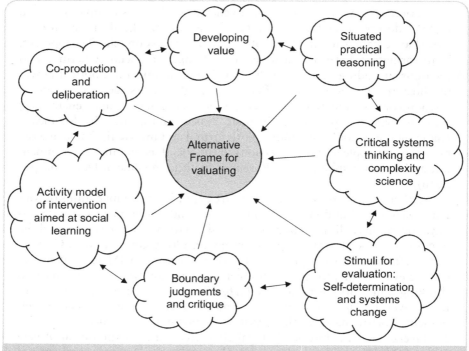

FIGURE 5.1. Multiple interdisciplinary influences on an alternative framing of evaluating.

lowing key influences: (1) situated, practical reasoning, (2) systems thinking and complexity science, (3) boundary critique, (4) co-production and
deliberation, (5) activity model of intervention, and (6) self-determination
and systems change as stimuli for evaluation. Within and across these influences, we witness a rethinking of evaluating from a task of determining
value to one defined by developing value. We close the chapter with discussion of what it means to redefine evaluating as a practice of developing
value.

SITUATED, PRACTICAL REASONING

The conventional frame for evaluating reflects a long-standing cultural
assumption that scientific knowledge and scientific reasoning define the
only kind of rigor and exactitude that can be called rational (Dunne &
Pendlebury, 2003). The epistemology of professional practice in the mainstream frame is technical rationality: "instrumental problem solving made
rigorous by the application of scientific theory and technique" (Schön,

1983, p. 21). The alternative frame both draws on and revitalizes an older form of rationality, knowledge, and reason known as practical judgment. Situated, practical judgment, also called practical wisdom, is discussed at length in the philosophical (e.g., Edmondson & Hülser, 2012), business (e.g., Intezari & Pauleen, 2019), and popular (e.g., Schwartz & Sharpe, 2010) literatures.

Practical knowledge is the kind of knowledge required to answer the question, "What should I/we do?" in circumstances where the available stock of technical knowledge is of little direct help. Practical reason is required precisely in those situations that are neither standard, typical, nor conventional, situations we would call predicaments (or in ethics, dilemmas), rather than clearly defined problems. It is a form of reason employed in concrete, immediate situations or cases that have this character. It is not a kind of instrumental reason focused only on the effectiveness and efficiency of various means to given ends, but it involves "deliberation about the end itself—about what would 'count' as a satisfactory, or at least not entirely unacceptable, outcome to a particular case" (Dunne & Pendlebury, 2003, p. 199). Practical reason attends carefully to the normative, institutional, and organizational context in which decisions and choices are made and action is taken (Majone, 1989). Viewed as a form of practical reason, evaluating in the alternative frame is simultaneously a matter of empirical inquiry, a case for deliberation, and a judgment of practice (i.e., what to do) (De Munck & Zimmermann, 2015). Questions that this approach to evaluating addresses include the following:

- Given what we know and what we can imagine is possible, what should we do now?
- How well did our efforts accomplish the multiple goals and desired outcomes agreed on by several stakeholder groups?
- How, if at all, should our goals and desired outcomes change in light of shifting or differing value perspectives?
- What assumptions underlie our understanding of the problem and our efforts to address it?
- Who gains and who loses from what we plan to do or have done?
- What should we do to address potential exclusion and marginalization?

In addressing these questions, evaluating is more a communicative undertaking than a technical one, a matter of coping with ambiguity in relation to a range of technical, political, moral, and ethical considerations through communicative processes of dialogue, argumentation, and learning (Sanderson, 2009). Innes and Booher (1991) explain that

[t]he basic idea of communicative rationality is that emancipatory knowledge can be achieved through dialogue that engages all those with differing interests around a task or problem. For dialogue to produce emancipatory knowledge, the stakeholders must be equally informed, listened to, and respected, and none can be accorded more power than others to speak or make decisions. . . . Participants bring their praxis to the table because their experience and know-how are as much part of getting at truth as are logic and science. If such a group, following such principles, can reach consensus after thorough discussion, then the conclusions of their deliberations can be regarded as both rational and ethical. (p. 418)

This communicative orientation to evaluation research is, in our judgment, aligned with a social constructionist theory of social problems (Blumer, 1971; Spector & Kitsuse, 1977). In this theory, social problems are not objective conditions and functional social arrangements but a product of social processes—the degree to which something is perceived to be a problem and the kind of problem it is understood to be is a function of a process of collective activities involving alleging, asserting, and claiming. The social constructionist theory of social problems argues that problems arise through a series of stages: claims making (involving stakeholders including activists and experts, as claims makers); media coverage; public reactions; policymaking; the social problems work of implementing policy; and policy outcomes. "At each of these stages, individuals reconstruct the troubling condition to reflect their cultural and structural circumstances, so that social problems and social policies can be understood as products of continually shifting arguments and interpretations, emerging through interactions between those making claims and their audiences" (Best, 2013, p. 237). This dynamic, constructionist view of social problems contrasts with assumptions about social problem solving characteristic of the conventional framing of evaluation.

Practitioners of the alternative framing of evaluating appeal to practical judgment as precisely the kind of reason demanded when dealing with wicked, ill-structured problems or messes. As first argued by Rittel and Webber (1973; see also Churchman, 1967; McMillan & Overly, 2016), wicked problems are characterized by the fact that they are defined or structured in multiple ways, making it difficult to sort out definitive cause-and-effect relationships. They are distinguished by the presence of overlapping stakeholder groups with different perspectives on the problem and different standpoints on solutions. They are enduring and bewildering problems; that is, they cannot be solved once and for all. Consider, for example, the problem of homelessness. Multiple stakeholding groups— operators of local shelters, medical professionals, related social service nonprofit agencies, local government officials, the police, local business owners, those who are homeless, members of the community—are likely to see the problem and its solution differently. Hence, simply providing more low-barrier shelters or more sympathetic police patrols and offering more counseling for addictive behaviors and mental illness are hardly likely to "end" the "problem" of homelessness once and for all. Table 5.1 displays several key characteristics of wicked problems as encountered by planners, policy analysts, and evaluation researchers.

The activity of situated practical reasoning can be depicted visually, as shown in Figure 5.2. Management scholars Intezari and Pauleen (2014)

TABLE 5.1. Some Features of Wicked Problems	
Characteristic	**Description**
Nature of a problem	Problems are discrepancies between a current state of affairs (e.g., in education, health, criminal justice, social services) and the way things ought to be. There is no single, clear explanation for any given discrepancy because individual problems are composed of multiple, interacting causal factors. Any individual problem is itself interconnected with others and can be considered a symptom of another problem.
Problem formulation	Wicked problems cannot be formulated definitively. Any attempt at formulating why a particular state of affairs (i.e., what is) is problematic requires conceiving of what ought to be. Analysis of what ought to be requires conceiving of potential solutions or alternatives. This makes the formulation of problems inseparable from the formulation of potential solutions or responses.
Problem solving	There is no point at which one stops solving a wicked problem. Solving a problem and the process of understanding a problem are interdependent; thus, different understandings lead to different solutions. What constitutes a fixed solution in one understanding may not be a solution from a different understanding of the problem.
No value-free or true–false solutions	There are no true or "correct" answers to a wicked problem. Understanding and addressing such problems require political and normative judgment of some solution or response as better or worse, good enough, and so on. Judgment of a solution depends on agreement with how the problem was understood. This makes wicked problems continuously open to new understandings, framings, and responses.
Problems are unique and solutions are consequential	There are not classes or types of wicked problems such that a class of problems can be dealt with in a uniform way. Each problem is essentially unique. Solutions to wicked problems have potentially irreversible consequences on people's lives and surrounding conditions. Attempts to address one problem have consequences for understanding and addressing other problems, which the problem at hand may interconnect with.
Responsibility for those attempting to formulate and address wicked problems	Since there are no right ways to formulate and solve wicked problems and any attempt to do so has consequences, those working to address such problems face a dilemma. They can't get it right from a plurality of viewpoints, yet they must try, for any attempt has consequences.

Note. From Rittel and Webber (1973).

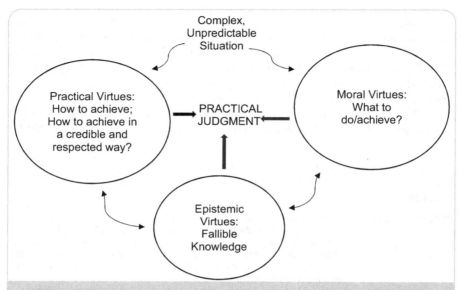

FIGURE 5.2. Practical judgment illustrated. Adapted from Intezari and Pauleen (2014, p. 397).

contrast practical judgment, or what they call a wise response to a situation, with a solely knowledge response: "While a 'knowledge response' is constructed solely of knowledge and can be fostered by knowledge management, we define a 'wise response' as the embodied individual/organizational practice that brings along with knowledge a set of moral, epistemic, and practical virtues" (p. 397).

SYSTEMS THINKING AND COMPLEXITY SCIENCE

The growing interest in systems thinking and complexity sciences across the social sciences generally (e.g., Byrne & Callaghan, 2014) is evident in the field of evaluating social interventions as well (Bamberger, Vaessen, & Raimondo, 2015; Gates, 2016; Mowles, 2014; Reynolds, Forss, Hummelbrunner, Marra, & Perrin, 2012; Reynolds, Gates, Hummelbrunner, Marra, & Williams, 2016; Walton, 2014). This interest stems, in part, from concerns about the linear and reductionist tendencies in social science methodologies, which arguably fall short of facilitating understanding and action in the face of multifaceted and dynamic issues. There are a variety of theoretical approaches and methodologies within the umbrella of systems thinking and complexity science. Such variety calls for caution in making sweeping claims about these fields. We highlight a few ideas drawn from these fields that scholars are using in relation to an emerging frame for evaluating.

First, complexity does not simply mean difficult or multifaceted, as used in everyday life. Systems thinkers and complexity scientists tend to use the term differently. In systems thinking (Reynolds & Holwell, 2020), complexity refers to a problem situation (a "problem" is a situation needing improvement or an opportunity to be addressed). Complexity characterizes the interconnectedness of multiple factors that influence a situation of interest and the plurality of perspectives, values, and interests brought by the people involved in and affected by the situation. In complexity science, the word *complex* typically refers to systems. The natural and social worlds are assumed to be composed of systems, some of which are labeled "complex adaptive systems" if they exhibit certain properties (Byrne & Callaghan, 2014). Regardless of whether one ascribes complexity to situations or systems, the key is that systems thinking and complexity science both embrace complexity and advance a systemic approach to making sense of it. A systemic response differs from a systematic response. The traditional systematic response to complexity, stemming from Newtonian science, is to reduce the situation or system to its component parts; understand each part separately; and then, put these understandings back together to understand the whole. However, given dimensions of complexity, such as interrelationships that generate emergent properties, such a reductionist approach can be problematic. Complex situations and systems cannot simply be reduced to and studied in terms of their parts alone, for, as is commonly stated, "the whole is greater than the sum of its parts." Therefore, systems thinking and complexity science advance systemic approaches that aspire to understand the whole system or situation while accounting for boundaries.

Second, the situations (including interventions) of greatest interest to systems thinkers are characterized by a need for a multidisciplinary approach to making sense of them; continually changing data; differing perspectives and conflicts over values; as well as disagreements not only on what actions to take but also on what the results of those actions are likely to be and what constitutes progress. Taken collectively, these characteristics point to the impossibility of completely understanding (i.e., studying, mapping, modeling) a complex situation or system. The alternative, systemic and complexity-oriented response, uses systems methodologies (e.g., Reynolds & Holwell, 2020) and complexity-congruent theories, concepts, and methods (Byrne & Callaghan, 2014). Systems thinking offers guidance in making sense of complex interrelationships and feedback loops in engaging with multiple, often conflicting, perspectives on situations; and in challenging our frameworks of understanding and practice (Reynolds, 2007, p. 3).

Third, complexity science uses several analytic concepts that are not commonly employed in the conventional frame (e.g., nonlinearity, phase and space attractors, system trajectories). Understanding the relevance of complexity-informed thinking to the alternative frame of evaluating thus requires careful study of this analytical vocabulary as well as knowing how to adapt it to the activity of studying social interventions. For example, in complexity theory, complex systems do not have a sole future (Byrne & Callaghan, 2014), thus the study of how systems change moves from consideration of a single, predictable linear pathway to multi-potential paths or future states. This complicates the matter of prediction and control. Prediction will involve identifying possible future states and determining what might lead to any one of these possible states. Adapting this idea to the practice of evaluating leads us to view processes of learning and acting about the performance (value) of social interventions as iterative, ongoing, and defying any predetermined moves from point *A* (the start of an intervention) to point *B* (the planned outcomes of the intervention).

Fourth, evaluating acquires a different character when informed by systems thinking and complexity science. As noted in Chapters 3 and 4, in the conventional frame, evaluating is *purposive*—it is a matter of establishing the purpose (or goals), intended beneficiaries, and performance criteria for determining the achievement of those goals for the beneficiaries. It is assumed that an intervention's purpose is defined in relation to the manner in which the problem is framed and goals are chosen. The purpose of the intervention is endogenous in the sense that it is inherent ("fixed" or "set") in the design of the intervention and the views of primary stakeholders. The assumed purpose constitutes the scope of the value of the intervention.

In the emerging alternative frame, the scope of the value of an intervention is more fluid and dynamic. Purposes are pluralistic and exogenous, stemming from outside the intervention (as designed or intended) and from the various ways the intervention can be framed using different boundaries, values, and evidence bases. As such, purposes are unstable, changeable, and negotiable. Evaluating therefore requires ongoing inquiry about purposes amidst changing circumstances and from different viewpoints rather than from a presumed fixed purpose(s). This kind of evaluative inquiry incorporates consideration of stakeholder values, interests, and perspectives and individual and group-level normative ideals about how the situation or system both is and should be. Evaluating is thus a matter of *purposeful* action (Reynolds, 2007), that is, action aimed at adapting to changes in situations and values.

Fifth, in contrast to a solution-driven approach to evaluation characteristic of the mainstream frame, the emerging orientation as informed by systems thinking is more problem-focused. More attention is paid to problem-structuring methods. Problem-solving and solution-driven approaches tend to assume that all relevant issues, goals, constraints, limits, and so on that make up a problem can be identified and defined in advance of problem solving. On the contrary, problem-structuring methods assume that there is no single uncontested representation of what constitutes the problem and thus focus on facilitation of the participatory exploration of ideas and actions (Midgley, 2000). In addition, while acknowledging that problem definition draws on evidence, this emerging orientation emphasizes that the act of defining a problem is often a political process of exercising power and framing evidence to persuade others to pay close attention to one specific interpretation of a problem (Cairney, 2019). Wicked problems characterized by multiple actors, multiple perspectives, incommensurable or conflicting interests and values, and key uncertainties are prime candidates for problem-structuring methods (Mingers & Rosenhead, 2002; Smith & Shaw, 2019).

Sixth, the emerging orientation generally steers clear of efforts to find "best practice" solutions that are supposedly transportable to multiple sites and circumstances. It aligns with frameworks such as Problem-Driven Iterative Adaptation (PDIA) that rest on the following four principles (Andrews, Pritchett, & Woolcock, 2012, 2016):

1. Develop local solutions for local problems: Solve locally nominated and defined problems in performance (as opposed to transplanting preconceived and packaged "best-practice" solutions).

2. Foster positive deviance: Create an authorizing environment for decision making that encourages positive deviance and experimentation (as opposed to designing projects and programs and then requiring agents to implement them exactly as designed).

3. Try, learn, iterate, adapt: Embed experimentation in tight feedback loops that facilitate rapid experiential learning (as opposed to enduring long lag times in learning from ex post "evaluation").

4. Engage champions: Engage broad sets of agents to ensure that reforms are viable, legitimate, relevant, and supportable (as opposed to a narrow set of external experts promoting the top-down diffusion of innovation).

Evaluating from systems and complexity orientations can take the form of entirely new ways of thinking about evaluation. This is evident in Patton's (2011, 2018) explanations of developmental evaluation and principles-based evaluation, in Bob Williams's (Williams & van't Hof, 2016) work combing evaluation with strategy development and organizational change, in Jonathan Morrell's focus on evaluation uncertainty (*https://evaluationuncertainty.com*), and in the guidelines on using systems thinking in evaluation prepared by the Systems in Evaluation Topical Interest Group of the American Evaluation Association (2018). Other examples of how evaluators draw on systems thinking and complexity science can be found in the 2021 issue of *New Directions in Evaluation* (Gates, Walton, & Vidueira, in press).

BOUNDARY CRITIQUE

In the alternative framing of evaluating, researchers and evaluators recognize that social problems of poverty, homelessness, immigration, educational achievement, public health, environmental degradation, and so
on are continuously changing and subject to differing perspectives such
that any attempt to bound them is temporary. For every problem, there are
pluralistic and contested definitions, and any definition implies a solution
option and, therefore, a political and normative stance about what should
be done (Gates, 2016). Furthermore, most social problems are interconnected, and any policy or program to address one problem inevitably influences others. Critical systems thinking and its principles and process of
boundary critique raise questions and offer guidance within this alternative
frame. Critical systems thinking, a particular version of systems thinking,
emphasizes

> (a) Critical awareness—examining and re-examining taken for-granted
> assumptions, along with the conditions that give rise to them; (b) Improve-
> ment—defined temporarily and locally, but in a widely informed manner, tak-
> ing issues of power into account; and, (c) Methodological pluralism—using
> a variety of methods in a theoretically coherent manner, becoming aware of
> their strengths and weaknesses, to address a corresponding variety of issues.
> (Boyd et al., 2007, p. 1320)

Drawing on boundary critique, the emerging orientation of evaluating
problematizes the notion of social betterment or improvement. For something to be called an improvement, the boundary of an analysis is crucial.
As Midgley (2000, p. 137, following Churchman, 1970) explains, "What is
to be included or excluded is a vital consideration: something that appears
to be an improvement given a narrowly defined boundary may not be seen
as an improvement at all if the boundaries are pushed out. Essentially,
defining the boundaries of improvement is an *ethical* issue, requiring the
exercise of value judgments."

In the alternative framing of evaluation, two primary concerns are
(1) how different stakeholders in a project or intervention view and frame
problems, strategies, solutions, and outcomes and (2) how these different
perspectives can engage one another in a meaningful way. As Williams
(2015, p. 10) explains: "perspectives influence what we consider relevant or
irrelevant; they determine what is 'in' our framing—the way we understand
a situation—and consequently determine what lies 'outside' that framing."
The central question is who controls setting the boundary of the evaluative
inquiry. This is addressed through a process of boundary critique (Ulrich,
1983, 1987, 1988a, 1988b) whereby the borders of concern or what is relevant to a given evaluation are determined. For example, in an evaluation

designed using Principles of Kaupapa Māori (the Māori epistemological framework; see *www.rangahau.co.nz/research-idea/27*) and boundary critique, the evaluation team was composed of a local community-owned health service, Māori subtribes, and a government research agency (Hepi et al., in press). The project commissioners initially contracted the team to examine whether the risk of waterborne illness had decreased as a result of changes to drinking water supplies within a particular village area. They challenged this narrow boundary defined by the experts who had commissioned the project in which health was understood as the absence of disease. Instead, they adopted a Māori worldview that valued self-determination and health as a matter of community ownership and control. Adopting the latter boundary, among other alterations to the original scope of work, led to an evaluation that examined a wider set of activities and assessed their value in relation to supporting or hindering the village's ownership and control over the natural resources and processes vital to their health and well-being.

Setting the criteria for evaluating the instrumental worth or value of what is being evaluated, as described in Chapter 4, is a boundary decision. What differs in the alternative framing of evaluating is that (1) boundary setting is intimately linked to value judgments—the values adopted and promoted by stakeholders will direct drawing boundaries that determine what facts and evidence are considered relevant and (2) boundary critique is raised to a prominent, visible, and critical level. Ulrich (1988a, p. 416) argued that the field of evaluation has shown "an amazing helplessness, if not indifference, with respect to the problem of value judgments." While it pursues the goal of applying evaluation knowledge to public decision making so as to secure improvement, it has failed to develop "convincing heuristic tools for identifying and rationally unfolding the normative content of any concept of improvement, definition of 'the problem,' or solution proposal" (p. 416).

The justification of choices among boundaries should be conducted through rational arguments among those involved in and affected by an intervention. Stakeholder participation is therefore crucial to boundary setting. Ulrich and Reynolds (2010, p. 287) argue that engaging in boundary critique serves several critical ends, notably:

- Helping us to become aware of, and think through, the selectivity of our claims as a basis for cultivating reflective practice.

- Allowing us to explain to others our bias; how our views and claims are conditioned by our assumptions.

- Making it possible to see through the selectivity of the claims of others and thus to be better prepared to assess their merits and limitations properly.

- Improving communication by enabling us to better understand our differences with others. When we find it impossible to reach shared views and proposals through rational discussion, this is not necessarily because some of the parties do not want to listen to or have bad intentions but more often, because the parties are arguing from a basis of diverging boundary judgments and thus cannot reasonably expect to arrive at identical understandings of fact and value.

- Promoting among all the parties involved a sense of modesty and mutual tolerance that may facilitate productive cooperation.

The emerging orientation of evaluating replaces the mainstream orientation's quest for epistemological certainty that defines the pursuit of empirical evidence of what worked with acceptance of practical confidence arising through a process of critical reflection on boundaries. Boundary critique is not an operationalized process; that is, it does not follow a set of prescribed procedures. Rather, it is a discussion guided by a set of heuristics that help explore four dimensions of problem situations—sources of motivation, control, knowledge, and legitimacy as displayed in Table 5.2. Parties to an evaluation ask and answer the 12 questions shown in the table in two ways, a descriptive, mode—"This is the way it is"—and an ideal mode—"This is the way it ought to be." The dialogue facilitates analytical understanding of perspectives as well as a practical focus on ways to improve a situation (Ulrich & Reynolds, 2010).

Gates (2018) combines the use of critical systems heuristics with the idea of adaptive action from Eoyang and Holladay (2013) to argue that evaluating in the alternative frame is a matter of developing contrasting maps of a situation or intervention. Evaluating involves an iterative cycle guided by three questions: (1) What is? (2) What should be? and (3) What next? The first two questions involve using contrasting understandings and evidence bases. Gates (2018) describes this as "quality-as-mapped," and it involves

> comparing a descriptive map of what is with a normative (or ideal) map of what should be to generate an evaluative judgment, critique, and conversation. Determining value in quality-as-mapped involves rendering multiple evaluation judgments based on different boundaries and framings to develop a more comprehensive and pluralistic understanding of the value of an evaluand while explicitly acknowledging the boundaries and framings used and who or what is and might be excluded and marginalized by these boundaries and framings. This is distinct from taking a descriptive approach to valuing that involves identifying criteria of interest to relevant stakeholders and reporting performance on each of these criteria. (p. 213)

Evaluating in this approach involves two phases. The first phase involves contextual, situational, and problem mapping, modeling, and analysis as well as examining multiple stakeholder and value perspectives

TABLE 5.2. Critical Systems Questions

Relevant groups	Sources of influence	Boundary judgment	Questions
The involved	*Motivation*	Beneficiary	1. Who ought to be/is the intended beneficiary?
		Purpose	2. What ought to be/is the purpose?
		Measure of improvement	3. What ought to be/is the measure of success?
	Control	Decision maker	4. Who ought to be/is in control of the conditions of success?
		Resources	5. What conditions of success ought to be/are under the control of the decision makers?
		Decision environment	6. What conditions of success ought to be/are outside the control of the decision makers?
	Knowledge	Expert	7. Who ought to be/is providing relevant knowledge and skills?
		Expertise	8. What ought to be/are relevant knowledge and skills?
		Guarantor	9. What ought to be/are regarded as assurances of successful implementation?
The affected	*Legitimacy*	Witness	10. Who ought to be/is representing the interests of those negatively affected but not involved?
		Worldview	11. What ought to be/are the opportunities for the interests of those negatively affected to have expression and freedom from the dominant worldview?
		Emancipation	12. What space ought to be/is available for reconciling differing worldviews among those involved and affected?

Note. Adapted from Ulrich and Reynolds (2010, p. 244) with permission. The boundary questions were first published in Ulrich (1987, p. 279), and their arrangement in the present table form originates in Ulrich's table of boundary categories (1983, p. 258) along with a table he suggested for recording the process of unfolding the boundary questions (1996/2014, p. 44).

on "what is." The second phase involves normative mapping, systems modeling, values deliberation, and other means of examining ways to improve the current situation, intervention, or system. Following the first and second phases, there is an evaluative process of contrasting what is with what should be to examine the value of some intervention or to identify future actions. Evaluators can also use these phases in exploring and structuring a problematic situation of interest or designing interventions to move from what is to what should be.

CO-PRODUCTION AND DELIBERATION

The alternative framing of evaluating builds on and extends notions of participatory and collaborative approaches to evaluation (e.g., Cousins & Whitmore, 1998; see also Shulha et al., 2016) that directly involve stakeholders in the process. In the evaluation literature we find four arguments for the importance of involving stakeholders in significant ways in evaluating: (1) It improves the quality of the evaluation research, (2) it enhances the likelihood of the use of findings, (3) it potentially empowers nonevaluator participants and increases their sense of ownership of the evaluation, and (4) participation/engagement of stakeholders is simply an intrinsic good in a democracy. As is evident from the prior discussion of boundary critique, the rationale for participant involvement in the emerging framing of evaluating extends these arguments. Stakeholder involvement is allied with the focus of participatory action research on promoting social change. Evaluating is thus viewed as a type of co-production—an iterative, dynamic, and collaborative process involving multiple and diverse types of expertise, knowledge, and actors producing context-specific knowledge to answer questions such as "How did we do?' and "What should we do now?"

Originally introduced by the late Eleanor Ostrom (1996), co-production has multiple meanings in policymaking, governance, and research in different fields. Here we focus on it as a means of redefining the relationship between professionals evaluating a public service and citizens. Mutuality and reciprocity replace the relationship of a client or consumer depending on expert appraisal. Citizens are not merely beneficiaries in receipt of expert services but collaborators who contribute their knowledge, experience, skills, and capabilities to creating social innovation. Co-production differs from a transaction-based method of service delvivery in which citizens consume professional services provided by governments, foundations, consulting firms, and nongovernmental organizations. Co-production is also an exploratory space and a generative process that leads to different, and sometimes unexpected, forms of knowledge, values, and social relations.

Co-production is also closely allied with democracy as a way of life, but in a unique way. Evaluation in the mainstream frame is championed by its apologists for its function of feeding in to and informing democratic discussion of social direction as that discussion and debate unfolds in the formal, institutional political sphere of decision making. This is evident in the oft-quoted goal of how evaluation of public programs serves the broad goal of social betterment, as well as in efforts to build evaluation capacity in institutions, agencies, and governments. In contrast, co-production is less concerned with the politics of democratic decision making in formal institutions in a democracy. Instead, co-production aligns with the idea of returning politics to the people, to the sphere of everyday practices, interactions, and understandings, and hence, to viewing democracy not as composed of all the features of formal politics but as a way of life—as John

Dewey put it. This is the realm of cooperative civic work of "a public—a mix of people whose interests, backgrounds, and resources may be quite different" (Dzur, 2008). Public work means something more than the idea of public deliberation. It raises the expectation that citizens act as co-creators of a public world; citizens making a public life together (Dzur, 2008). As politics returns to the people, the independent professional stance characteristic of much evaluation practice—wherein the evaluator serves as an outside expert rendering a judgment of value—gives way to a role for the evaluator as a facilitator of public discussion in ways that share power and responsibility with citizens (Schwandt, 2017, 2018).

The public work of evaluating unfolds not only through analysis as described in the notion of quality-as-mapped, but also through deliberation of boundaries and direction as explained previously. The National Research Council (1996) explains the two processes:

> Analysis and deliberation can be thought of as two complementary approaches to gaining knowledge of the world, forming understandings on the basis of knowledge, and reaching agreement among people. Analysis uses rigorous, replicable methods, evaluated under the agreed protocols of an expert community—such as those of disciplines in the natural, social, or decision sciences, as well as mathematics, logic, and law—to arrive at answers to factual questions. . . . In deliberation, people confer, ponder, exchange views, consider evidence, reflect on matters of mutual interest, negotiate, and attempt to persuade each other. Deliberation includes both consensual communication processes and adversarial ones. (p. 73)

In discussing the characteristics of public decision making, Thomas Webler (1998), a professor of environmental decision making, adds that analysis is not simply about facts, and deliberation is not simply about values. Values inform the way analyses are done, by whom, and when. And we often deliberate the facts of the matter, as is evident in any courtroom proceeding.

ACTIVITY MODEL OF INTERVENTION AIMED AT SOCIAL LEARNING

Thinking and acting in evaluating informed by systems practice are not distinct activities but are related to one another in a recursive fashion. That is, they bring each other forth, and collectively they can be understood as conceptually or theoretically informed practical action (Ison, 2010). Thoughtful, practical doing is what Aristotle called *praxis*. This activity has been described in similar ways by Schön (1995) as reflection-in-action, by Dewey (1933) as inquiry, as a form of "doing" under conditions of complexity and uncertainty, and in traditions of action research (Midgley, 2000). Rather than linking evaluating to a linear process of program design–program implementation–program evaluation, the emerging orientation regards evaluating as part of a structured, systemic, collaborative inquiry by multiple stakeholders into a situation experienced as complex and uncertain, coupled with action to change or transform the situation. Systems theorist and practitioner Ray Ison (2010) explains that transformation of a situation results from simultaneous changes in understandings (knowledge in action) and practices; a situation at $State_1$ is transformed to $State_2$ and so on and, with each iteration, stakeholders build their stakeholding in the situation.

In the emerging frame, evaluating as part of a broader inquiry-based social practice aimed at social learning is understood as concerted action by multiple stakeholders in complex and uncertain situations. Scholars of urban planning and management science John Friedmann and George Abonyi (1976, p. 933) argue that social learning is composed of four dynamically interrelated processes: (1) the actors' image of the situation, (2) social values that are normative guides to the actors' strategy for action, (3) political strategy, the course of action chosen as most likely to produce a desired result, and (4) social action, practical matters taken to implement the strategy. Any change in one of these aspects will necessarily affect the others.

The interplay of these processes of the social practice of learning can be clearly seen when one considers actors' perspectives or framings of a situation (Williams & Hummelbrunner, 2011; Williams & van t'Hof, 2016). Different stakeholders (groups of people that share a common role in a situation) have particular stakes in a situation (motivations that underpin their behaviors as well their sense of risk and opportunities), which leads them to see the situation in a particular way and place a premium on a particular way of acting in that situation. For example, consider again the situation/social problem of homelessness mentioned earlier. Members of law enforcement are likely to frame the situation of homelessness in ways quite different than those volunteers who staff a homeless shelter on a nightly basis.

When the focus is on evaluating as social learning, the role of the evaluator shifts from solely providing information to actually facilitating change and adaptive management (Eoyang & Berkas, 1999). This requires evaluators to assess communication and information flows in the intervention and to design the evaluation to facilitate use of data in these ongoing exchanges. Social learning is similar to models of team science that move "beyond simple linear methods of drawing association, to methods that enable multiple sources of data from different aspects of the scientific enterprise to inform the evaluation. Such multimodality may require modeling such different perspectives in the composition of the evaluation team itself" (Norman, Best, Mortimer, Huerta, & Buchan, 2011, p. 80). Social learning draws on critical pedagogy, participatory action research, soft systems methodology, and other group reflection–learning–action approaches (see the Methods Appendix in Chapter 6 for an introduction to some of these methods). Some constraints on and risks to learning in groups include defensive routines and group think, suppression of dissent, ignoring of dis-confirming evidence, cognitive and group errors, and time delays (Sterman, 2006).

Finally, in viewing evaluating as part of an activity model of interven-tion in a system, the emerging orientation places a particular emphasis on what participation in evaluation means. As noted above, in the mainstream orientation, participatory evaluating is driven primarily by epistemological and practical concerns. In the emerging orientation, participation is more sharply attuned to matters of authority (e.g., who defines the problem, who decides what constitutes good evidence, who determines what constitutes a valuable outcome and how), as well as power relationships within interven-tions and conflicts built into the structure of society (e.g., structural rac-ism). Power is seen as a critical determinant of the level and effectiveness of participation (Gregory, 2000). Power is a concern in the micropolitics of relationships between evaluation experts and stakeholders and between stakeholders of different social status. It is also evident at the much larger macropolitical level where, for example, social steering mechanisms focused on concerns about efficiency, cost–effectiveness, performance measure-ment, and "governing by numbers" (Rose, 1991), particularly in education and health fields, begin to intrude into all aspects of social life. These con-cerns about the distinctly moral-political dimensions of participation are evident in forms of evaluation practice labeled empowerment (Fetterman, Kaftarian, & Wandersman, 2015), culturally responsive (Hood, Hopson, & Frierson, 2015), and transformative (Mertens, 2009).

SELF-DETERMINATION AND SYSTEM CHANGE AS STIMULI FOR EVALUATION

An additional influence on the emerging frame comes from two distinct areas of evaluation practice that challenge the idea of evaluation as a mod-ernist undertaking and question the concept of improvement within the context of the status quo. Recall that the conventional frame for evaluating rests on the rationale that it contributes objective knowledge and rational feedback to policymakers and practitioners for improving society, where improvement occurs through a process of incremental change in policies and practices. Scholarship and practice on indigenous approaches and sys-tem change reframe this impetus for evaluation each in different ways.

Indigenous Research and Evaluation Approaches

Self-determination, the process by which a group or community directs its own vision and controls for its ways of living, serves as a central motiva-tion for evaluation in indigenous communities. These forms of evaluation criticize whose and what interests ultimately are, and should be, served by evaluating, and they reframe evaluating from indigenous (non-Western, non-Northern) perspectives. As part of an effort by the American Indian Higher Education Consortium, LaFrance, and Nichols (2010) conducted a study of the perceptions of evaluation within American Indian tribes to build an indigenous evaluation framework. In reporting what they heard during focus groups, they describe the following:

> Many stories illustrated how evaluation has come to be associated with exploitation, oppression, loss, and deficiency. Some expressed the view that evaluation, as taught in a Western tradition, focuses on assessing against non-Indian standards. When these standards become the definition of success, evaluation fails to recognize strengths in the community. . . . An important recommendation arising from these discussions was that, to counter this negative legacy, it was critical that evaluation be redefined. Rather than conveying judgement, evaluation should be viewed as an opportunity for learning. (p. 18)

Globally, multiple efforts have been made to develop and share what is emerging from indigenous evaluation—"done by, with and for indigenous people and informs decolonization" (Cram & Mertens, 2016, p. 166). This work directly opposes the colonization of land and people that shaped the history of Western science, including the evaluation field, and calls for framing evaluating based on furthering the well-being and control of indigenous groups over their lives. Marlene Brant Castellano (1997), Professor Emeritus of Indigenous Studies at Trent University in Canada, discusses three kinds of Aboriginal knowledge, two of which go beyond what is typical in social science-based evaluation: "traditional knowledge: handed down through the generations; empirical knowledge: gained through careful observation; and revealed knowledge: acquired through dreams, visions, and spiritual protocol" (cited in Cram & Mertens, 2016, p. 174). Some evaluation practitioners and scholars may regard indigenous evaluation as connected with transformative, culturally responsive, and social justice-oriented approaches given their shared interest in centering the voices, perspectives, and values of those most marginalized in society and advancing the well-being of these groups. However, Cram and Mertens (2016) argue that more is at stake: "The transformative paradigm emphasizes a commitment to social justice and equity, whereas the transformation desired by indigenous peoples includes decolonisation, sovereignty, and the return of stolen resources" (p. 170). Given this focus on self-determination, indigenous evaluation draws on existing "collective processes of reflection and decision-making that exhibit . . . connectedness with one another; with the earth, the oceans and rivers, animate and inanimate life as all have a life force; and with a spiritual world" (pp. 169–170). In our view, indigenous approaches provide an illustration of the emerging alternative frame for evaluating.

Approaches to System Transformation

Another effort to reshape evaluating that is gaining popularity in philanthropy among other areas is that of systems change and transformation. These efforts question the status quo and current social order. Over the last few decades, some philanthropies have shifted from traditional solutions to social issues toward strategies to change systems. Grantmakers for the Effective Organizations and Management Assistant Group (2016) explain, "A philanthropy cannot focus on one issue or set of grantees and achieve long-term change. Instead, grantmakers are trying to influence the bigger picture in all its complexity" (p. 4). Curtis, Vanstone, and Weinstein (2019), at the Australian Centre for Social Innovation, suggest a similar shift: "The norms of traditional philanthropy, e.g. short term, discreet investments and a board of experienced professionals, tend towards sustaining existing systems rather than transforming them to something different" (p. 7).

As discussed by Kania, Kramer, and Senge (2018), system change refers to shifting the conditions or factors that hold a problem, pattern, or trend in place. They offer a model focused on three levels of changing a system: (1) a structural level of explicit change of policies, practices, and resource flows; (2) a semi-explicit level of relationships, connections, and power dynamics; and (3) a transformative, implicit level regarding mental models or internally and culturally held understandings and assumptions (p. 4). Interest in leading system change work within philanthropy has sparked ways of reframing evaluating from a traditional focus on programs and interventions to evaluating within ongoing processes of system change and adaptive management. Learning guides evaluations of system change:

> Something we're learning is that the discussions and collective learning among stakeholders is where the value lies. It's what develops our skills to work with complexity in planning, actions, network design, and governance. Systems mapping isn't a technical fix, which a lot of people want it to be. It is really shifting the way we 1) look at complex social issues and the key dynamics involved and 2) engage a more diverse set of actors that are intentionally connected and aligned to have broader impact. (Grantmakers for Effective Organizations and Management Assistant Group, 2016, p. 5)

Evaluating system change is an open question explored by foundations and scholars alike. For example, the Rockefeller Philanthropy Advisors (2019) workshop of funders exploring this question drew from a systemic change evaluation framework developed by Margaret Hargreaves, which includes the following phases or characteristics: "systemic understanding of problems, developing a systemic theory of change, adaptive implementation, iterative learning cycles, assessing pattern shifts, and building sustainable capacity for monitoring, evaluation and learning" (p. 10).

DEVELOPING VALUE

In *determining* value, characteristic of the mainstream framing of evaluating, what constitutes an intervention's value (i.e., success, quality, performance) can be established in advance as a set of desired ends (objectives, goals, criteria, standards, or benchmarks) against which the intervention as a means is evaluated. This presupposes a particular relationship between means and ends in which ends can be defined with some level of agreement and certainty, and then the evaluative task can focus on the means—the policies, programs, projects, or practices carried out to realize such ends.

In *developing* value, this relationship between means and ends is fundamentally problematic and in need of radical challenge and reconsideration. If researchers and evaluators acknowledge the complexity of the social world, then problematic situations and interventions to address them require ongoing learning and action, both of which are always developing. Means and ends cannot be separated with examinations focusing on one or the other; rather, means and ends are intricately linked such that current actions reveal ends-in-the-making and shifts in desired ends call for immediate shifts in current actions (De Munck & Zimmerman, 2015). This poses an affront to results- and outcomes-based notions of accountability in which "doing good" and "succeeding" mean achieving what one set out to achieve and learning consists of improving means within given ends. As discussed in Chapter 3, the mainstream frame for evaluating emphasizes single-loop learning, which involves answering whether current goals are being achieved, strategies are being followed, and processes are working effectively. While this is an important question, it typically leads to answers that help to make minor adjustments in the short term, with little examination of whether the current goals, strategies, and procedures are indeed the right things to be pursuing. The alternative frame for evaluating emphasizes double-loop learning by encouraging reflection and critique of goals and underlying assumptions. Additionally, it seeks to raise questions about the normative perspectives from which any goal or action is considered right along the lines of "What makes this the right thing to do?" This is known as triple-loop learning; it moves beyond learning for making course corrections (as in single- and double-loop learning) to learning for discovering new courses of action that may have been out of view until overturning longstanding assumptions and perspectives.

Furthermore, in the emerging frame for evaluating, evaluative judgments about interventions are regarded as unstable, time bound, and variable across levels of a complex situation or system. Thus, reaching the judgment that citywide homeless shelters successfully provide housing locally is met by the fact that homelessness actually increases in other parts of the city over time and results in fewer shelters statewide as the homeless population relocates to the city with shelters. Value judgments vary depending on the purpose and perspective one takes on a situation or intervention, as we discussed earlier. Hence, in the emerging orientation, evaluative judgments are understood differently:

1. As previously noted, evaluative judgments are emergent and iterative in relation to different framings of what is evaluated and the situation under consideration.
2. More than simply reflecting a synthesis of the facts of the matter taking into account value preferences of stakeholders, evaluative judgments require the explicit consideration of matters of power, authority, and marginalization.
3. Such judgments are not pronouncements or resolutions but a form of action and reflection on the world in order to change it.
4. Evaluating is less like program auditing or gauging performance against a standard and more like an activity of moral-practical reasoning.
5. The aim of evaluating is to answer the question: "Given what we know and what we can imagine is possible, what should we do now?"

In the language of Reynolds (2007; drawing on Friedmann, 1987), these ideas align with the notion of "purposeful" evaluation—a complex, time-dependent process that involves, in addition to the action of evaluation itself, political strategy and tactics, theories of reality (which tell us what the world is like), and the values that inspire and direct our action in the world. Taken together, these elements constitute a form of evaluating as a social practice. Evaluating is very much a pragmatic endeavor in which evaluative judgments are tested by putting them into practice and seeing if the results are satisfactory, whether they enable helpful responses to novel problems or situations, and whether living in accordance with those judgments yields satisfactory results (Anderson, 2019).

The intellectual influences discussed above can be visually presented as a scheme of considerations influencing the way evaluative questions are answered, as shown in Figure 5.3.

SUMMARY

As a sense of urgency grows for ways to effectively address the interconnectedness of social, economic, political, and cultural circumstances and problems, discrete, goal-focused interventions and narrowly framed evaluations of planned processes and intended outcomes will likely be insufficient at best to effect change and innovation. An alternative mode of evaluating

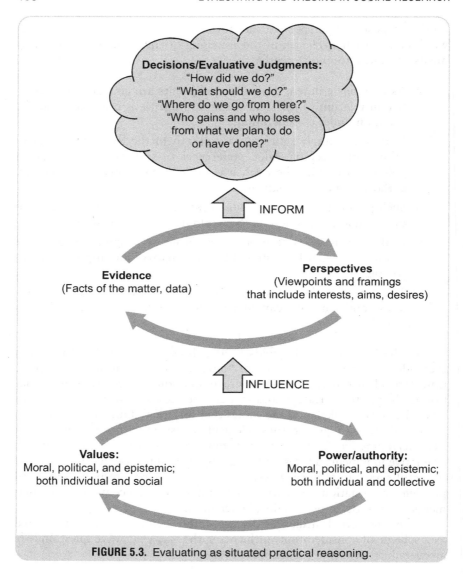

FIGURE 5.3. Evaluating as situated practical reasoning.

is needed, one that helps ask and answer difficult questions about whether and how to foster system change, adaptation, and innovation. This chapter sketched a picture of an alternative framing of evaluating as a social practice that draws on multiple resources across fields and disciplines, including practical reasoning, systems thinking and science, deliberative valuation, and social learning. Evaluating in this frame both questions and seeks to change the existing social order; is guided by stakeholder deliberation;

facilitates problem finding, learning, and action; views values as shaping both means and ends in an iterative fashion; and regards evaluative judgments as situated in processes of learning and action.

IMPORTANT RESOURCES ■ ■ ■ ■ ■ ■ ■ ■ ■ ■ ■ ■ ■ ■ ■ ■ ■

■ Ison, R. (2017). *Systems practice: How to act in situations of uncertainty and complexity in a climate-change world* (2nd ed.). London: Springer, 2017.

A comprehensive and very accessible examination of systems thinking and how that translates into theory-informed practical action. Part I explains why systems thinking is sorely needed. Part II uses a juggling metaphor to introduce readers to systems practice and how a systems practitioner works. Part III explores what constrains the use of systems practice and argues for innovation in practice via systemic inquiry. Part IV develops an argument for systems practice that can be utilized from personal to societal levels.

■ Williams, B., & van't Hof, S. (2016). *Wicked solutions: A systems approach to complex problems.* Self-published by Bob Williams. May be purchased at *www. gum.co/wicked* as well as on Amazon Books.

A user-friendly workbook for researchers, evaluators, and managers explaining the three basic systems concepts—interrelationships, perspectives, and boundaries—and how these dimensions of systems thinking can help one design suitable ways of tackling wicked problems.

■ Reynolds, M., & Holwell, S. (Eds.). (2020). *Systems approaches to making change: A practical guide* (2nd ed.). London: Springer.

Provides an overview of several different systems approaches, including System Dynamics, the Viable System Model, the Soft System Methodology, and Critical Systems Heuristics.

■ Gates, E. F. (2016). Making sense of the emerging conversation in evaluation about systems thinking and complexity science. *Evaluation and Program Planning, 59,* 62–73.

A paper directed to the audience of professional evaluation practitioners that explains how ideas and concepts from the literature in systems thinking and complexity science are influencing evaluation practice.

■ Rockefeller Philanthropy Advisors. (2019). *Assessing systems change: A Funders' Workshop report.* Download the report at *www.rockpa.org/wp-content/ uploads/2019/10/Assessing-Systems-Change-A-Funders-Workshop-Report-Rockefeller-Philanthropy-Advisors-August-2019.pdf.*

Summarizes and provides links to resources from a three-day workshop led by Margaret (Meg) Hargreaves, Glenn Page, and Zenda Ofir on how to monitor and evaluate systems change. Also see information on the broader initiative led by Rockefeller called *Scaling Solutions toward Shifting Systems* aimed at exploring the question, "Can we encourage collaborative, longer-term, adaptive resources to fund and accelerate scalable solutions targeting systemic changes around pressing global issues?"

■ Centre for the Evaluation of Complexity Across the Nexus (CECAN)

Based in the United Kingdom, a collaboration between researchers and practitioners in government, industry, and other sectors that provides training, methodological briefs, case studies, and research services regarding evaluating policy amidst complexity, particularly in the food, energy, water, and environmental domains. Visit the website at *www.cecan.ac.uk*.

BRIDGE TO PRACTICE

Imagine being tasked with evaluating the following network-based, educational initiative using the ideas discussed in this chapter. This six-page open-access article by David Dockterman (2018), "Insights from 200+ years of personalized learning" (*www.nature.com/articles/s41539-018-0033-x*) provides the context. Consider the following questions:

- How would you describe the purpose(s) and problem(s) addressed by the initiative?
- Which stakeholders might you engage with and what deliberative processes could you use to understand the initiative?
- What purposes or questions might evaluation(s) of this initiative serve?
- Which methods might you draw on to help address these purposes or questions?

Problematic Situation: Shifting Education from Standardized to Personalized

Dockterman (2018) argues that the educational system in the United States needs to shift from an outdated model of standardization in which instruction is designed and delivered for average age-based cohorts to a model that is personalized to each student:

> The instructional model of our age-graded system is based on the assumption of sameness with exceptions. Publishers of instructional materials and teachers construct lessons for the group and differentiate to accommodate the outliers. They provide layers of typically predetermined intervention to capture lagging students and occasionally offer extra challenges or gifted programs to stave off the boredom of children who are ready to progress ahead of their peers. . . . A personalization-based pedagogy, on the other hand, starts with the assumption that each student is different. Variability, across multiple dimensions (not just domain knowledge and skill), is inevitable. . . . To sustain this new approach, a new organizational and accountability system must mesh with the new pedagogy. (p. 4)

Along with others nationwide, Dockterman (2018) asks, "What kind of scalable educational structure can support and encourage a pedagogy more directed toward meeting variable learner needs?" (p. 4).

In an innovative response to this question, a former school superintendent, former school principal, and several educational technology specialists came together to form an initiative to inspire and support districts and schools in shifting to student-centered or personalized learning. Learning is "student-centered" when it foregrounds individual interests and needs, focuses on developing competencies, occurs in flexible spaces and modalities, and is owned by the participants (Nellie Mae Education Foundation, 2015). Student-centered approaches are called "personalized" because they center on student needs and identities (Wolfe, Steinberg, & Hoffman, 2013). Teachers apply these principles by designing curriculum and instruction that is individualized and relevant, flexibly paced, and grounded in formative assessments (Hinton, Fischer, & Glennon, 2013).

The initiative is a partnership between an educational technology group and a state department of education. According to its founders, the core purpose of the initiative is to address the need for a statewide, coordinated program to facilitate networking, learning, and implementing personalized learning. The initiative includes research to examine ongoing district and school infrastructure and practices to identify opportunities to initiate, expand, or deepen efforts to personalize learning; provide resources, regular news, and training for member districts and schools that are interested in or already working to personalize learning; create and promote experience- and video-based tours of personalizing learning efforts in classrooms; advocate for personalized learning in district and state meetings about educational policies; and on an ongoing basis, engage with national and international partnerships and organizations working on similar initiatives to shift the educational system from standardized to personalized learning. Facing limited funding and a passion to both learn from and expand their work, the leadership team put out a request for proposals to evaluate this initiative. The call described the initiative, as above, and invited evaluation proposals that would help the team learn from and improve their work and gather evidence of the value of their work. The evaluative evidence would be used to build momentum within and across the network to, hopefully, invite additional schools and districts to join and to inform funding proposals.

CHAPTER 6

Evaluating as a Multifaceted Investigation of Value

In Chapters 3, 4, and 5, we discussed multiple ways in which the activity of evaluating is framed, and we drew attention to assumptions in each of those framings about what constitutes a social problem, how evaluation is linked to social problem solving, how stakeholders should be involved in evaluation, what and whose criteria should be used as a basis for evaluation, and so on. Perhaps the most pronounced contrast we identified was between the ideas of *determining* value versus *developing* value. One interpretation of the purpose of evaluating in social research is that evaluative judgments are a matter of determining the value of interventions on the basis of agreed-upon criteria. Determining means establishing, settling on, and concluding. Thus, evaluative judgments take the form of relatively determinate answers to questions such as "Are we doing things right?"; "How did we do?"; and "Did we accomplish what we set out to accomplish?" The phrase "determining value" is also shorthand for the idea that evaluating is a matter of using rigorous evidence to reduce uncertainty about whether an intervention reliably works to produce intended outcomes.

Another interpretation of evaluating views making evaluative judgments as a much more fluid, contested, open-ended, and dynamic undertaking. In other words, agreeing on the value some action (intervention, plan, project, program) has is always to some extent an uncertain, unfolding, conditional, and developing matter that not only looks at where we have been (i.e., "How did we do?") but also where we might go and what might be the consequences of our choices. The phrase "developing value" is also shorthand for the idea that evaluating is as much a matter of making sense of value perspectives as it is about gathering evidence.

On the one hand, framing evaluating as a matter of developing value is well suited to decision-making situations where facts and values are disputed; the problem in question is incapable of definitive formulation; and action and learning are ongoing, with continuous adjustments as knowledge and circumstances change and the future unfolds. On the other hand, while framing evaluating as developing value is materially and substantively distinct from the framing discussed in Chapters 3 and 4, it is not uncommon that evaluating aligned with the notion of developing value will also make use of some of the ideas and practices associated with determining the value of planned interventions. In this chapter, we use the example of ReThink Health—a philanthropic initiative to transform the systems that shape health and well-being in the United States—to illustrate a multifaceted investigation of value.

A variety of groups working on complex, dynamic social and environmental issues or pursuing structural and systemic change engage in evaluating informed by features of the emerging alternative frame (e.g., Center for Community Health and Evaluation, 2020; Richardson & Patton, in press; Scally et al., 2020). This case provides one illustration of what this alternative looks like in practice. The case draws from a study conducted by Gates and Fils-Aime (in press) of evaluation—both the purpose of evaluation and methods used—within ReThink Health. They found a blend of system change evaluation paired with more traditional, project-based evaluation work. ReThink Health uses a wide variety of methods for both researching and evaluating, some of which are more closely aligned with what one might find in the conventional framing of evaluating others uniquely developed by ReThink Health to address characteristics of the emerging alternative frame for evaluating discussed in Chapter 5. After introducing the philanthropic initiative, we highlight several features of the ReThink Health initiative, including its focus on (1) purposive and purposeful systems change; (2) co-developed change processes; (3) cycles of problem framing, learning, and action; and (4) methods for boundary analysis, evidence generation, and values deliberation. We then turn to the role and character of evaluating within this initiative, distinguishing evaluating for purposes of learning and field-building; discrete evaluations to examine progress against the theorized change processes; and ongoing evaluating as situated in deliberation and learning.

THE RIPPEL FOUNDATION'S RETHINK HEALTH INITIATIVE

The Rippel Foundation shifted from a traditional approach to social change work through grantmaking to research and development work designed to create and sustain conditions for health and well-being in the United States. As part of this shift, in 2007, Rippel launched the ReThink Health Initiative, which "sought to enable a genuine metamorphosis within the health system" (as cited in Sastry & Penn, 2014, p. 267). Their work is influenced by well-regarded systems thinkers and scholars, including Peter Senge (1990), author of *The Fifth Discipline: The Art and Practice of the Learning Organization,* and Nobel Prize winner Elinor Ostrom's *Governing the Commons: The Evolution of Institutions for Collective Action* (2015). Bobby Milstein, co-founder of ReThink Health, spent two decades at the U.S. Centers for Disease Control and Prevention prior to joining Rippel. He also leads Rippel's efforts to rethink evaluation for system change. Milstein works closely with Jane Erickson, who leads Rippel's Organizational Learning and Evaluation team with several colleagues.

Purposive and Purposeful Change

Conventionally framed, social interventions have clear goals and are part of a well-planned approach to addressing a social condition, problem, or need. Both planners and evaluators assume that if the intervention is well designed and implemented, it probably can (and hopefully will) solve or remedy the targeted problem. Evaluating assesses various aspects of the intervention, including the needs and characteristics of target populations, intervention design and implementation, outcomes and impacts, and cost–effectiveness (Rossi et al., 2019). In contrast to this more purposive approach to evaluation and more illustrative of the emerging alternative frame, the work of ReThink Health seeks to generate systems change and conceives of social intervention as an ongoing activity co-produced with others.

ReThink Health aims to transform health ecosystems and explore what is possible amidst future unfolding conditions that shape health and well-being in the United States. Its work began with questioning underlying assumptions and trends in public health, health care services, and medicine, as well as broader societal trends. As explained by Milstein (2019), the widespread and common-sense use of the term *health* is both narrow and problematic. *Health,* which originally meant a "state of being whole, sound, or well," has come to be associated with health care industries and services recasting health as "efforts to maintain or restore physical, mental, or emotional well-being especially by trained and licensed professionals" (p. 7). The work of ReThink Health builds on a foundational relationship between health and wealth, understood as well-being. It regards health and wealth in a feedback loop—"a vicious or virtuous cycle" (p. 2)—in which declines of one lead to declines in the other and increases of one lead to increases in the other. ReThink Health also challenges the reliance on health care as primarily relying on the professional expertise of health care providers. It expands the idea of health care using the concept of system stewardship as explained below. Questions that motivate the foundation's work include "How do we produce health, wealth, and well-being?" (Milstein, 2019, p. 2) and "What can we do, with others, to alleviate urgent needs and secure the vital conditions that all people need to survive and thrive?" (Milstein, 2019, p. 4).

In this way, ReThink Health began with a morally and politically motivated commitment to alter the systems and conditions that shape health and well-being in the United States. Systems change serves as an internally ascribed purpose to their work but also undergoes continual framing and reframing as the meanings and processes for systems change are purposefully developed within each initiative. Moreover, Rippel staff members do not view themselves as scientific experts operating out of an established evidence base or intervention model. Rather, they view their role and charge as leaders, collaborators, learners, and partners who work closely with multiple stakeholders to explore and influence the structures and conditions that shape health and well-being.

Rippel draws on a model of systems change introduced by researchers at the consulting firm FSG. The model, displayed in Figure 6.1, portrays six interdependent conditions that play important roles in holding a social problem in place (in this case, the problem of public health and well-being) and that must be addressed to achieve systems change. Structural, explicit

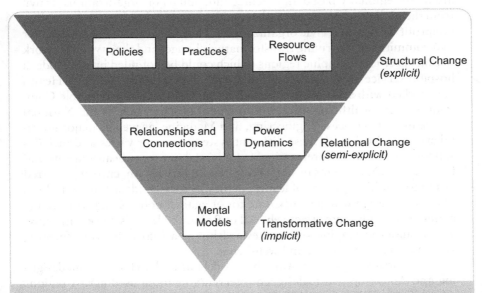

FIGURE 6.1. Six conditions of system change. From Kania, Kramer, and Senge (2018). Reprinted with permission from FSG.

conditions are evident in policies, practices, and resource flows in organizations. Relational conditions are both tacit and explicit (hence semi-
explicit) and refer to connections and communications, interactions, and
power dynamics among individuals and groups. Finally, genuine transformative conditions are quite implicit in that they deal with changing mental models—deeply held beliefs and assumptions. This focus on systems
change serves as an internally driven (i.e., purposive) model to organize
the work of ReThink Health. Yet, that model becomes purposeful as it is
interpreted, made real, and adapted for use in the initiatives that Rippel
co-develops with its partners.

Change Process Co-Developed with *System Stewards* and Guided by the *Pathway*

In conceiving of systems change as a process that necessarily involves co-
development with others, ReThink Health draws on two approaches. First,
they work with and foster *system stewards* in their work regionally and
nationally. The concept of being a steward draws on the work of Peter Block
(2013), who argues that stewards exhibit commitments to the ideas that
"purpose must be larger than oneself and one's organization; power must be
built and distributed with others, not consolidated; wealth must be invested,
not withheld, to create long-term value as well as address short-term urgent
needs" (as cited by ReThink Health, n.d.-a., Foundation website). Stewards
are often regionally based and include individuals or organizations drawn
from the philanthropic sector, policymaking arenas, the corporate as well as
nonprofit worlds, and civic organizations. They share a sense of concern for
and commitment to driving transformative change, and they typically work
within specific geographic regions (which could be bounded by a zipcode, a
hospital service area, a neighborhood, etc.). Additionally, ReThink Health
has worked with state groups, including the California Accountable Communities for Health Initiative, and national groups, such as the National
Academies of Sciences, Engineering, and Medicine, as well as major hospital systems. Work with these different system stewards varies and includes
supporting stewards in reframing narratives about what health means and
the role of local residents in supporting community health; crafting a shared
vision for multiple groups of leaders across sectors; or identifying windows
of opportunity in which to advocate for or against policies and strategizing
about how to advocate effectively. All of ReThink Health's work with stewards is about leveraging system stewardship as a vehicle for transforming
systems to produce health and well-being.

Supporting a system stewardship model rather than focusing on designing and delivering select, designed interventions to be used across regions
allows for focusing the system change work on strengthening existing (or
newly formed) relationships as well as engaging in region-specific delibera-

tions about the means and desired ends for system change. Sastry and Penn (2014) further describe this approach: "The goal was to create a disciplined way for each community to explore how they could improve everyone's health by involving local stakeholders—including business, government, and social sector leaders who rarely collaborate systematically to plan a joint future. Each effort would be driven by a community that invited the program team. Together, they would take on pressing questions, needs, opportunities, and desires driven by the stakeholders themselves" (p. 268). ReThink Health focuses on developing a viable, sustainable process of fostering stewardship for systems change and is less concerned with the immediate outcomes or results of these efforts. This approach is grounded in a conviction that changes in outcomes or results are temporary and fleeting if the design and workings of underlying system conditions are set up to produce contrary outcomes. For example, an initiative to change the consumption patterns of sugary beverages within a targeted region through marketing campaigns and other efforts may produce successes. However, successes will not last if the underlying issues that influence this pattern of consumption are not changed (e.g., access to healthy food, safe spaces for physical exercise, advertising).

Beginning from the premise that the public health ecosystem is not working well and needs to be transformed, ReThink Health also grounds its work in a vision and process for making the system better called the *Pathway for Transforming Regional Health*. This *Pathway* is based on what they call a hypothesis of how system stewards contribute to changes in the systems of interest:

> Rippel's best hypothesis is that as stewards mature in their ability to facilitate cross-sector collaboration and alignment, they are able to create a new ecosystem for health and well-being in their regions; an ecosystem known for producing equitable outcomes. This hypothesis is backed by both empirical and anecdotal evidence. . . . As our team works with stewards, we all get more and more knowledgeable about what the Pathway ought to include. With the passing of time we have refined our hypothesis, making it stronger and better for stewards who want to use it as a framework for transforming the regions they serve. Refinement will continue as we take on each new initiative and project. (ReThink Health, n.d.-c, Stewards' Pathway)

This *Pathway,* depicted in Figure 6.2, provides a common framework for ReThink Health's work with system stewards that can be used across regional- and national-level initiatives. The *Pathway* is composed of five phases: (1) coming together, (2) exploring regional goals, (3) building an interdependent portfolio, (4) making the portfolio happen, and (5) living a new ecosystem (ReThink Health, 2019b).

The *Pathway* is not a static framework but rather something that continually gets tested, refined, and altered with each co-developed initiative. It

Phase 1: Coming Together	Phase 2: Exploring Regional Goals	Phase 3: Building an Independent Portfolio	Phase 4: Making the Portfolio Happen	Phase 5: Living a New Ecosystem
• Focus on identified problem or need, typically for a limited period of time • Each individual or group contributes but does not change their ways of working or self-interests	• Widen working relationships and establish group routines • Begin to articulate a shared vision • Explore sharing information and responsibility across multiple issues and initiatives	• Work together routinely to shared vision • Use vision to guide investments and actions • Negotiate and begin to enact an interdependent portfolio of interventions	• Abandon business as usual • Align their work with a wider portfolio of interventions • Act through new roles and new mindsets to bring their portfolio to life	• New institutions, markets, and accountability mechanisms emerge • Organizations coordinate to produce fair and just opportunities for health and well-being • Integrate continuous monitoring and improvement in system design

FIGURE 6.2. *Pathway* for transforming health and well-being through regional stewardship. From ReThink Health (n.d.-b). Adapted with permission from The Rippel Foundation.

reflects a developmental approach to systems change that unfolds through a set of 10 "essential practices" that stewards should commit to throughout their work together (ReThink Health, n.d.-c, Stewards' Pathway). These 10 practices call on stewards to do each of the following:

- Articulate and routinely pursue a clear, compelling, shared vision for the region.

- Ensure that stewards' efforts, including governance and management activities, are aligned to achieve their shared vision.

- Seek to expand the diversity and number of other stewards involved.

- Increase their commitment to the regional effort, relative to their vested interests.

- Create the conditions for robust, routine, and transparent resident leadership.

- Use common measures and integrate data. Share knowledge and use it to reflect on and refine their practice.

- Develop a comprehensive theory of system change.

- Design an interdependent portfolio of interventions.

- Develop a long-term financial plan for implementing the portfolio of interventions and related integrative activities.

- Secure long-term financial sustainability. (ReThink Health, 2019a, pp. 2–4)

ReThink Health assumes that in the early stages of their work, stewards have less collaborative capacity to work across boundaries, but that over time collaborative capacity will increase across four dimensions: shared vision, broad stewardship, sound strategy, and sustainable financing to generate system change.

Change Process as Cycles of Problem Framing, Learning, and Action

ReThink Health frames itself as an ambitious action research and development initiative weaving iterative cycles of learning, action, and evaluation into ways it works internally as well as with partner groups. Rippel endorses a systems approach to change and breaks away from the traditional approach of identifying a need or problem bounded by geographical region and target population, followed by developing or using an evidence-based intervention model where learning and evaluating focus on improving or assessing the effectiveness of the model.

ReThink Health guides a change process with system stewards to determine what the problems, issues, concerns, or needs are within the existing set of interconnected and dynamic circumstances shaping health and well-being. The process has been described as follows: "participants . . . start by examining the current health system within the region to identify existing or potential failure modes, in essence creating a list of things they did not want to occur. Working within a carefully designed process, they then come up with new ideas for collaborations, policy changes, and shared priorities" (Sastry & Penn, 2014, p. 268). A key feature of the foundation's work in facilitating this change process is that the problems and interventions are not predefined by ReThink Health, but rather are identified, discussed, and prioritized by the regionally based stakeholder groups. ReThink Health developed a variety of resources for stewards to use that are publicly available on their website (n.d.-e, Stewards' Resources). *Ventures* and *Vistas* are examples of developing value through cycles of problem framing, adapting, and learning.

Ventures was a multiyear initiative funded by the Robert Wood Johnson Foundation that supported six established multisector partnerships. Each partnership received a small grant of $25,000 for their involvement, technical assistance, individualized coaching from ReThink Health staff members, and cross-learning during virtual meetings and in-person convenings with other teams in *Ventures*. For example, the Trenton Health Team was a citywide partnership and state-designated Accountable Care Organization that grew into a regional hub during its involvement with *Ventures*. Another initiative, based in King County, Washington, was composed of a team of leaders from the public, nonprofit, and philanthropic sectors who created an initiative called "You Belong Here" to broaden resident and other stakeholder engagement in health in the region (Mt. Auburn Associates, 2019). ReThink Health's work with each regional stewardship team was tailored to the priorities of that team. Using an emergent design process, ReThink Health did an initial site assessment to establish the scope of work, followed by continuous development and refinement of frameworks, tools, and processes that the team could use (Mt. Auburn Associates, 2019). Across *Ventures* initiatives, ReThink Health sought to "identify 'exemplary practices' that would advance learning about more mature efforts to transform health and well-being among local leaders and national catalyst organizations focused on this work" (Mt. Auburn Associates, 2019, p. 4).

On the basis of evaluating this initiative, Rippel learned that it was the networks of actors with distributed leadership rather than multisector partnerships that were the real drivers of change. As a result, the Foundation launched another initiative called *Vistas* in order to understand how networks of actors successfully organize to drive change along the Pathway. This initiative explores whether and how stewardship contributes to changes in stewards' mindsets and actions and connections between these changes and shifts within broader networks of stewards. Efforts to understand what happened and what can be learned from *Vistas* are currently underway.

Boundary Critique, Values Deliberation, and Evidence Generation

Conventional models of intervention focus on a robust program design and on implementing this design with fidelity as preconditions to rigorous evaluation aimed at generating evidence of the association between the intervention and intended effects and minimizing error and uncertainty in these estimates. ReThink Health wholly departs from this way of thinking and turns to a wide variety of methods and tools to support its work that align with features of the alternative frame discussed in Chapter 5, including boundary critique, values deliberation, and evidence generation.

In working with stewards in *Ventures* and *Vistas,* ReThink Health discovered the need to facilitate discussion across stakeholders coming from various disciplinary, institutional, and role perspectives about what is wrong with the current circumstances shaping health and well-being in a given region. Typically, boundaries are set narrowly around health as the absence of disease and an outcome of quality health care systems. In order to broaden the scope of the phenomena of health and well-being and to invite questioning and dialogue about the various influences at work, ReThink Health staff developed the *Wellbeing Portfolio* (ReThink Health, 2019b). This visual tool helps in identifying vital conditions, urgent services, and civic muscle. Vital conditions for health include basic needs for health and safety; humane housing; lifelong learning; thriving environment; meaningful work and wealth; and reliable transportation. Urgent services include acute care for illness or injury; homeless services; addiction and recovery services; environmental clean-up; criminal justice and emergency services; unemployment and food assistance. Ways to build civic muscle, an individual's or a group's sense of belonging and power to influence, include things like reducing discrimination, providing social support, and training in advocacy (ReThink Health, 2019b). This tool provides an accessible way of framing the problem areas that groups could work on and invites reflection and engagement with questions of where and how to set boundaries regarding what to address.

Social and political values play several roles in the work of ReThink Health. Because their work involves challenging the status quo with respect to the meanings of health and well-being and cultivating system stewardship, it involves challenging and changing societal and regional values. In traditional health care, urgent services are overvalued, whereas preventative care and maintenance of vital conditions tend to be undervalued. The processes and tools used by ReThink Health help generate reflection, conversation, and learning around what is and should be valued to enhance health and well-being. One tool, used mostly in their regionally based, stewardship work is the *Public Narrative*:

> Narrative is the skill of creating a shared story around our common values to motivate others to join us in action. It involves three core components: personal stories that illustrate our own values ("story of self"); collective stories that illustrate shared values ("story of us"); and stories that illustrate both the challenges a group faces and the hopeful actions groups can take to address those challenges ("story of now"). In this tool, we focus specifically on the first narrative: Story of Self. (ReThink Health, 2015a, p. 2)

The tool provides a framework and process for stewards to surface and share their personal stories and values, which are then woven together as a shared set of values. Values identification and deliberation are also part of ReThink Health's frameworks and tools.

To ensure that analyses and deliberations about where to intervene are informed by evidence and scenario testing, ReThink Health (n.d.-b) uses a *Dynamics Model*. The model comes from system dynamics modeling, which broadly involves "gathering information, mapping cause-and-effect relationships related to the community's health and other important outcomes, then generating and testing different hypotheses about changes that the community proposes" (Sastry & Penn, 2014, p. 269). As used widely in public health, "a system dynamics model consists of an interlocking set of differential and algebraic equations developed from a broad spectrum of relevant measured and experiential data. . . . Modeling is an iterative process of scope selection, hypothesis generation, causal diagramming, quantification, reliability testing, and policy analysis" (Homer & Hirsch, 2006, p. 453). ReThink Health's Dynamics Model can be used by system stewards to individually and collectively examine questions such as "How are local health systems structured? How and when do they change (or resist change)? Where is the greatest leverage to enhance performance? What trade-offs may be involved? What if nonexperts could test scenarios for themselves" (ReThink Health, 2015b, p. 1). The model was developed using national data on multiple aspects and influences on health and well-being, including population health, health care delivery, health equity, workforce productivity, and health care costs, and then the model was adjusted in scale to characterize small- and midsized American cities (ReThink Health, 2015b). Users of the model adjust different boundaries, such as geographical focus, age, insurance, and income, to mirror characteristics of their region. Then they explore different scenarios by selecting from a menu of initiatives (e.g., improving routine preventive and chronic care for physical illness, reducing crime, improving hospital efficiency) and examining potential consequences of these initiatives within the dynamic model. This process brings data into planning, makes boundary choices explicit, and facilitates consideration of multiple scenarios so that groups can then deliberate about which initiatives to pursue within a particular region and time frame. The Dynamics Model can facilitate finding potential "multi-solvers," which regionally based teams then consider to decide what is desirable to try to change.

Evaluating for Learning and Field Building

Conventionally, externally commissioned evaluators gauge whether interventions are accomplishing what they set out to accomplish. Learning focuses on single-loop questions to provide feedback on whether planned activities and results are occurring and sometimes to inform changes to the activities if desired results are not realized. Audiences for evaluations are typically funders, program leaders and implementers, and other key decision makers who can use evaluation data to make decisions or direct changes in interventions. ReThink Health sought to challenge this way of circumscribing the scope and audience for evaluation in several ways.

First, ReThink Health establishes an evaluation and learning agenda focused on progress toward system change. Rippel does not operate within constraints such as health priority areas, specific geographical regions, or predetermined kinds of interventions or models. Instead, a focal question guides Rippel's work: How can we influence transformative change to produce health and well-being for all? (ReThink Health, n.d.-a, Foundation website). In the style of research and development, they develop learning priorities within this overarching question and create initiatives that provide opportunities to develop this learning. They then frame evaluations as a way of examining how well they are progressing and what they are learning in answering that question.

They privilege triple-loop learning followed by double- and then single-loop learning. Triple-loop learning focuses on exploring underlying values, assumptions, and ways of working that frame and shape the decisions made and the consequences of these decisions. This learning is concerned with the question, "What makes this the right thing to do?" In its founding, ReThink Health engaged in this kind of learning, and today it facilitates conversations with systems stewards in the early phases of their work together. As an organization, Rippel has established a learning agenda with questions, norms, and processes for creating, retaining, and sharing knowledge generated. Deliberation and prioritization of vision, values, and learning then inform double-loop learning concerned with identifying and understanding what are the "right" things to do to bring about desired changes. Their externally commissioned evaluations focus centrally on this question, typically drawing on a blend of developmental and realist evaluation approaches, and addressing variations of the question, "What works, for whom, how, and in what circumstances?" Lastly, when working with stewards in *Ventures* and *Vistas,* they hold coaching and feedback sessions that include single-loop learning discussions of what adjustments need to be made to address emerging obstacles as well as what new ways of thinking or working may help overcome these obstacles.

Second, ReThink Health includes expected audiences for its learning and evaluation work, such as their funders, board of directors, partners/ system stewards who work with them, and the regional communities where system stewards work. However, the primary and consistent audience that cuts across any individual initiative is the broader field of those working to change systems that affect health, including organizations and individuals in public health, philanthropy, and health care. A continuous commitment to contribute something to this field-level conversation and knowledge generation drives their evaluating efforts above all. Field-building is framed as a cooperative, rather than competitive, effort of learning from and ideally generating learning that could inform others' work.

Evaluating to Examine Progress against Theorized Change Processes

Evaluating in the conventional frame tends to focus on questions of an intervention's effectiveness in relation to targeted goals and outcomes. The expanded conventional frame positions evaluating as centered on values-based criteria and standards and opens up questions beyond stated goals and intended results to a wider set of issues such as contextual relevance, equitable opportunities, meaningfulness of experience for participants, and sustainability of outcomes. Standards tend to be established to compare the intervention on selected criteria in relation to other interventions or other kinds of benchmarks. In the case of ReThink Health, the *Pathway* is used to gauge progress against a working idea of how system stewardship develops over time and influences change in systems.

On a regional level, ReThink Health uses a *Pulse Check* survey based on the *Pathway* to assess the developmental phase and nature of stewardship practices. It also guides stewards in self-assessing their progress (Erickson et al., 2017; ReThink Health, n.d.-d, Pulse Check). Evaluation data are gathered, analyzed, and used to refine understanding of each phase of the *Pathway.* These project-level evaluations follow traditional evaluation thinking in that they generate data about project processes, outcomes, and learnings. However, they differ in their dual focus on gauging progress in relation to an envisioned change process and on modifying this model of change to reflect learning. For example, on the *Pulse Check* survey, participants rate their team and region's progress in relation to indicators such as the following:

- Stakeholders are able to access diverse, long-term financing sources to support new interventions that improve health and well-being.

- Collaborative groups are pursuing a more comprehensive regional portfolio of interventions.

- The region has an enhanced set of policies, programs, practices, and investment priorities.

- Leaders are thinking more clearly about how to achieve a shared vision by working together across boundaries.

- There is a clearer and more compelling value proposition in the region around which the stakeholders have aligned.

- There is a stronger forum of influential stakeholders who have a shared vision and goals for the region. (Mt. Auburn Associates, 2019, p. 12)

Results assembled across initiatives are then used to understand the course of change, such as the time it takes for certain changes to occur. ReThink Health tends to focus on assessing their and stewards' progress in terms of movement on the *Pathway,* with less emphasis on whether they and stewards accomplish changes in health conditions, outcomes, or trends in stewards' regions.

Evaluating as Situated Deliberation and Learning within Initiatives

Within the *Ventures* and *Vistas* projects as they unfolded, ReThink Health staff members built in evaluation processes to engage stewards in collectively deliberating about and learning from what they were doing, how it was going, and what they should do next. In addition to their externally commissioned evaluations, ReThink Health hosted and facilitated sensemaking sessions with stewards and with the funding agency to engage in collective evaluative thinking. For example, in a sensemaking session, they used emergent learning maps to capture information on the following: what we learned from what has already happened, what we think will make us successful in the future, key moments looking back from which we can learn, and upcoming opportunities to test our hypotheses in action. The emphasis on *we* sensemaking and deliberation aligns with Schwandt's (2018) reframing of evaluative thinking from an individual cognitive activity to a group process:

> Because boundaries are not given, we have to "do" something about boundaries when we make judgments of how to act in the world. Thus, "what should *we* do?" is a practical, situated, time- and place-bound question. Developing

good answers to that question is what practical reasoning in evaluation is all about—a commitment to examining assumptions, values, and facts entailed in the questions: "What do we want to achieve/Where are we going?" "Who gains and who loses by our actions, and by which mechanisms of power?" "Is this development desirable?" "What, if anything, should we do about it?" (p. 134)

Rather than prepare and disseminate reports for later use, these sessions provide direct discussion of what is being learned, notes from these sessions, and high-level analysis of insights to be distributed to those involved.

SUMMARY

The case of ReThink Health provides a glimpse into what evaluating informed by the alternative frame may look like. In our judgment, one of the biggest obstacles facing Rippel in its evaluation efforts within ReThink Health has been the lack of an alternative framework and language for talking about what evaluating entails. Much of what involves bringing together values, perspectives, and interests with data, evidence, or scenarios to take stock of where one is and discuss where to go next is cast as learning through evaluation. By naming and beginning to articulate the emerging alternative frame, we hope to recast evaluating beyond its conventional bounds and support possibilities already underway for a more iterative, dialogic, and continual role of evaluating in social change and intervention work. The work of the Rippel Foundation currently includes a second major initiative, *Foresight,* co-developed with 17 philanthropies across the United States and motivated by the question, "What could a transformed system that produces health and well-being look like?" *Foresight* works with leaders across the nation on envisioning and designing a future for health (*https://foresightforhealth.org*). This future-oriented initiative centers on questions of "what should we do" and may exemplify evaluating from the emerging alternative frame. It is too soon to tell at the time of writing. We hope that as this and many other initiatives unfold in the space of system change and transformation, they continue to evolve the theory and practice of evaluating.

APPENDIX 6.A. Methods Appendix

This appendix presents a set of methods that complement those discussed in Chapter 4 but are more oriented toward evaluating informed by systems thinking and complexity science. The list below is partial and provides only brief introductions to each method. Resources are provided for readers to examine each method in greater detail (see also Williams & Hummelbrunner, 2011).

ADAPTIVE ACTION

Glenda Eoyang, founder of Human System Dynamics and author with Royce Holladay of *Adaptive Action: Leveraging Uncertainty in Your Organization* (Eoyang & Holladay, 2013), developed "adaptive action" as a method for engaging with dynamical change. Designed for practitioners, the approach centers on asking and answering three questions:

- What? (e.g., What do you see? What changes have occurred? What is the same as before?)
- So what? (e.g., So, what surprises you? So, what do your observations mean?)
- Now what? (e.g., Now what will you do? Now what will we do together?)

The approach is paired with a theoretical model that defines a complex adaptive system using three concepts—containers, differences, and exchanges. The questions are meant to be used in an iterative learning cycle and at any scale (e.g., individual reflection, group discussion, organization review, societal critique).

AGENT-BASED MODELING

This approach to modeling draws on the theory of complex adaptive systems and assumes that system-level behaviors or patterns emerge from interactions between agents in the system. Distinct from system dynamics modeling in which the units tend to be the variables or factors interacting to influence a system or situation, agent-based modeling examines semiautonomous agents as the units of interest. Each agent is thought to be following some set of rules, whether consciously or not; collectively, as agents follow various options within these rules, predictions can be made about higher-order, system-level behaviors or patterns. In his short guide, *Agent-Based Models* (2008), Gilbert describes the unique advantages of this approach:

> In comparison with variable-based approaches using structural equations, or systems-based approaches using differential equations, agent-based simulation offers the possibility of modeling individual heterogeneity, representing explicitly agents' decision rules, and situating agents in a geographical or another type of space. It allows modelers to represent in a natural way multiple scales of analysis, the emergence of structures at the macro or societal level from individual action, and various kinds of adaptation and learning. (p. 1)

CRITICAL POLICY ANALYSIS

Frank Fischer, professor emeritus of political science at Rutgers University, has published several books and numerous articles developing what he calls argumentative, deliberative, and critical approaches to policy analysis. These works include *Confronting Values in Policy Analysis: The Politics of Criteria* (Fischer & Forester, 1987), *Reframing Public Policy: Discursive Politics and Deliberative Practices* (Fischer, 2003), *The Argumentative Turn in Policy Analysis and Planning* (Fischer & Forester, 1993), and *The Argumentative Turn Revisited: Public Policy as Communicative Practice* (Fischer & Gottweis, 2012). As practical guidance for critically evaluating a policy or program, Fischer and Gottweis (2012) developed a set of questions that cover what they call four levels or discourses of evaluation: (1) a program verification level concerned with realizing intended objectives and outcomes; (2) situational validation concerned with the relevance of a program to a problem situation; (3) societal validation concerned with the societal and systemic arrangements within which a program functions (or seeks to change); and, most critically, (4) social choice concerned with the ideologies and value conflicts relevant to the program and whether alternatives should be considered. Each level includes a goal for analysis and several guiding questions. Analysis can be carried out in any order but should address all levels and questions to provide a full evaluative picture.

DELIBERATIVE VALUATION

Jasper Kenter, an interdisciplinary researcher in sustainable development, conservation, and environmental management based at the University of York, along with colleagues, has a body of work examining how economic and deliberative methodologies can be used to develop what he calls "shared values" and incorporate these into decision-making processes. Shared values, such as transcendental values, cultural and societal values, communal values, and deliberated values, are typically endogenous to a deliberative process. They cannot be identified in advance but emerge and are articulated through group participation, dialogue, and prioritization. The Deliberative Value Formation model (Kenter, Reed, & Fazey, 2016) provides a theoretical model of the various types of values that may be generated or discussed during a deliberative process; the factors that influence deliberation; and the potential outcomes of deliberation. Such a model could inform the design and planning as well as research on or evaluation of a deliberative process.

INTERACTIVE PLANNING

The method of interactive planning begins with desired ends, that is, where an organization or group wants to be in the future. Developed by Russell L. Ackoff, who was an organizational theorist and professor emeritus at the University of Pennsylvania, interactive planning is based on the premise of "design of a desirable present and the selection or invention of ways of approximating it as closely as possible" (Ackoff, 2001, p. 3). This approach is distinguished from reactive planning, which tends to focus on finding the deficiencies, gaps, or weaknesses and then addressing them one by one, and preactive planning, which tries to predict what might happen in the future and prepare in the present. Interactive planning involves two phases and six steps (a–f). First, the idealization phase involves (a) "formulating the mess" or situational analysis followed by (b) "ends planning" to determine what the organization would ideally like to be. Second, the realization phase realization involves (c) means planning to explore how to get from the present to the desired future state, (d) resource planning to identify what supports are needed, (e) design of implementation or specification of specific people and processes, and (f) design of controls to embed monitoring, evaluation, learning, and adaptation. For further information, see Ackoff's "A Brief Guide to Interactive Planning and Idealized Design" (2001).

MOST SIGNIFICANT CHANGE

Developed by Dart and Davies (2003), this is a participatory method for monitoring and evaluation involving a systematic process of gathering and reviewing stories of change from those affected by an intervention. This method focuses on domains of change that are "not as precisely defined as would be the case for performance indicators . . . the domains are deliberately left loose, to be defined later by the actual users" (p. 138). The process generally involves identifying types of stories to collect; gathering the stories in formats authentic for those sharing the stories; determining which stories are the most significant (hence the name); sharing the stories with various stakeholders or audiences; and facilitating learning about what is valued and the value of an intervention in relation to the stories considered most significant (Davies & Dart, 2005). Most significant change could also be used to develop value by using the stories gathered to inform the next set of actions focused on cultivating similar changes as evidenced in the stories.

NORMATIVE CASE STUDY

David Thacher (2006), an associate professor at the University of Michigan and scholar who takes an interpretive and humanistic approach to public policy analysis, mostly in the area of criminal justice policy, writes about an approach to conducting case studies that examines questions about values, norms, and ethics— normative case study. He developed this approach as a "viable method that social scientists can use to answer the calls for normative study that have become common in sociology and other fields" (Thacher, 2006, p. 1669). At the heart of a normative case study is the desire to contribute to normative theory—theory about what ideals we should pursue and what obligations we should accept. This is done by blending case study methods to gather empirical observations with analytic processes that help to identify, describe, critically examine, as well as facilitate reflection and deliberation about normative issues.

PROCESS TRACING AND CONTRIBUTION ANALYSIS

Barbara Befani, an independent researcher specializing in innovative methods for impact evaluation, and John Mayne, an independent advisor on public-sector performance and evaluation, advance several novel theory-based approaches to assessing the impacts of interventions. Process tracing is an approach that utilizes a theory of change to explain the causal processes and mechanisms by which an intervention works to produce particular outcomes and impacts. It takes a case-based approach to causal inference, which typically means focusing on causal processes within one or several interventions without comparison groups. It also adopts a generative view on causality, meaning causation can be investigated through modeling and testing causal mechanisms. Contribution analysis is an approach that involves developing a theory of change and challenges to it; gathering existing evidence in support and in challenge to the theory of change; and using this evidence to develop an argument about the role an intervention or set of interventions played in contributing to some empirically verified outcomes or impacts. Befani and Mayne (2014), among others, combine process tracing and contribution analysis to develop a rigorous nonexperimental approach to impact evaluation that is compatible with systems and complexity approaches to change. For further reading, see Befani and Mayne (2014), "Process Tracing and Contribution Analysis: A Combined Approach to Generative Causal Inference for Impact Evaluation"; Befani and Stedman-Bryce (2017), "Process Tracing and Bayesian Updating for Impact Evaluation"; as well as searching for other independent works by Barbara Befani and John Mayne.

SUCCESS CASE METHOD

Developed by Brinkerhoff (2003) in the context of professional training evaluation, the success case method involves identifying successful and unsuccessful cases to illustrate what works and what does not work within a company after the enactment of a training program. A comparison of the journalism method of finding and then empirically verifying the story shows that the success case method typically involves five steps: (1) focusing the study; (2) creating a model and operational definition of successful transfer of training into changed professional practice; (3) conducting a survey to gather best and worst cases of training transfer; (4) gathering data through interviews, document review, and other methods to verify and capture the stories; and (5) communicating these results (Brinkerhoff, 2003, pp. 29–39). Coryn, Schröter, and Hanssen (2009) expanded the method by adding a time-series design.

SOFT SYSTEMS METHODOLOGY

Peter Checkland, author of *Systems Thinking, Systems Practice* (1999), developed a methodology to be used participatorily by groups to inquire about and act to address a problematic situation of interest. At the core, soft systems methodology assumes that when people encounter situations they view as problematic and in need of change, they bring different worldviews, perspectives, values, and interests to the situation. These worldviews are not static; rather, they are continuously changing or may be changed. In order for some group to come together to take what Checkland calls "purposeful action" to change the situation, it is incredibly helpful if they first examine how they individually and collectively understand the situation (i.e., what is) and what needs to be changed (i.e., what could or should be). To do this, the soft systems methodology offers a seven-step process that includes developing rich pictures, typically unstructured, hand-drawn illustrations of what's happening; identifying possible relevant systems in the situation and how they could be changed; and deliberating about the desirability and feasibility of changes.

SYSTEM DYNAMICS MODELING

Developed by Jay Forrester (1961) and John Sterman (1994) and taught in the Sloan School of Management at Massachusetts Institute of Technology, system dynamics modeling provides a way to depict the interrelationships and feedback processes that influence a system or situation. The method begins with causal loop diagramming to illustrate the interconnected relationships between variables or factors and the directionality of each relationship. Directionality is typically depicted as positive/reinforcing—that is, as one variable increases, so does the other—or negative/balancing—that is, as one variable increases, the other decreases. After the initial causal loop diagram is constructed, a more extensive mathematical model can be built in which each variable and relationship is quantified using data or estimations. This process allows researchers and practitioners to examine a large number of interrelationships and feedback loops at once. System dynamics can be used to explain the behaviors of a system or patterns in a situation; identify potential places to intervene, coined as leverage points by Donella Meadows (1999); and play out different assumptions and scenarios to imagine possibilities in the face of uncertainty.

CHAPTER 7

Valuing, Evaluating, and Professional Responsibility

> Many professionals shy away from a notion of professional competence
> that would include its normative core in addition to its technical core, as
> such a notion obviously entails questions of value judgment and ethical
> responsibility. They have learned in their training that a good professional,
> not unlike a good scientist, maintains a stance of professional objectivity
> and neutrality, a requirement that (they assume) is more easily met by
> restricting themselves to the choice of adequate means for reaching
> "given" ends while avoiding questions related to the choice of ends, as
> ends are not theirs to judge.
>
> —ULRICH (2011, p. 13)

INTRODUCTION

Value is a conception of the desirable or what should be. What is desirable or valuable in the professional practice of research and evaluation in fields related to applied social science where the focus is on the use of data and evidence in formulating, implementing, and assessing the interventions intended to change people's lives for the better? This chapter aims to answer this question by offering an account of what professional responsibility entails; we offer one perspective on the normative core of professional competence in applied social research and evaluation. We do not approach the question through the familiar sociological investigations of the origin of professions, the role of professional organizations, or contemporary studies of professionalism. Nor do we explore the extensive discussion of evaluator competencies that has been ongoing in professional evaluation societies for the past several years (Schwandt, 2015; United Nations Evaluation Group, 2016). These are important issues and have been addressed elsewhere in the field of evaluation as a professional practice (e.g., Meyer & Stockmann, 2016; Schwandt, 2017, 2019b). In fact, in this chapter we are addressing not only the audience of readers who identify as professional evaluators, but all researchers engaged one way or another in examining and evaluating social interventions.

The account we offer here begins with the practical realities in which many researchers and evaluators find themselves. These include the challenge of reconciling their formal technical training and awareness of professional norms with the messiness of the real world of research where personal, societal, institutional, and professional values are all at play. A world where decisions about "What should we do?" must be technically sound, morally defensible, and politically feasible. A world where multiple stakeholders in the research endeavor and their perspectives and what they value are at issue, including but not limited to those funding a study; those working on the research team; institutional administrators; individuals and groups with vested interests and responsibilities in the settings in which a study takes place (e.g., program, school, organization, partnership, community); those whose lives and circumstances are immediately meant to be bettered through the work; and the wider local, societal, or global good to which the inquiry is meant to contribute. A world often characterized by the toxic state of public discourse, highly polarized debates and misinformation campaigns. A world where racism in all its forms persists (Kendi, 2019). These practical realities of power and vested interests cannot (and should not) simply be put aside to focus on so-called real scientific work. Social research in applied science fields is always, at once, an empirical and normative undertaking.

What does a morally committed social science look like? Not surprisingly, but perhaps unsatisfyingly at first glance, there can be no professional code of conduct that recommends the "right" choices researchers must make in every situation. Rather, as Ulrich (2011) implies in the opening quotation, professional conduct is a matter of researchers and evaluators assuming ethical responsibility for their practice(s) and that involves active questioning, reflecting, deliberating, and justifying the ways they think about the work they do, the choices they make and why they make certain choices and not others, and who or what may benefit or lose by their ways of thinking and their choices. However, this ethically responsible posture is not simply a matter of individual researcher or evaluator responsibility. Rather, active questioning and critical reflection takes place within the organizational circumstances and practical situations in which researchers and evaluators find themselves and in deliberative dialogues with stakeholders to discuss whether they would think and act in similar or different ways. Researchers and evaluators also turn to their respective professional communities as a source for collective reflection on questions of the union of normative and empirical commitments. How and how carefully and seriously these reflections and discussions unfold lie at the heart of individual and collective professional competence.

There is yet another, related, dimension to the idea of a morally committed social science (including the practice of evaluating) besides acting
ethically in this way. It has to do with how we see ourselves and others as
democratic citizens. Drawing on their work in democratic theory, democratic dialogue, and civic leadership, education professors Joel Westheimer
and Joseph Kahne (2004, p. 239) asked, "What kind of citizen do we need
to support an effective democracy?" They claim that there are three visions
of citizenship that answer this question: the personally responsible citizen,
the participatory citizen, and the justice-oriented citizen. The personally
responsible citizen is committed to core democratic values and character
traits (e.g., honesty, integrity, self-discipline) and to acting responsibly
in her or his community. The participatory citizen is more aligned with
progressive thought, embracing the notion of a strong democracy and its
requirement for multiple kinds of civic participation. The justice-oriented
citizen is more inclined to emphasize the need for the critical assessment
of social, political, and economic structures, redressing areas of injustice,
and working toward systemic change. Of course, these are ideal types, and
in any one individual, aspects of each type of citizen may be combined.
Nonetheless, we find the distinction instructive, for it suggests different
models for learning responsible professional behavior as a researcher or
evaluator. The distinctive set of goals of each type suggests different kinds
of educational programs for the professional preparation of researchers and
evaluators. For example, as Westheimer and Kahne note, a program of
studies in the ethical education of researchers targeting the development of
researchers as responsible citizens will generally look quite different from
one that focuses primarily on developing capacities and commitments for
participatory citizenship or activist change agents. Our own bias is toward
programs of study that combine the progressive interest in features of a
strong democracy (Barber, 1984)—particularly civic participation—with
the social justice orientation. Our advocacy for developing researchers and
evaluators committed to civic participation and social justice coupled with
critique of unjust arrangements and practices should not, however, be mistaken for preparing these professionals as activists—that is, teaching them
how to take political action and engage in community organizing. As we
explain below, we seek to decenter researchers' and evaluators' claims to
authority, instead emphasizing that what they bring to investigations are
capacities for collaboration, for skeptical scrutiny, and for fostering the
incorporation of scientific (and evaluative) thinking into democratic deliberation (Dzur, 2008).

To anchor this work of developing a morally committed social science,
we offer a set of five professional commitments. These commitments reflect
changing norms specifically for the practice of evaluating, a practice that is
aligned with the alternative framing discussed in Chapter 5. However, they
are applicable to all forms of research unfolding in social science-related

applied fields. At the close of the chapter, we briefly address the implications of these commitments for the educational preparation of social researchers, for the practice of research on evaluation, and for agencies commissioning evaluative studies. We invite readers to consider whether their perspective on researching and evaluating is more in keeping with yesterday's practice or with emerging trends.

KEY COMMITMENTS

Commitments signal responsibility and both a willingness and a resolve to do something. Thus, they are about human agency, about our capacities to act in the world. In what follows, we discuss commitments to (1) supporting learning and acting through evaluating, (2) focusing on the primacy of practice, (3) embracing an epistemology and politics of participation, (4) accepting professional expertise and responsibility as a civic matter, and (5) critically questioning the normative ideas of improvement (e.g., social change, problem solving, development) and the underlying theories of social change that prompt social interventions and research as well as evaluations on these interventions.

Evaluating to Learn and to Act

Evaluating is being refocused on agency and practice. It has to do with human activity, with doing. If we (1) accept the proposition that learning is a social process, a participative undertaking situated within unique contexts and circumstances, and (2) believe that evaluating ought to contribute to that kind of learning, then (3) evaluating must come to be seen less as a kind of auditing of performance against a set of criteria and more as a type of reflection-in-action. It is an activity akin to a Deweyan chain of acting–reflecting–learning–acting anew, and so on. Moreover, "if we agree with Dewey that evaluative judgments are geared toward action in the future, then an evaluative judgment must integrate the future it anticipates, as well as the fact that it is itself a determining factor in that future" (De Munck & Zimmermann, 2015, p. 123).

Evaluating centered on agency takes the form of a practical argument focused on answering the questions "What should be done?" and "Where do we go from here?" and not simply "What is the case?" This does not mean that evaluating as a kind of point-in-time stocktaking to answer the questions, "Are we doing things right?" and "What are we accomplishing?" is not important. That kind of analytical information about the success of proposed solutions to social problems is useful particularly when those problems are carefully specified, there is a well-devised and implemented plan for action, and outcomes are clearly agreed upon in advance and are readily measurable. However, that kind of evaluating does not tell us what to do. Nor is it best for coping with perdurable challenges such as the eradication of disease, climate change, migration, food security, and economic inequality. Those kinds of challenging situations demand that we abandon assumptions of linear relationships between interventions and outcomes, notions of learning as a solely cognitive individual affair, and traditional approaches to planning in favor of recognizing uncertainty that accompanies complexity and engaging in adaptive planning and management. Those circumstances require a form of evaluating that is more compatible with the evolution of solutions. That, in turn, requires creating a joint problem space in which stakeholders engage in negotiation, collaborative problem solving, and together try to find out what can be reasonably said about and done in the situation at hand.

This is a kind of evaluating that also supports learning about how adaptation and innovation work. This means that researchers and evaluators should select evaluation tools to support characteristic actions of adaptive management. In the blog of the Global Learning for Adaptive Management Initiative, Tiina Pasanen (2020) explains that a critical feature of adaptive management is its concern with intentionally building opportunities for structured and collective reflection, ongoing and real-time learning, course correction and decision making, in order to improve effectiveness (see also Pasanen & Barnett, 2019). Owen Barder (2012) of the Overseas Development Institute observes that adaptive management embraces a focus on variation (space for experimentation, inclusion of sources of diversity and innovation, and tolerance for failure), fitness (distinguishing good, socially useful changes from bad in view of some path to desired outcomes), and effective selection (how choices are made to cause good changes to succeed and bad ones to be suppressed). Barder also explains that evaluating focused on the support of experimentation, adaptation, and learning need not mean abandoning a concern with results. Monitoring and reacting to results are necessary to effective adaptation. But what it does mean is that results cannot be only a matter of the prespecification of activities and outputs of planned interventions.

There is more to evaluating in support of adaptive management than simply focusing on a program or project in its development phase, so to speak. This is so because design and planning are ongoing processes of constantly reacting to emerging results and what is being learned. In addition, evaluating supports flexibility in changing projects and programs using evidence (managerial, operational, programmatic, financial) from multiple stakeholder perspectives. Figure 7.1 displays possible relationships between evaluating and organizational planning/management, depending on the state of knowledge about causes of a problem and knowledge and stability of context. Evaluation in the conventional frame (e.g., an experimental study of a vaccine) as discussed in Chapter 3 unfolds in Quadrant #2. In Quadrant #1 where knowledge of the causes of a problem are well understood but the context is unstable or uncertain, evaluation supports the testing, close monitoring, and rapid feedback of tried-and-true approaches to the problem (cash transfers, for example, are known to have specific, sustainable impacts). Quadrant #3 is a very difficult situation for an organization, and it should seek to move out of that set of circumstances by using evaluation to support situation analysis and structured problem solving. Quadrant #4 is where evaluation would directly support problem-driven iterative adaptation, namely, experiment–iterate–learn–adapt. Figure 7.1 is a heuristic device to aid thinking rather than a description of reality. There may be differences in perception of where to place a given situation on these two axes regarding knowledge of the problem and its operating environment. The situation itself unfolds over time, as does what we know about it, which may mean moving from one quadrant and orientation to another.

Finally, while the emerging conception of evaluating certainly attaches great importance to evidence, it is not exclusively preoccupied with evidence, as is the case with evaluating informed by the ideology of evidence-based policy and practice. In the emerging perspective, evaluating is equally focused on the normative, participatory, and interest-driven aspects of both policymaking and evaluating itself.

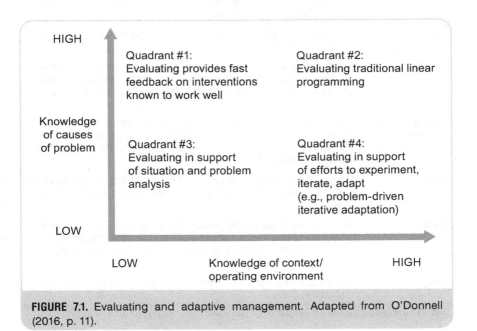

FIGURE 7.1. Evaluating and adaptive management. Adapted from O'Donnell (2016, p. 11).

Primacy of Practice (*Praxis*)

Researchers and practitioners understand the concept of practice in several different ways (e.g., Dunne, 1993; Taylor, 1995). Here we adopt an interpretation emphasizing that practice is like Dewey's notion of inquiry—a purposeful, flexible engagement with the world, a union of knowing and doing. This is in keeping with the Aristotelian notion of *praxis* as how one lives as a citizen and human—one's moral-political conduct in everyday life—wherein there is no outcome separable from its practice. In the view of Hendrik Wagenaar and Noam Cook (2003, p. 149), apologists for the idea of deliberative policy analysis, practices are "the ways people negotiate in a structured and meaningful way the challenges they encounter in life's course." They point out that practice entails several interrelated elements, as displayed in Table 7.1.

TABLE 7.1. Interrelated Elements of Practice	
Action	The core element. People negotiate the world by interacting with it and acting upon it. Action is not explicitly goal-oriented but is triggered holistically by everyday situations.
Community	Action as practice means participation in a community. Practice is socially situated, and the notion of community signifies the social configurations in which aspirations, values, and purposes are formulated and activities are identified as worthwhile, meaningful, etc.
Knowing	Knowledge/knowing is tied to action. What people know gives form and direction to what they do.
Dialectic	Practice is not a matter of implementing algorithms. Problems and their solutions, opportunities, and constraints emerge because actors must constantly negotiate the details of everyday life. There is a reciprocal, dialectical relation between problems and solutions.
Criteria, standards, and warrants	Practitioners employ criteria, standards, and warrants (CS&W) to judge the feasibility and rightness of actions. There is a reciprocal relationship between CS&W and the concrete situation at hand; hence they are local, flexible, and negotiable.
Emotion	Emotion is not considered the enemy of reason. Rather, certain situations must be sufficiently meaningful and important to merit the risk and effort of active involvement.
Values	Aesthetic, moral, social, and political values play a role in the search for problems and solutions in practice situations. They tell us what is worth paying attention to and serve as reasons for what we do in concrete situations.
Discourse	Discourse is a key vehicle by which the practical, active negotiating of reality takes place.

Note. From Wagenaar and Noam Cook (2003, pp. 149–156).

It bears emphasizing that the primacy of practice does not mean the valorization of practice or that all practice is intrinsically good (compare Dahler-Larsen, 2019, pp. 95ff.). Practices—active engagements with the world—can be judged as good or bad, right or wrong-headed on the bases of pragmatic, aesthetic, moral, and political criteria and standards internal to a given practice, as well as by means of comparison to the criteria and standards of other practices (Ivaldi, Scaratti, & Nuti, 2015).

The practices of interest in evaluating (besides the practice of evaluating itself) include those of planning, management, educating, social service work, and so forth. They are of interest in a specific way, however. These practices are not simply the executive (i.e., the decision making) arm of knowledge production; the site where scientific knowledge is put to use, or the location where lay knowledge is replaced by scientific, technical reason. On the contrary, practice is *sui generis* "a way of engaging with the world in its own right; a way of moving about that is much more attuned to the pluralistic, open-ended, moral-political character of the everyday world" (Wagenaar & Noam Cook, 2003, p. 141). This means that the dilemmas encountered in teaching, in providing social services or health care, in managing and administration, and so forth are real human predicaments and not primarily technical problems that have scientific (i.e., evidence-based) solutions. As Schwandt (2005, p. 99) argued elsewhere, practitioners are "always on the 'rough ground' where values, personalities, evidence, information, feelings, sensitivities, emotions, affect, ambiguities, contradictions, inconsistencies, and so forth are simultaneously in play as they try to do the right thing and do it well." Praxis is not reducible to technical rationality or instrumental action (Flyvbjerg, 2001).

Observing the centrality of practice with respect to evaluating and researching means that practice comes first. Ulrich (2001) explained this idea in the following way: The typical understanding of the relationship between evaluating/researching and practice—as found, for example, in the mainstream framing of evaluating—is that good practice (P) is a function (f) of research and evaluation ($R\&E$), or $P = f(R\&E)$. This assumption is quite apparent in the evidence-based policy and practice movement and the concomitant search for best practices based on rigorous research. Research and evaluation methods determine what is good practice. In the alternative framing of evaluating, the relationship is reversed, or $R\&E = f(P)$. In other words what is good research and evaluating ought to be a function of the practice we are striving for. Thus, for example, if the practice we are aiming at is adaptive management, then the means of research and evaluation must be suited to the requirements, realities, and exigencies of that practice. Relatedly, it becomes incumbent on the researcher/evaluator to make clear what kind of practice the choice of methods and methodologies is likely to promote.

Epistemology and Politics of Participation

Evaluating, like politics, is about values as well as facts and interests. We agree with Thomas Dietz (2013), a researcher on matters of human ecology and cultural evolution, that "it is a form of cognitive bias to think that disagreements are mostly about facts. It is a comfortable bias because it leads us to believe we can resolve disagreements by better information about facts" (p. 14085). Evaluating must therefore take into account the values and perspectives held by stakeholders (including the evaluator). It does so by helping stakeholders to surface and discuss implicit and embedded values and their consequences for what should be done. This discussion is not simply a matter of adopting a process ensuring that the favored criteria of different stakeholders are included as the basis for evaluative judgments. Bringing to light different perspectives and values is a more complicated and contested undertaking, for it requires accepting a pluralist knowledge politics. Stephen Healy (2003, 2009), whose work involves critical posthumanist science studies, defines pluralist knowledge politics as (1) recognizing that professional expertise has often exercised a form of epistemic sovereignty over what counts as legitimate knowledge, and instead encouraging difference in multiple, legitimate ways of knowing, that is, epistemological pluralism; (2) regarding knowing and knowledge as matters of practice—knowledge shapes the world in ways that both facilitate and constrain action; and (3) accepting that "encouraging difference . . . becomes not only a matter of involving all with a legitimate interest, but also crucially of facilitating processes in which all relevant perspectives and insights . . . are accounted for" (Healy, 2003, p. 691). An epistemology of participation raises issues related to deliberation and the role of emotion, power, and rejection of an adversarial approach to argument.

Deliberation

This pluralism in knowledge and values is the chief reason for deliberation. As Albert Dzur (2008), political scientist and philosopher, explains, given conditions of value pluralism, no single, overarching moral point of view can guide planning and policymaking. Reaching agreements in societies characterized by value pluralism must therefore depend on procedural norms that ensure inclusive, equal, rational, respectful, sincere, and honest debate. Deliberation is also necessary because what is to be counted as pertinent data (i.e., the facts of the matter) will vary depending on perspectives. This is not to say that there are facts and so-called alternative facts, but that what different stakeholders perceive as relevant data will likely vary based on the stakes each has in the situation. Stakeholders are groups of individuals who have a common role in a situation (e.g., the police, the managers of a homeless shelter, nonprofit agencies funding the shelter). Stakes are motivations that underlie stakeholder behavior and perspectives and include honor, fairness, ideas of professional obligation, purpose, social role, and so on (Williams & van 't Hof, 2016).

The notion of participation central to this way of thinking of evaluating is reflected in the idea of a "knowledge democracy:" "a society in which a wide diversity of actors hold relevant knowledge to address important societal problems. . . . In such an ideal democracy, dominant and nondominant actors have equal access and ability to bring this knowledge forward in order to contribute to solutions for societal problems" (Bunders et al., 2010, pp. 125–126). Evaluation theorist Ernie House (House & Howe, 1999) draws broadly on the idea of a knowledge democracy to offer an approach called deliberative democratic evaluation grounded in three principles: inclusion of stakeholder views, values, and interests; dialogue among evaluators and stakeholders to foster mutual understanding; and extended deliberation of evaluative conclusions with and by all parties to the evaluation. Additional principles of dialogue and deliberation directing public engagement are displayed in Box 7.1.

It is not uncommon to find the deliberative process framed almost entirely in cognitive terms—focusing on reasons, bias control, valid arguments, and evidence—as well as cognitive appeals to civility, to being "reasonable," and to acting in good faith. However, the current climate of highly polarized debates, coupled with awareness of politically motivated

---

BOX 7.1. PRINCIPLES FOR SUCCESSFUL PUBLIC ENGAGEMENT PROCESSES

- Encourage multiple forms of speech and communication to ensure that all kinds of people have a real voice.
- Make listening as important as speaking.
- Connect personal experience with public issues.
- Build trust and create a foundation for working relationships.
- Explore a range of views about the nature of the issue.
- Encourage analysis and reasoned argument.
- Help people develop public judgment and create common ground for action.
- Provide a way for people to see themselves as actors and to be actors.
- Connect to government, policymaking and governance.
- Create ongoing processes, not isolated events.

Note. From McCoy and Scully (2002, pp. 120–126).

reasoning, casts significant doubt on the strength of these kinds of exclusive appeals to cool reason. From research on politically motivated reasoning (Kahan, 2016) we learn that we typically cannot persuade people on the other side of a political debate (e.g., over climate change, concealed carry law, immigration policy) with evidence. Rather, people will use their minds to protect the group(s) to which they belong from evidence they do not wish to consider. In other words, the motivation of an individual to conform to the identity-defining group of which he or she is a member is stronger than the motivation to reason about the evidence.

Emotion

In his popular book decrying the toxic state of public discourse and what to do about it, James Hoggan (2016) claims that we need to give up the idea that facts are enough and instead engage in dialogue and deliberation by talking to others' hearts, not just their heads. He emphasizes the importance of emotional dialogue and moral narratives in public deliberation. To do that, he argues, we ought to be having conversations about values— about matters of hope, fear, and mistrust. Philosopher Martha Nussbaum's (1994) work on the idea of a "therapeutic argument" offers a suggestion for what this might mean for a morally committed social science. Adapting her idea would mean the arguments of researchers and evaluators would (1) have a practical goal directed at the stakeholder(s)' good; (2) be value-relative, that is, respond at some level to the wishes and needs of the stakeholder(s); and (3) be responsive to the particular case at hand, to the stakeholder's concrete situation. In sum, reasonableness requires both logic and values.

Power

Researchers, policymakers, evaluators, and other stakeholders concerned about development and change must also explicitly acknowledge how various configurations of power influence the dialogue and deliberative process. John Gaventa (2005), at the Institute of Development Studies, who is well known for his effort to map the kinds of power relations at work in efforts to engage citizens in research, planning, and evaluating at global, national, and local levels observes:

> Despite the widespread rhetorical acceptance of participation, rights and deepened forms of civil society engagement, it is clear that simply creating new institutional arrangements will not make them real and will not necessarily result in greater inclusion or pro-poor policy change. Rather, much will depend on the nature of the power relations which surround and imbue these new, potentially more democratic, spaces. (p. 5)

Based on extensive conceptual work growing out of empirical studies of civil society participation in development in five countries, Gaventa (2006) designed the power cube depicted in Figure 7.2. The cube is a power analysis tool for examining and mapping how power operates in various political spaces, and it is a means to assess the possibilities for transformative action in those spaces. Researchers and evaluators can use the cube to examine how power is expressed and used, that is, power over, power to, power with, and power within.

Deliberating facts and values, while taking into account a power analysis, is a distinctly different activity than relying on polls, surveys, key informant interviews, or focus groups to gather general attitudes or values of stakeholder groups. These are means of tallying up citizens' perspectives, interests, or preferences. They are not procedures for significantly and critically engaging them. In contrast, the activity of co-production or deliberation facilitates changes in understanding, behaviors, practices, decisions, and values. In their discussion of a model for deliberative value formation, Jasper Kenter, an interdisciplinary researcher specializing in public and stakeholder participation in ecological economics, along with fellow transdisciplinary colleagues (Kenter, Reed, & Fazey, 2016), argues that "deliberation encourages participants to learn from each other, to form reasoned opinions, evaluate positions and reach informed decisions, implying that social learning is a central component of group deliberative processes" (p. 198). Of course, one should not be naive about the realpolitik of citizen participation and deliberation in policymaking, planning, researching, or evaluating. Political scientist Mary Scudder (2020), for example, argues that democratic deliberation must go beyond the usual paean to inclusion

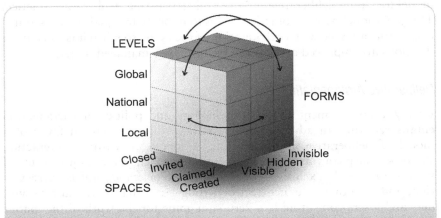

FIGURE 7.2. The power cube. From Gaventa (2006, p. 25). Adapted with permission from the Institute of Development Studies.

to consider how and the extent to which citizens' perspectives are in fact taken up—that is, critically engaged and not simply included or heard—by others in deliberation, as well as how we should address the risks of taking up undemocratic inputs in deliberation. She claims that focusing on uptake (fair consideration) and the critical appraisal it aims to ensure is a way of avoiding the reproduction of simplistic and essentializing binaries of privileged and marginalized, silenced and silencer. Having reviewed the literature on the potential contribution of deliberative methods in the health sector, Julia Abelson and colleagues (2003) noted several significant challenges to engaging citizens in deliberation. These include how to mitigate strong vested interests that may try to use the deliberative process to sway the process or outcomes; how to achieve fair representation when citizens do not wish to participate, and how to ensure accountability to participants for the outcome of the deliberation.

Communications studies scholars Carcasson and Sprain (2016) served as deliberative practitioners with the Colorado State University Center for Public Deliberation designing deliberative forums. The Center was formed "in response to the limitations of the dominant expert and adversarial models of public discourse, particularly in terms of their inability to address wicked problems effectively" (p. 43). They explain that "deliberative engagement seeks genuine interaction and communication across perspectives. Unfortunately, bringing multiple perspectives together in the same room to address difficult issues can be problematic, especially in a fractured political environment dominated by distrust, polarization, and cynicism" (p. 47). To address these and related difficulties associated with deliberative processes, they describe a framework they call deliberative inquiry as a practical guide to help citizens better handle wicked problems and generate new possibilities for action. Figure 7.3 displays their process model for doing deliberative inquiry and structuring deliberative practice. The goal for deliberative practitioners is to improve the quality of discourse concerning an issue with each iteration of the cycle, so when it is time to act decisions are improved and wicked problems are managed better.

Deliberative Argumentation

Finally, a commitment to the epistemology and politics of participation entails rejecting an adversarial approach to disagreement in favor of a model of deliberative argumentation. A focus on reasoned interaction stands in sharp contrast to an adversarial approach that assumes points of view are mutually exclusive—one perspective or standpoint is correct or right and the others are incorrect or wrong—and that there must be winners and losers competing in a zero-sum game for the truth of the matter (Makau & Marty, 2013). In the training course he designed on participation, consensus building, and conflict management, Delli Priscoli (2003,

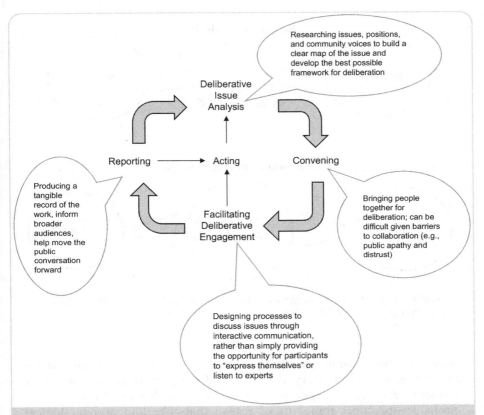

FIGURE 7.3. The deliberative cycle. From Carcasson and Sprain (2016, p. 52). Adapted with permission from Oxford University Press.

p. 9) notes that "public involvement and conflict management programs attempt to create an environment where the alternative viewpoints are synergized into creative solutions that have not been previously conceived, rather than canceling out one another." Figure 7.4 displays the difference between an adversarial model where pressures are to move to the extremes of competing perspectives versus a reasoned interaction model where the goal is to find a shared middle ground.

Recognizing that perspectives and framings of what is considered valuable and important will differ and often conflict among and between stakeholders, the evaluator aims to create circumstances where stakeholders can engage each other across differences. In addition, in deliberative argumentation, acceptable decisions are subject to reasonableness standards rather than the logician's analytic construct of rationality. The latter argues that the validity of an argument rests on its being self-evident and certain—and

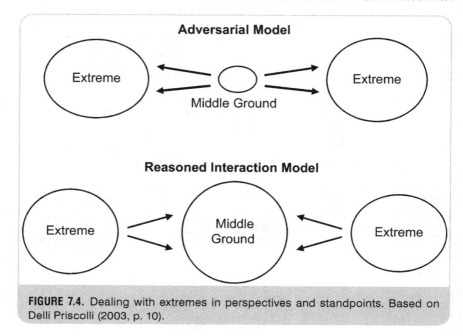

FIGURE 7.4. Dealing with extremes in perspectives and standpoints. Based on Delli Priscolli (2003, p. 10).

we can see this assumption underlying the evidence-based decision-making movement. On the contrary, the limits and strengths of an argument in a model of deliberative argumentation are made within the domain of the probable—practical standards of reason that take into account logical analysis, moral imagination, and emotion (Makau & Marty, 2013).

Expertise and Responsibility

Social researchers who conduct evaluation are employed in both the private and public sectors. Some are academics, or at least affiliated with research centers at academic institutions, but many are also employed in the business services sphere at firms such as KPMG and Deloitte Consulting; in research, development, and service agencies such as WestEd, American Institutes for Research, and Abt Associates; in smaller private consulting firms; as evaluation and monitoring managers or officers in not-for-profit agencies and foundations; and in the civic and governance spheres as employees or contractors with national (e.g., National Institute of Justice, Centers for Disease Control) and international agencies (e.g., USAID, United Nations Development Programme). Increasingly, as sociologist Steven Brint (1994, 2015) has argued, the professional work of these researchers has focused on the technical core of that work—that is, on their specialized skills and formalized knowledge. Brint explains that the dominant professional ideology arising in the mid-20th century and continuing to the present is that of expert professionalism, with its emphasis on formal rationality (problem solving by the application of technical criteria and methods). That has come to largely replace an older ideology that underscored the professional's social responsibility and substantive rationality (decision making subject to value choices and an appeal to ethical norms): "Expertise is now a resource sold to bidders in the market for skilled labor. It is no longer a resource that requires an extensive sphere of occupational judgment about purposes" (Brint, 1994, p. 15).

Civic-Led Framework for Social Responsibility

While not denying that technical skill and expertise are important, the emerging perspective on evaluating is once again drawing attention to the ethical and public responsibility of evaluation researchers. In so doing, it draws upon insights from the work of political scientists, philosophers, and systems thinkers to develop new means to engage with the publics it serves. The central concern is one of replacing a technocratic, expert-led framework of professional responsibility with a democratic, civic-led framework as depicted in Table 7.2 (Reynolds & Schwandt, 2017).

This civic-led framework for responsibility includes several key aspects. First, this means exploring the possibility of a new organizational form for professional work. As management and labor relations scholars Adler, Heckscher, McCarthy, and Rubinstein (2015) explain, even the most strongly institutionalized professions of medicine and law are increasingly under intense pressure to conform to instrumental rationality, bureaucratic standards, and market norms of self-interest. As a result, the notion of a

TABLE 7.2. Two Frameworks for Professional Responsibility		
	Technocratic, expert-led framework	Democratic, civic-led framework
"What"—Purpose	An arrangement to provide objective, value-free knowledge	An arrangement to serve the public as (participant) citizens rather than as clients
"How"—Processes need to achieve the purpose	By (1) depoliticizing issues and treating them as problems to be solved (2) disempowering publics, and (3) aligning with bureaucratic government agencies rather than civil society	By means of sharing knowledge and tasks through meaningful conversation and deliberation
"Why"—Rationale	To promote professional interests in instrumental rationality by embedding expertise in a modern organizational culture of control and standardization	To promote value rationality by contributing to transforming, renovating, reconstructing, and co-creating civil society

profession's responsibility to higher social purposes is diminishing. These authors call for a new organizational form, called "collaborative community," that can restore the value-rational interests of the professions: "This organizational form must enable a wider scope of collaboration within and across professions and deeper dialogue with stakeholders outside the professions" (p. 310). The ReThink Health Initiative of the Rippel Foundation discussed in Chapter 6 is one example of an emerging collaborative community of health professionals, researchers, evaluators, health delivery organizations, philanthropies, and city and county health departments.

Second, a civic-led framework does not mean abandoning experts or expertise, but rather "a strategic reduction of the expert's authority. Rather than proclaiming truth about this or that problem . . . [the] expert would be much more of an interpreter and would recognize any project of interpretation as something that can be carried out collaboratively" (White & Taket, 1994, p. 735). The evaluation researcher will also act as a facilitator of public learning and civic engagement, assisting citizens to examine their own interests and perspectives and make their own decisions (Fischer, 2003). In the mainstream framing of evaluation, expert-developed interventions are evaluated by other experts, albeit with input from major stakeholders. The experts with their specialized knowledge reside in their consultancies, academic offices, and evaluation agencies, while citizens with their local knowledge inhabit their neighborhoods and communities. This framing underemphasizes civic agency and the citizen as problem-solver (neither merely service recipient, stakeholder, nor information provider) and the producer of public goods. It does not concern itself with evaluators as citizens and with citizens, along with other professionals, as co-creators of a public world making a public life together (Boyte, 2103, 2014; Boyte & Kari, 1996).

For the field of evaluation, this means focusing directly on the civic nature of the professional's responsibility related to evaluating and defining the normative characteristic of evaluation professionalism as citizen centric. This entails (1) recognizing that citizens have a stake in professional decisions, which may include the stakes researchers and evaluators have as citizens themselves; (2) working collaboratively with citizens, enabling them to deliberate and make decisions on issues that affect them; and (3) sharing authority, knowledge, power, and responsibility with citizens and engaging in ethical examination of difficult questions. Dzur (2008) defines this political ethic of professionalism as "democratic professionalism": "Sharing previously professionalized tasks and encouraging lay participation in ways that enhance and enable broader public engagement and deliberation about major social issues inside and outside professional domains" (p. 130). In this idea of co-creation and public work, there is something far more at stake than a model of rational decision making unfolding in participatory approaches to evaluating. The difference is that there is learning about value—an essential aspect of practical action—that leads to "transformations of relationships and responsibilities, networks and competence, and collective memory and memberships" (Forester, 1999, p. 115).

Third, given that social research is unavoidably selective and partial, social inquirers have a professional and moral responsibility to handle this selectivity and partiality critically. This means replacing the disinterested stance of the social researcher with a type of professional integrity that involves "the professional's awareness (or alertness, reflective stance, critical distance, etc.) regarding the institutional patterns at work [in shaping the research agenda, research questions, preferred evidence, etc.], along with the worldviews, values, and interests that shape them and which put pressure on professionals to adapt to them, whether consciously or not" (Ulrich, 2011, p. 10). Rather than aspiring to be neutral or impartial, on the one hand, or taking a clearly partisan stance in favor of some particular perspective, values, and interests, the responsibility of the professional is to critique. This specifically means continuously calling attention to whose and which sociopolitical values are and should be influencing a research or evaluation study and potential consequences of that framing for other groups and interests (Gates, 2018). It also means openly acknowledging the fallacy that a professional evaluator or social researcher can serve all interests equally (Levin-Rozalis, 2015).

Role of the Social Critic

This sense of responsibility aligns with the role of the social critic more than the change agent or researcher-as-activist, accepting that expertise is more a matter of asking questions and facilitating deliberation than providing answers (Schwandt & Gates, 2016; Ulrich, 2001). As displayed in Box 7.2, political scientist Brooke Ackerly (2000) identifies three efforts that the researcher-as-social-critic promotes. Following an idea advanced by Dewey, she adds that

> [t]he roles of the social critic include the promotion of ongoing evaluation not just of values and practices but also of decisions. . . . Critics who inquire promote the examination of values, practices, and norms that are commonly unquestioned either because people cannot question them due to some form of coercion, due to force of habit, or because they don't know another way is possible. . . . The social critic must not only question existing practices and values, research versions of practices and values from past or other cultures, analyze her own findings and those of others, and provide evaluation herself, but also promote the community's collective evaluation process. . . . With this in mind, social criticism is as much an attitude as a practice. Critics manifest this attitude through skeptical scrutiny. They also manifest it by encouraging critical engagement of others through fostering deliberative opportunities. (p. 123)

BOX 7.2. THREE EMPHASES OF THE WORK
OF THE SOCIAL CRITIC

- **Inquiry**—Questioning, researching, analyzing, and interpreting values, practices, and norms to solicit the variety of perspectives informing a situation; especially attending to the views of those who have been silent as a function of coercion, neglect, or oppression
- **Deliberative opportunities**—Promoting and hosting deliberative opportunities among different and multiple perspectives
- **Institutional change**—Representing the silent or proposing institutional changes that allow those silenced or marginalized to participate themselves; proposing institutional changes that affect the ability of the powerful to exploit inequalities

Note. From Ackerly (2000, p. 123).

The evaluator *qua* social critic also raises questions about the ethical bases of interventions. The ethics of ends raises the question of "What ought we to do?" because ethical choices are focused on assessing whether the right values and norms are being pursued in or through a given intervention. In the field of international development, for example, Des Gasper (2012, p. 5) notes that central questions here include: What is good or "real" development? What is the good life which development policy should seek to facilitate? What really are benefits? How are benefits and costs to be shared within the present generation and between generations? Who decides and how? What rights of individuals should be respected and guaranteed? Human development theorist and founder of work on development ethics, Denis Goulet (1988, p. 157), has argued that this kind of ethical thinking must become "the means of the means: a moral beacon illuminating the value questions buried inside instrumental means appealed to by decision-makers and problem-solvers of all kinds." Gasper (2012) adds that this examination of values must be accompanied by epistemological reflection of the processes of authoritative knowledge production—how different cognitive and social values come to guide choices, and how those values are influenced by power relations. Evaluating the ethical bases of interventions can also involve appraising both alternative societal paths—that is, arguments for the major value choices (as well as trade-offs among values) involved in interventions designed to address social and economic development among, for example, economic growth, the provision of basic needs, cultural survival, and ecological balance (Gasper, 2012). It can also mean evaluating valuing schemes—arrangements for putting a certain idea of valuing and evaluating into effect—including results-based management, evidence-based policy and practice, social impact investing and social value determination, performance management, and organizational learning.

Systems theorists and practitioners Richard Hummelbrunner and Martin Reynolds (2013) reinforce this view, arguing that social research and evaluating ought to focus on triple-loop learning. Whereas single-loop learning asks, "Are we doing things right?" and double-loop learning asks, "Are we doing the right things?" triple-loop learning asks, "What makes this the right thing to do?" Examining this question requires "critically reflecting on the rules and relations of power that affect behaviour and cognition patterns," including those of "evaluation commissioners and evaluators themselves" (p. 2). This critically reflective orientation also fits well with what Schwandt (1997) identified as a value-critical framework for evaluating, the aim of which is "improving praxis by enabling practitioners to refine the rationalities of their practices" and which "can only be achieved by helping practitioners develop a kind of educative, critically reflective self-knowledge that enables them to question the beliefs and unstated assumptions that sustain a particular practice of education, management, health care, and so forth" (p. 35). This professional role for evaluating also bears similarity to Schwandt's (2008) conception of evaluation as a social conscience in an experimenting society:

> This is a society in which we ask serious and important questions about what kind of society we should have and what directions we should take. This is a social environment indelibly marked by uncertainty, ambiguity, and interpretability. Evaluation in such an environment is a kind of social conscience; it involves serious questioning of social direction; and it is a risky undertaking in which we endeavor to find out not simply whether what we are doing is a good thing but also what we do not know about what we are doing. (p. 143)

Improvement Revisited

A final core commitment is to problematize the notion of improvement used throughout the practice of evaluation and applied social research. In the field of program evaluation practice in democratic societies, it is common to find reference to social betterment as the guiding rationale for evaluation (Henry & Mark, 2003a; Mark, Henry, & Julnes, 2000). The term refers to improved social conditions, the reduction of social problems, or the alleviation of social distress (Henry, 2000). For the most part, this noble aim is largely unexamined in any detail. Even more problematic, however, is a tension endemic to program evaluation practice (and to all applied social research more generally) between whether the goal of improvement is best achieved by evaluation practice serving participatory democracy and active citizenship or the enlightened political and policymaking elite of the administrative state (Datta, 2011). Some who practice evaluation are persuaded that the means of evaluating ought to give pride of place to the meanings, definitions, and experiences of marginalized groups; critique approaches to problem definition and problem solving (i.e., policies and programs) that further the unjust treatment of these peoples; and address power inequities and the impact of privilege on efforts to achieve social justice (see, e.g., transformative evaluation [Mertens, 2009] and culturally responsive evaluation [Hood, Hopson, & Kirkhart, 2015]). Other evaluators argue that establishing the normative ends of society as reflected in the choice of social policies and programs is a political task best left to politicians and citizens (Chelimsky, 2014; Shipman, 2012). This latter group typically limits evaluating to means–end reasoning about whether a given social intervention achieved its intended aims.

The tension is evident in different schools of thought on how to conduct evaluating. Participatory and collaborative approaches are relational and dialogic, with evaluators working in partnership with nonevaluators (e.g., stakeholders in the program such as program managers and program beneficiaries) to produce evaluation knowledge jointly (Cousins, 2019; Cousins & Chouinard, 2012). When used in the fields of public health and community development, these approaches often also link community assessment, program implementation, and program evaluation (Whitmore et al., 2006). Nonparticipatory approaches to evaluation that aim to influence policymakers' judgments about the significance of a social problem and the effectiveness of a remedy (intervention) to address the problem favor the use of causal methods, including randomized controlled field trials and quasi-experiments (Mark & Henry, 2006) as well as evidence synthesis methods (e.g., Tripathi, Kingra, Rathinam, Tyrrell, & Gaarder, 2019).

In the realities of the everyday world of evaluation and in terms of the identity and reputations of individuals practicing program evaluation, these different political stances on how best to achieve social betterment through researching and evaluating are not unimportant matters. Yet, regardless of their respective stances, both protagonists in the debate present themselves as moral actors—that is, people who are endeavoring to do the right thing; to do good. Failing to recognize that fact by claiming moral superiority on one side of the debate is problematic, as is the mistaken effort to make a dispute about a political stance into a methodological debate. By doing so, one ignores the fact that any methodology can be co-opted and used to further either injustice or justice. The political debate obscures a more profound issue about improvement as the guiding aim of evaluating. The debate conceals the idea that opposing political stances on achieving social improvement are boundary judgments determining what each side in the debate considers relevant and irrelevant to investigating a situation or intervention. As such, neither perspective can simply be asserted as if it were self-evidently true as a justification for researching and evaluating. On the contrary, each perspective in the debate must be subject to critical reflection. As Ulrich (2001) explains,

As researchers we must make it clear to ourselves, and to all those concerned, what values our research is to promote and whose values they are; for whether we want it or not, we will hardly ever be able to claim that our research serves all interests equally. We cannot gain clarity about the . . . validity and relevance of our research unless we develop a clear notion of what kind of difference it is going to make and to whom. (p. 9)

As noted in Chapter 5, this involves the critical handling of boundary judgments that can be done in three different ways (Ulrich, 2000):

1. As *self-reflective questioning*—asking: What are my boundary judgments? How do they differ from others with whom I work/interact? What ought to be my boundary judgments so that I can justify them vis-à-vis all those concerned?

2. As *dialogical questioning*—asking: Can we agree on our boundary judgments? Why do our opinions or claims differ? What different boundary judgments make us see different facts and values? Can we find common boundary judgments? If not, can we at least understand and respect why we disagree?

3. As *controversial questioning*—asking: Don't you claim too much? Can I challenge an opponent's claims by making visible to others the boundary judgments on which these claims depend? Can I argue against an opponent's allegation that I do not know or understand enough to challenge the claim in question? How can I make a cogent argument even though I am not an expert and indeed may not be as knowledgeable as the opponent with respect to the issue at hand?

Furthermore, regardless of the political leanings of evaluators, if the goal of evaluation is improvement, it must at the very least be implicitly connected to a theory of social change. And this is rarely examined. The conventional project approach to social change looks like this:

In a situation that needs changing we can gather enough data about a community and its problems, analyze it and discover an underlying set of related problems and their cause, decide which problems are the most important, redefine these as needs, devise a set of solutions and purposes or outcomes, plan a series of logically connected activities for addressing the needs and achieving the desired future results, as defined up front, cost the activities into a convincing budget, raise the funding and then implement the activities, monitor progress as we work to keep them on track, hopefully achieve the planned results and at the end evaluate the Project for accountability, impact and sometimes even for learning. (Reeler, 2007, p. 6)

The mainstream framing of evaluation clearly aligns with this way of viewing social change, and it also shares the set of characteristics displayed in Box 7.3.

BOX 7.3. ASSUMPTIONS OF THE CONVENTIONAL THEORY OF CHANGE

- Project interventions themselves introduce the change stimulus and processes that matter and are the vehicles that can actually deliver improvement. Existing, indigenous social change processes are largely not amenable to conventional analysis.
- Problems are discernible to the planners and evaluators upfront out of cause-and-effect analysis; solutions to problems are posed as predetermined outcomes.
- Participatory processes during planning get stakeholders on board, paving the way for ownership.
- Unpredictable factors either from within or outside of the project are inconveniences to be dealt with along the way.
- Desired outcomes, impacts, and results are translatable into detailed action plans and budget and pursued in a logical and linear way.

Note. Adapted from Reeler (2007, p. 7).

Betterment or improvement might align equally well with a transformative theory of social change. The SDG Transformation Forum (*https://transformationsforum.net/totc*) distinguishes transformative change from both incremental change (doing more of the same) and reform change (changing the boundaries of how an intervention is organized and delivered but retaining underlying goals and power structures). Transformative change is marked by central characteristics, including (1) its core questions—"How do I make sense of this?"; "What is the purpose?"; "How do we know what is best?"; (2) its purpose—to innovate and create previously unimagined possibilities; (3) its archetypal actions—visioning, experimenting, and inventing; and (4) its exploration of shifts in power structures. Crises—whether political, economic, social, environmental, or a combination of same—precipitate the interest in transformative change. Climate change, the decline of biodiversity, a pandemic, the rapid expansion of cases of dementia, changes in immigration patterns, persistent unemployment, and so on are all examples of crises. Working with transformative change is a matter of facilitating the unlearning of ideas, practices, and values that underpin the crisis and that hold back effective ways to address it. These practices include evaluation, governance, finance, and innovation. The U-Process displayed in Figure 7.5 captures this idea. Doug Reeler (2007) of the Community Development Resource Association explains:

> The practice here is of surfacing the hidden roots, revealing the repeated patterns of behaviour, culture, habits and relationships that unconsciously govern the responses to the experience of crisis that people have. Further work requires bringing to light the deeply hidden and no longer appropriate values,

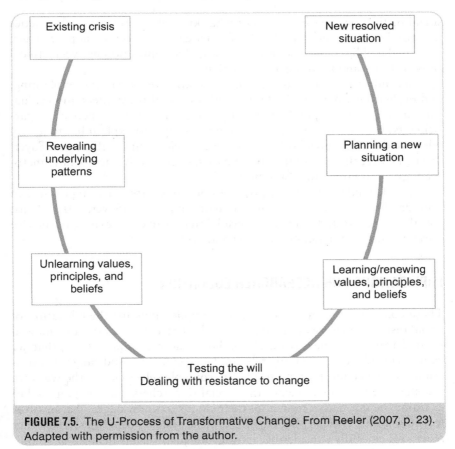

FIGURE 7.5. The U-Process of Transformative Change. From Reeler (2007, p. 23). Adapted with permission from the author.

beliefs or principles governing people's behaviours and habits—those that are real rather than the stated values and beliefs. (p. 23)

CODA

The vision of a morally committed social science reflected in these five commitments is just that, a vision. It is a direction we believe researchers and evaluators who address social problems and their solutions should take, not necessarily a direction currently taken. It begins from several assumptions.

First, "moral-political content is *internal* to the conduct of social research, not something that can be culled and dealt with exclusively by people in roles other than social researcher" (Howe & MacGillivary, 2009, p. 565, original emphasis). Moral-political content includes questions about researcher and evaluator identities and practices as they become part of social institutions, raising issues of what kind of institutions and societies it is good to have and what kinds of practices it is good to support. Thus, there is the obligation to act on an inescapable connection between ethical responsibility and knowledge production.

Second, rather than the common practice of observing, explaining, and evaluating what people do, the task of social researchers and evaluators should be to cooperate with people in shaping some practice. As participants, we will find ourselves having not simply to explain but to justify what we do and to invite others to accept or reject our justifications (Sayer, 2011). Hence, the importance of employing deliberative democratic methodology in research and evaluation.

Third, while answers to positive questions surely are important, in everyday life normative questions are more important (Sayer, 2011). Thus, social researchers and evaluators must learn how to engage those normative questions in the practices they study and participate in.

IMPLICATIONS FOR RESEARCHER EDUCATION

These commitments carry at least four implications for the education of social researchers for work in applied fields. These implications extend well beyond training in new research methods and techniques. First, that we cannot consider all potentially relevant facts, concerns, and values in a situation and hence must attend to the unavoidable selectivity of the ways we investigate and evaluate means that social researchers must be prepared to examine the normative content of their claims to knowledge. That involves learning about critical pragmatism, critical systems heuristics, and other means for carefully considering, setting, and justifying the choice of boundaries and values as illustrated in Chapter 5.

Second, consequently, social researchers must acquire skills in designing and managing deliberative participatory processes, consensus building, conflict management, and interest-based negotiation. The last-named "involves parties in a collaborative effort to jointly meet each other's needs and satisfy mutual interests. . . . This approach to negotiation is frequently called 'integrated bargaining' because of its emphasis on cooperation, meeting mutual needs, and the efforts by the parties to expand the bargaining options so that a wiser decision, with more benefits to all, can be achieved" (Delli Priscoli, 2003, pp. 48–49). The apt image for the outcome of researching and evaluating may be less that of problem solving through the application of method and more the preparation of legal brief—an argument for why one course of action should prevail.

Acquiring the skills in question will involve a change in the way we prepare researchers and evaluators who work in applied fields of study. The teaching philosophy of deliberative pedagogy, which is focused on helping students acquire the mindsets and skills needed for participatory decision making in the face of wicked problems, provides one means (Carcasson, 2017). In their introduction to a collection of essays exploring this model of teaching, communications scholars and educators Longo, Manosevitch, and Shaffer (2017) explain that

> deliberative pedagogy is a democratic educational process and a way of thinking that encourages students to encounter and consider multiple perspectives, weigh trade-offs and tensions, and move toward action through informed judgment. It is simultaneously a way of teaching that is itself deliberative and a process for developing the skills, behaviors, and values that support deliberative practice. Perhaps most important, the work of deliberative pedagogy is about space-making: creating and holding space for authentic and productive dialogue, conversations that can ultimately be not only educational but also transformative. (p. xxi)

Third, traditional training in becoming better methodologists must be supplemented with education in how to become better moral agents. Learning to be a moral agent does not simply mean learning to be responsible for one's actions as a professional. It also means learning how to address and answer value-rational questions. What this means is less unnerving and daunting than it first may appear, for it does not mean acting as a moralist who passes moral judgment. Professor of urban planning Robert Lake (2014), drawing on the pragmatists' idea that social scientific inquiry and ethical inquiry are interconnected aspects of a joint enterprise (Anderson, 1998), argues that democratically inclusive empirical inquiry "provides usable evidence to answer the value-rational questions regarding material circumstances (What are we doing?), the justification of moral principles (What should we do?), and progress toward desired outcomes (How should we do it?)" (p. 664).

Fourth, researchers whose work is primarily a matter of evaluating policies and programs will need specific training in two additional areas: (1) how to integrate evaluation into the day-to-day management of organizations versus the typical role of serving as an isolated, outside expert, and (2) how to focus more broadly on a system rather than a single intervention and hence to understand that in their work they are accountable to a community in all of its diversity and not just to those who fund the intervention that they are evaluating (Carden, 2017).

IMPLICATIONS FOR RESEARCH ON EVALUATION

The commitments we have discussed carry significant implications for the practice of research on evaluation (RoE)—empirical inquiry into some aspect of evaluation processes or products, theories, methods, or practices to test, challenge, or develop knowledge of the practice—that has been ongoing for the past 15–20 years (Coryn et al., 2011, 2016, 2017; Henry & Mark, 2003b). Many of these studies to date are descriptive accounts of various forms of evaluation practice; syntheses of existing literature in an evaluation issue or topic; and opinion surveys of the views of practicing evaluators. Very few studies address the central issue of valuing, and even fewer examine issues in professional ethics. Moreover, if RoE takes place solely within the mainstream frame for evaluating, as discussed in Chapter 3, there will be little genuine innovation and transformation of the practice. Recasting of the RoE agenda is needed considering emerging trends not simply in evaluation but in the ways in which funders and commissioners of interventions in both the public and not-for-profit sector are rethinking their work. For example, a study in the United Kingdom (Knight, Lowe, Brossard, & Wilson, 2017) of several charitable funders and public-sector commissioners "who were trying new collaborative, relational ways of working, moving beyond a target-driven culture" (p. 6) emphasized the importance of being collaborative; developing networks; recognizing the interdependence of individuals, organizations, and system structures; accepting failure and being honest about saying "we don't know"; and being straightforward about and accepting risk. The report argued that business as usual is simply unacceptable: "We are in a world of fictional 'transformations' that start with a problem, deliver a service and expect a result. This is both damaging and endemic" (p. 2).

Some topics for RoE that are more aligned with the emerging view of evaluating as explained in Chapter 5 include evaluating the efficacy of deliberative practices necessary to address relevant facts and values to be taken into account in evaluating; examining the fit of evaluative practice and tools to processes of innovation and adaptive management; exploring the consequences of evaluators acting as social critics and, at times, as partisan change agents; and moving beyond examining methods as a toolbox and linking particular methods to specific purposes and ways of framing situations or problems such as characterizing and attending to an intervention as simple, complicated, or complex.

SUMMARY

The emerging practice of evaluating is grounded in commitments that signify a new ethos of professional responsibility for researching and evaluating. That ethos is characterized as democratic professionalism—a sense of responsibility that regards the production of evaluation knowledge as a "relational public craft" (Boyte, 2007, p. 83). The democratic professional fosters a way of working together on co-owned, shared problems. He or she "seeks the public good with and not merely for the public" (Dzur, 2008, p. 129) by aiming to "assist citizens in their efforts to examine their own interests and to make their own decisions" (Fischer, 2000, p. 38). That responsibility rests upon an unavoidable pragmatic link between empirical and moral inquiry. It also reflects a profound sense of humility about professional inquiry, as together the evaluator and stakeholders consider critically such matters as what should count as relevant facts, knowledge, and sources of expertise or as an ethically defensible improvement, and who should benefit from such an improvement.

IMPORTANT RESOURCES ■ ■ ■ ■ ■ ■ ■ ■ ■ ■ ■ ■ ■ ■ ■

■ Dzur, A. (2008). *Democratic professionalism.* University Park: University of Pennsylvania Press.
   Dzur makes the case for democratic professionalism as an important way to bring professional knowledge to bear in addressing social problems in a climate where technocratic and bureaucratic decision making overlooks citizen input.

■ Flyvbjerg, B. (2001). *Making social science matter: Why social inquiry fails and how it can succeed again.* Cambridge, UK: Cambridge University Press.
   Flvvbjerg argues that to be of relevance and use, social science must drop all pretense to emulate the natural sciences. The social sciences must attend to problems in such a way that there is careful, critical consideration of issues of context, power, and values. It must become activity performed for publics in public.

■ Makau, J. M., & Marty, D. L. (2013). *Dialogue and deliberation.* Long Grove, IL: Waveland Press.
   This book explores what it means to communicate effectively across disagreement and other forms of difference. It begins with an extensive critique of adversarialism and the relentless pursuit of self-interest and its implications for effective communication. The second section of the book explores dialogic communication as an alternative to adversarialism and what that entails with respect to enabling people to express their thoughts, feelings, and experiences informing their perspectives and values. The third section of the book offers an extended discussion of the practice of deliberation and deliberative arguments.

BRIDGE TO PRACTICE

Metaphors can help researchers make meaning of their work, professional identities, and the worlds they inhabit as practitioners of research and evaluation. In reflecting on the commitments posed in this chapter or others that guide you in your work, choose a metaphor to illustrate what being a social researcher engaged in evaluating means to you. Or perhaps choose two metaphors: one that represents how you saw your role in the past and another illustrating the role you envision for yourself after reading this chapter.

1. Select a metaphor and describe what it means to you.

2. Draw an illustration of the metaphor and incorporate key commitments.

3. Metaphors reveal and conceal: Identify what your metaphor reveals about what it is like to be a social researcher and what it conceals.

4. Share your metaphor with others and discuss which metaphor best captures the kind of professional role and work you aspire to.

Ray Ison (2010, 2017), in his book *Systems Practice: How to Act in Situations of Uncertainty and Complexity in a Climate-Change World*, provides one illustration of this activity. He employed the metaphor of a juggler to characterize what thinking and acting as a systems practitioner means to him. Ison claims that a systems practitioner metaphorically juggles four balls at once: one concerned with what it means to be a systems practitioner (e.g., the difference between an embodied versus a disembodied knower); a second concerned with engaging situations (e.g., naming them as wicked or tame problems or complex and uncertain situations); a third ball, concerned with adapting one's practice to the circumstances at hand (What are the relevant tools, techniques, and methods for effecting action in this situation? Who should be involved? What are the politics and practical realities?, etc.); and a fourth ball focused on managing one's overall performance in a situation (think of terms such as controlling, coping, informing, facilitating, encouraging, delegating, communicating, etc.). Other metaphors that might characterize what it is like to be a researcher evaluating social interventions or change initiatives include space (research practice is about opening up or developing new areas of knowledge); travel (research practice is a journey of exploration); and navigating a labyrinth.

Glossary

Adaptive management—An iterative approach to decision making and learning in the face of uncertain and continuously changing circumstances; emphasizes exploring alternatives to meeting goals and objectives by gathering real-time data about changing circumstances and the consequences of decisions or actions, then using this learning to inform the next decisions and actions.

All-things-considered judgment—A common way of making judgments in which one weighs reasons for and against a particular choice, conclusion, or course of action. When used in evaluating, it can be stated as "a policy, program, etc. (X), is considered valuable when every way in which X could be valuable is weighed one against the other."

Applied ethics—The study of ethics in particular situations, professions, or institutions; for example, research ethics, journalism ethics, medical ethics, managerial ethics.

Bias—Usually thought to be synonymous with the term *prejudice*; there are three senses of the term: (1) a characteristic or tendency in individuals that prevents or makes difficult unprejudiced consideration or judgment; (2) individual preferences that prevent impartiality and objectivity; (3) mistakes in reasoning. *See* **Cognitive bias.**

Bioethics—The application of ethical theories and principles to moral issues or problems in health care.

Boundary/boundary judgments—In systems thinking, a term that is used in two ways: (1) a border of a system or situation, set by someone (e.g., observer, researcher, program leadership), that distinguishes the system/situation from the environment, the whole system/situation from its parts, and so on; (2) judgments about what is (or should be) included and excluded in an investigation that determines what facts and values are considered (ir)relevant, (un)important, and has implications for who or what is excluded and marginalized.

189

Boundary critique—A process in critical systems thinking that refers to a systematic way of examining alternate boundaries/boundary judgments and potential consequences. Involves surfacing current boundaries used to understand a system or situation; critically assessing these boundaries and considering alternatives; setting boundaries, temporarily and situationally; and, sometimes, justifying boundaries by the processes used to arrive at them. Because boundaries have consequences for who or what is included, excluded, and marginalized in a system or situation, boundary critique is one approach used by researchers, stakeholders, and citizens to critically examine boundaries.

Causal attribution—In evaluating impact, establishing a causal link between the planned intervention and observed outcomes is critical. The evaluation seeks to attribute the outcomes to the intervention and not to some other factors, often by using an experimental or quasi-experimental design.

Causal contribution—In circumstances where causal attribution is not possible or appropriate, the focus is on whether and how an intervention contributes to some observed outcomes or impacts. Rather than using an experimental or non-experimental design that isolates an intervention from other potentially causal factors, other methods are used, such as contribution analysis.

Cognitive bias—A systematic error in thinking, a mental bad habit, caused by the tendency for the human brain to perceive information through a filter of personal experience and preferences and thus thwart logical or critical thinking.

Common Rule (Revised)—The Federal Policy for the Protection of Human Subjects (known as the Common Rule), which is the baseline standard for ethics for any government-funded research in the United States. It was revised in 2018. See *www.hhs.gov/ohrp/regulations-and-policy/regulations/finalized-revisions-common-rule/index.html.*

Complex—A term that is used to characterize a problem, situation, or system and that has a meaning distinct from complicated. Complex indicates that something is composed of multiple parts but that analyses of each part when combined cannot collectively account for the whole. This is because the interactions between parts produce emergent characteristics. Labeling something as complex means that it cannot be fully knowable, determined, or predicted through systematic analysis and typically calls for a shift to systemic analysis.

Complicated —A term used to characterize a problem, situation, or system to indicate that it is made up of numerous parts that together may be quite difficult to analyze, but systematic analysis of each part allows for analysis of the whole. Labeling something as complicated means that it can be knowable, determined, or predicted through systematic analysis.

Conflict of interest—A situation in which a person has a financial, personal, political, or other interest that is likely to bias his or her judgment or decision making concerning the performance of his or her ethical or legal obligations or duties.

Co-production of knowledge—A form of knowledge production in which non-scientific and nontechnical groups and individuals as well as experts come together, with their different perspectives, viewpoints, and ways of viewing the world, and in an interactive process generate new knowledge.

Criteria—In evaluating, the dimensions of value (merit, importance, quality, etc.) of what is being evaluated that determine what the evaluation will focus on and the kinds evidence needed to assess value. Common criteria for evaluating programs and policies are effectiveness and efficiency. Criteria selection is important because it determines what is worth examining about what is being evaluated and what is not.

Critical systems heuristics— Originally developed by Werner Ulrich and elaborated by Martin Reynolds, a framework for reflective professional practice based on the idea that boundary judgments are socially constructed and that professionals have an ethical responsibility to carefully and transparently set boundaries used in their work. The framework guides a process of boundary critique by examining a set of 12 boundary judgments or questions that together comprise a reference system that bound an analysis and explicate the set of assumptions within which a claim is made.

Critical thinking— An intellectually disciplined process, requiring cognitive skills as well as particular attitudes and dispositions, of conceptualizing, analyzing, interpreting, and making inferences from information as a guide to belief and action.

Deliberative arguments—Reasoned interaction tailored to a particular audience. These arguments involve discernment, reflection, narrative and moral imagination, and related critical thinking skills.

Democratic professionalism—Broadening and sharing professional tasks and notions of expertise to involve stakeholders, citizens, and others as participants. Participation is viewed not solely as a means to better professional practice or as data for scientific or evaluative research but as an important end in itself as a democratic practice.

Determining value—A static process of assessing, gauging, or judging value in terms of performance against predetermined criteria, desired ends, standards, or benchmarks.

Developing value—A dynamic process of examining, reflecting on, and deliberating the value of some means (e.g., decisions, actions, interventions) in relation to some ends that include questioning and altering both means and ends.

Disinterested social science—Scientific contemplation at a distance. It signifies that the social scientist is a dispassionate, disengaged observer of the social-political world.

Emergent—A property or characteristic of a complex system that presents itself based on the interactions of parts but cannot be found in any individual part.

Epistemic values—Also known as cognitive values, constitutive values, and sometimes scientific values. These values arise from the goals of scientific inquiry and are attached to cognitive outcomes such as true statements, justified beliefs or hypotheses, or genuine knowledge.

Epistemological—A term that refers to knowledge or understanding and how this knowledge comes to be regarded as knowledge.

Ethical dilemma—A situation in which a choice must be made between two or more options, none of which entirely solves the problem in an ethically satisfactory way. For example, one must choose between the lesser of two evils or the greater of two goods.

Ethical reasoning—The ability to reflect on the moral issue(s) at stake in a given situation and make a decision based on a careful and thorough assessment of the different options in light of the facts and circumstances and ethical theories and principles.

Ethical theory—A unified set of statements that attempt to explain moral intuitions or judgments about right/wrong, good/bad, and so on, and offer justifications for those decisions. Examples include Aristotelian virtue ethics, utilitarianism, and deontological ethics.

Ethics—Moral principles governing behavior in interacting with human beings, animals, and the environment.

Evaluand—A term of art used in the evaluation field to signify the object or intervention being evaluated, for example, a policy, program, project, or strategy.

Evaluating/evaluation—The activity of assigning value (e.g., merit, worth, significance, importance) to some action, which might include a program, project, strategy, social intervention, policy, and the like. It is sometimes referred to as **valuation**, in the sense of calculating economic (both market and nonmarket) value. Synonyms for evaluation used in other fields include appraisal, performance assessment, and rating.

Evaluative thinking/reasoning—An individual or collective process of interpreting and weighing up data in relation to values (e.g., criteria, standards, stakeholder framings) in order to inform a judgment, decision, action, or conclusion.

Evidence—Factual information bearing on whether a statement (such as a finding, conclusion, or hypothesis) is true or false, valid or invalid, warranted or unsupported. Sources of evidence include the senses (e.g., observation), reason (e.g., analogies), the testimony of others, interviews, records, and statistics.

Fact–value distinction—The doctrine that asserts one should not confuse claims about the way things are (facts) with claims about the way they should be (values). It assumes that (1) only facts are subject to reasoned argument, and (2) values are personal preferences and hence not subject to rational debate and cannot be justified in the same manner as facts.

Frame/framing—A particular way in which individuals, groups, and societies bound and define an event, question, problem, or situation that influences how it is perceived and evaluated. Frames can be understood as sense-making devices that establish the boundaries of a problem or situation (i.e., what is considered "in" and "outside of" the problem or situation).

Impartiality—A term that has two meanings: (1) to consider something without bias (e.g., be an impartial observer) and (2) to not indicate a preference for any particular view, position, values, and so forth (e.g., to not "take sides" or support one position over another).

Improvement—Taking something that exists, whether materially or conceptually, and making changes to it to make it better according to some ideas of what better means. It is typically regarded as incremental; that is, change occurs in piecemeal fashion over time rather than all at once and comprehensively.

Instrumental reason/rationality—The use of reason as an instrument to determine the best means to achieve a given end; also called technical reason/rationality.

Judgment—A considered, deliberate opinion based on good reasons and evidence.

Logic model—A framework used to visually model an intervention in a linear process in terms of inputs, activities, outputs, outcomes, and impacts.

Logic of evaluation—An analytic procedure for making valid, defensible value claims about the merit, worth, or significance of something based on (1) criteria that define dimensions of value; (2) standards that indicate levels of performance on criteria; (3) data that empirically examine value in relation to criteria and standards; and (4) ways of synthesizing data into an overall evaluative claim or claims.

Nonepistemic values—Also called contextual or noncognitive values, values that are said to arise from outside the aims of scientific inquiry and are commonly understood as social and political values.

Norm—A standard that encapsulates expectations and guidelines for thinking or behavior; what one *should* (or *ought to*) do or what *should be* done.

Normativity—The experience of designating some action or outcome as good or bad, according to a norm.

Objectivity—A term understood in multiple ways: (1) as a synonym for being value-free, (2) as being unbiased as a social scientist, and (3) as making sure one's claims are grounded in reasoned argument and empirical support and are open to critical scrutiny.

Perspective—A way of experiencing and making sense of a situation shaped by values, assumptions, motivations, and viewpoints as well as personal and social histories.

Planned interventions—A set of activities with established goals determined in advance of implementation of those activities; activities implemented according to plans and adjusted as necessary to accomplish goals.

Practical reason/rationality—The kind of reason involved in deciding how to act, what one is to do, and how one should behave in the situation one is in. It is contrasted with theoretical reason/rationality, which is impersonal and concerned with matters of fact and their explanation.

Praxis—Aristotle's term for human activity involved in thoughtful, practical doing (parenting, managing, caring for others, etc.). The kind of knowledge required for this kind of human activity was called *phronesis,* or practical wisdom.

Preponderance of evidence—An evidentiary standard most often used in research. It means that a claim (finding, conclusion) can be considered supported if the evidence shows that it is more likely true than false (i.e., probability >50 percent). Preponderance of evidence is contrasted with a much stricter standard referred to as proof beyond a reasonable doubt.

Problem structuring—A set of techniques, methods, or processes originating in operations research and used to explore an ill-defined, ill-structured, or wicked problem or situation, and to then bound the situation in a way that allows for further analysis of the problem and/or intervention to address the problem.

Professional ethical guidelines—A set of moral principles, norms, or values serving as standards for right conduct and set forth in codes of conduct of professional associations.

Professionalism—A term that refers, on the one hand, to the way one conducts oneself as a professional. In this sense, it signifies a particular set of attitudes and the qualities of one's personal behavior (e.g., honesty, open-mindedness, respect for others, integrity, professional skepticism). It is a normative value that directs one's actions. On the other hand, professionalism refers to a particular professional group's distinguishing moral character or its codes of conduct.

Publication bias—A bias that occurs when the results of a research project dictate whether or not to publish; most often it means bias toward publishing positive results.

Purposes, purposive versus purposeful—In systems thinking, the existence of two types of purpose: extrinsic (or purposive) and intrinsic (or purposeful). Extrinsic (or ascribed) purpose refers to the purpose of a system as seen by an observer or designer; such a system is designed intentionally to serve a purpose (e.g., a road network; a planned social intervention). This type of purpose is called "purposive." Intrinsic purpose can only be attributed to systems involving people and represents the will of the people in the system to act (e.g., a network model of a knowledge management system). This type of purpose is called "purposeful."

Quality—A term that is commonly used to signify an attribute, property or characteristic of someone or something. In evaluation, quality typically refers to a standard for something as evaluated against other similar things, as, for example, in the phrase "quality improvement." The quality vocabulary used in evaluation, measurement, and assessment is quite extensive (see Dahler-Larsen, *Quality: From Plato to Performance*, 2019).

Research ethics—Narrowly understood, a term that refers to procedures for responsible conduct (e.g., informed consent) in the relationship between researchers and research subjects or participants. A broader interpretation includes consideration of ethical concerns arising in researchers' conduct with colleagues, students, funders, and institutions.

Research misconduct—As defined by the U.S. Department of Health and Human Services Office of Research Integrity, fabrication, falsification, or plagiarism in proposing, performing, or reviewing research, or in reporting research results.

Research on evaluation—Empirical inquiry conducted to build knowledge about evaluation by investigating the ways evaluations are designed and conducted, the theories and methods used to guide evaluations, and other aspects of evaluation practice.

Single-, double-, and triple-loop learning—As distinguished in the organizational learning literature, three types of learning: (1) single-loop learning, which means studying the relationship between actions and results and modifying actions when results deviate from what is expected or desired (i.e., Are we doing the right things and getting the right results?); (2) double-loop learning, which builds on single-loop learning to also examine the assumptions, values, and ways of thinking, underlying actions and results to consider whether and what changes in assumptions are necessary (i.e., What makes these the right things to do and the right results?); and (3) triple-loop learning, which builds on the prior two by examining the assumptions themselves to uncover deeper patterns, frameworks, or assumptions (i.e., On what normative bases do we assume rightness, and what other normative bases could or should we consider).

Situated judgment—A claim, decision, or action made within particular circumstances bounded by a time frame, place, and set of assumptions.

Situation of interest—In systems thinking, a situation is a set of circumstances that is of interest to someone or some group and that one wishes to further study (e.g., explore, model, analyze) or act in (e.g., intervene, change). Situations are typically unbounded at first, meaning there is a lack of clarity, decision, or agreement on the part of someone or some group about what is part of/not part of the situation and what the situation means.

Social betterment—A phrase used in the evaluation field that describes the normative ideal that guides evaluating interventions. Roughly equivalent to the slogan "better evaluation, better knowledge, better society."

Social learning—A dynamic and situated approach to learning in which stakeholders examine how they perceive a situation; determine the facts, data, or information relevant to the situation; appraise different perspectives on the situation; and together consider what can be learned, decided, or acted on. In some areas of practice, social learning is an alternative to data-driven decision making or evidence-based practice.

Social responsibility—In this book, a term that refers to the fact that scientists are accountable for fulfilling their civic duty or contributing to the benefit of society. How that duty is to be defined and what benefit means are matters of dispute both within scientific communities and in society at large.

Stake—An investment, concern, or interest that some person or group has in something and that can be put at risk in certain situations.

Stakeholder—Individuals or groups that can affect or be affected by a situation or action.

Stakeholding—An activity signifying that individuals and groups actively create, promote, advance, and defend their stake(s) in something.

System change—A term used to describe a shift from a focus on discrete, social interventions to addressing the root causes of social issues by altering social, educational, and health systems.

System of interest—A term used in systems thinking in two ways, both of which are distinct from routine use of the term *system* in everyday language. Commonly, people refer to a system as a kind of entity or process, as, for example, a transport system, the education system, the nervous system, a system to manage data, and so on. System in this sense is simply a kind of phenomenon that exists in the world. In systems thinking, system of interest is used more precisely to mean (1) a set of interacting parts that together achieve a purpose and that has a basis in reality such that it can be investigated empirically through observation, analysis, and modeling and (2) a social construct or lens used to examine some phenomenon as a system in order to individually or collectively make sense of what is happening and identify ways to change what is happening. The first meaning is evident in the statement that "the world comprises multiple interacting systems that can be studied using scientific and systems theories and methods, where the focus is often on building a model of the system to inform explanation." The second meaning is more commonly associated with building many systems models from different perspectives and using different boundary judgments to inform practical understanding and action.

Systematic thinking, analysis, or practice (also known as analytic thinking)—Proceeding in a methodical and detailed manner typically according to a plan and focused on examining the parts of a situation or system; uses the language of problems and solutions.

Systemic thinking, analysis, or practice—A theoretical and practical ability to explore or inquire of a situation by attending to interactions, connections, perspectives, interrelationships, and dynamics; oriented to learning; proceeds in a holistic manner to understand the whole situation or system; uses the language of issues and accommodations.

Systems theory—The interdisciplinary study of systems.

Systems thinking—A way of understanding the world using the language of systems and systems concepts.

Technical versus adaptive challenges—Those challenges that with sufficient knowledge and expertise can be solved, typically by experts, versus those challenges that require new and ongoing learning and acting to address but not solve the challenge.

Transformation (transformative change)—A term found repeatedly in policymaking in government and nongovernmental agencies, philanthropy, businesses, and the grand challenges funded by major research universities. The term refers to an alternative to incremental, piecemeal change. It signifies rethinking and restructuring of social life involving both quantitative and qualitative changes to practices and institutions and innovative ways to address long-standing complex issues in education, social welfare, the environment, and public health. In the systems thinking literature, transformation is often associated with new ways of collaborative working (among individuals and across institutions, teams, disciplines, and cultures), co-production, and social learning.

Uncertainty—The lack of being sure or clear about something. Wicked problems exist in a dynamic and largely uncertain environment, which creates a need to accept risk, perhaps incalculable risk.

Valuation—The practice of estimating the worth of something such as knowledge, property, and life. There are specific valuation practices in particular fields, for example, in art appraisal, real estate, health care, and insurance. *See also* **Evaluating/evaluation.**

Value-free (value-neutral)—A standpoint generally taken to mean that scientific investigation should be conducted without any influence of a researcher's social, moral, or political values; that researchers should address only the facts of the matter, so to speak, and avoid incorporating their own normative judgments in their research and conclusions.

Values—Attitudes, ideals, and beliefs that individuals and groups hold and use to guide behavior and decisions.

Valuing—In this book, a term used in the verb form to refer to the fact that values are not simply stable conceptions of what is good, right, proper, and desirable that are directly applied to decisions. Rather, values are enacted. They are dynamic, realized in actions, wrestled with, articulated, debated, and so on in decision making.

Virtue—A morally good or desirable character trait, such as honesty, courage, compassion, modesty, and fairness.

References

Abadie, A., & Cattaneo, M. D. (2018). Economic methods for program evaluation. *Annual Review of Economics, 10*, 465–503.

Abelson, J., Forest, P.-G., Eyles, J., Smith, P., Martin, E., & Gauvin, F.-P. (2003). Deliberations about deliberative methods: Issues in the design and evaluation of public participation processes. *Social Science and Medicine, 57*, 239–251.

Ackerly, B. A. (2000). *Political theory and feminist social criticism.* Cambridge, UK: Cambridge University Press.

Ackoff, R. (2001). A brief guide to interactive planning and idealized design. Unpublished manuscript. Retrieved from *https://eaasos.info/Content/Downloads/AckoffGuidetoIdealizedRedesign.pdf.*

Adler, P. S., Heckscher, C., McCarthy, J. E., & Rubinstein, S. A. (2015). The mutations of professional responsibility: Toward collaborative community. In D. E. Mitchell & R. K. Ream (Eds.), *Professional responsibility* (pp. 309–328). New York: Springer.

Alkin, M. C. (2013). *Evaluation roots* (2nd ed.). Thousand Oaks, CA: SAGE.

Alkin, M. C., & King, J. (2017). Definitions of evaluation use and misuse, evaluation influence, and factors affecting use. *American Journal of Evaluation, 38*, 434–450.

Alkin, M. C., Vo, A. T., & Christie, C. A. (2012). The evaluator's role in valuing: Who and with whom. In G. Julnes (Ed.), Promoting valuation in the public interest: Informing policies for judging value in evaluation. *New Directions for Evaluation, 133*, 29–41.

Alonso-Coello, P., Schünemann, H. J., Moberg, J., Brignardello-Petersen, R., Akl, E., Davoli, M., et al. (2016). GRADE Evidence to Decision (EtD) frameworks: A systematic and transparent approach to making well informed healthcare choices. 1: Introduction. *BMJ, 353*, i2016.

American Anthropological Association. (2014). Statement on ethnography and institutional review boards. Retrieved from *www.americananthro.org/ParticipateAndAdvocate/Content.aspx?ItemNumber=1652.*

American Association of University Professors. (n.d.). Institutional review boards and social science research. Retrieved from *www.aaup.org/report/ institutional-review-boards-and-social-science-research*.

American Educational Research Association. (2011). Code of ethics. *Educational Researcher, 40*(3), 145–156.

American Evaluation Association. (2018). Guiding principles for evaluators. Retrieved from *www.eval.org/p/cm/ld/fid=51*.

American Sociological Association. (2019). Code of ethics. Retrieved from *www. asanet.org/code-ethics*.

Ammerman, A., Smith, T. W., & Calancie, L. (2014). Practice-based evidence in public health: Improving reach, relevance, and results. *Annual Review of Public Health, 35*, 47–63.

Amy, D. (1984). Why policy analysis and ethics are incompatible. *Policy Analysis and Management, 3*, 573–591.

Anderson, C. (1979). The place of principles in policy analysis. *American Political Science Review, 73*(3), 711–723.

Anderson, E. (1998). Pragmatism, science, and moral inquiry. In R. Fox & R. Westbrook (Eds.), *In face of the facts: Moral inquiry in American scholarship* (pp. 10–39). Washington, DC: Woodrow Wilson Center Press.

Anderson, E. (2004). Uses of value judgments in science: A general argument, with lessons from a case study of feminist research on divorce. *Hypatia, 19*(1), 1–24.

Anderson, E. (2019). Dewey's moral philosophy. In E. N. Zalta (Ed.), *The Stanford encyclopedia of philosophy*. Retrieved from *https://plato.stanford.edu/ archives/win2019/entries/dewey-moral*.

Andrews, K., Parekh, J., & Peckoo, S. (2019). How to embed a racial and ethnic equity perspective in research [A Child Trends working paper]. Retrieved from *www.childtrends.org/wp-content/uploads/2019/09/ RacialEthnicEquityPerspective_ChildTrends_October2019.pdf*.

Andrews, M., Pritchett, L., & Woolcock, M. (2012). *Escaping capability traps through problem driven iterative adaptation (PDIA)* (CID Working Paper No. 240). Cambridge, MA: Center for International Development, Harvard University. Retrieved from *www.cgdev.org/publication/escaping-capability-traps-through-problem-driven-iterative-adaptation-pdia-working-paper*.

Andrews, M., Pritchett, L., & Woolcock, M. (2016). *Doing iterative and adaptive work* (CID Working Paper No. 313). Cambridge, MA: Center for International Development, Harvard University. Retrieved from *www.hks.harvard. edu/centers/cid/publications/faculty-working-papers/doing-iterative-and-adaptive-work*.

Archibald, T. (2020). What's the problem represented to be?: Problem definition critique as a tool for evaluative thinking. *American Journal of Evaluation, 41*(1), 6–19.

Argyris, C., & Schön, D. (1978). *Organizational learning: A theory of action perspective*. Reading, MA: Addison-Wesley.

Aufderheide, P. (August 17, 2016). Does this have to go through the IRB? *Chronicle of Higher Education*. Retrieved from *www.chronicle.com/article/Does-This-Have-to-Go/237476*.

Australian Council for International Development. (2017). *Principles and guide-*

lines for ethical research and evaluation in development. Australian Council for International Development. Retrieved from *https://acfid.asn.au/sites/site. acfid/files/resource_document/ACFID_R DI%20Principles%20and%20 Guidelines%20for%20ethical%20research12-07-2017.pdf.*

Australian Institute of Aboriginal and Torres Strait Islander Studies. (2012). *Guidelines for ethical research in Australian indigenous studies.* Canberra, ACT: Australian Institute of Aboriginal and Torres Strait Islander Studies. Retrieved from *https://aiatsis.gov.au/sites/default/files/2020-09/gerais.pdf.*

Bailin, S., & Siegel, H. (2003). Critical thinking. In N. Blake, P. Smeyers, R. Smith, & P. Standish (Eds.), *The Blackwell guide to the philosophy of education* (pp. 181–193). Malden, MA: Blackwell.

Bamberger, M., Vaessen, J., & Raimondo, E. (2015). *Dealing with complexity in development.* Thousand Oaks, CA: SAGE.

Barber, B. (1984). *Strong democracy: Participatory politics for a new age.* Berkeley: University of California Press.

Barder, O. (2012, September 7). Complexity, adaptation, and results [Center for Global Development Blog]. Retrieved from *www.cgdev.org/blog/complexity-adaptation-and-results.*

Barnett, C., & Eager, R. (2017). New frontiers for evaluation in a fast-changing world. In R. D. van den Berg, I. Naidoo, & S. D. Tamondong (Eds.), *Evaluation for Agenda 2030* (pp. 294–310). Exeter, UK: International Development Evaluation Association.

Battiste, M. (2008). Research ethics for protecting indigenous knowledge and heritage: Institutional and researcher responsibilities. In N. K. Denzin, Y. S. Lincoln, & L. T. Smith (Eds.), *Handbook of critical and indigenous methodologies* (pp. 497–510). Thousand Oaks, CA: SAGE.

Becker, H. (1967). Whose side are we on? *Social Problems, 14*(3), 239–247.

Becker, H. (1971). Reply to Riley's "Partisanship and Objectivity." *The American Sociologist, 6*(1), 13–18.

Befani, B., & Mayne, J. (2014). Process tracing and contribution analysis: A combined approach to generative causal inference for impact evaluation. *IDS Bulletin, 45*(6), 17–36.

Befani, B., & Stedman-Bryce, G. (2017). Process tracing and Bayesian updating for impact evaluation. *Evaluation, 23*(1), 42–60.

Berman, G., Powell, J., & Garcia Herranz, M. (2018). *Ethical considerations when using social media for evidence generation.* UNICEF, Innocenti Research Brief, Series 2018–2020. Retrieved from *www.unicef-irc.org/publications/968-ethical-considerations-when-using-social-media-for-evidence-generation-research-brief.html.*

Bernstein, J., Hutler, B., Rieder, T., Faden, R., Han, H., & Barnhill, A. (2020). An ethics framework for the COVID-19 reopening process) (Working Paper, John Hopkins Berman Institute of Bioethics). Retrieved from *https://bioethics.jhu. edu/research-and-outreach/covid-19-bioethics-expert-insights/resources-for-addressing-key-ethical-areas/grappling-with-the-ethics-of-social-distancing.*

Bernstein, R. (1998). The retrieval of the democratic ethos. In M. Rosenfield & A. Arato (Eds.), *Habermas on law and democracy* (pp. 287–305). Berkeley: University of California Press.

Best, J. (2013). Constructionist social problems theory. *Annals of the International Communication Association, 36*(1), 237–269.

Bickman, L., & Rog, D. J. (Eds.). (2009). *The SAGE handbook of applied social research methods* (2nd ed.). Thousand Oaks, CA: SAGE.

Bird, S. J. (2014). Socially responsible science is more than "good science." *Journal of Microbiology and Biology Education, 15*(2), 169–172.

Bledsoe, K. L., & Hopson, R. K. (2009). Conducting ethical research and evaluation in underserved communities. In D. Mertens & P. E. Ginsberg (Eds.), *Handbook of social research ethics* (pp. 392–406). Thousand Oaks, CA: SAGE.

Block, P. (2013). *Choosing service over self-interest* (2nd ed.). San Francisco: Berrett Koehler.

Blumer, H. (1971). Social problems as collective behavior. *Social Problems, 18*, 298–306.

Boruch, R. F. (1997). *Randomized experiments for planning and evaluation: A practical guide.* Thousand Oaks, CA: SAGE.

Boser, S. (2007). Power, ethics, and the IRB: Dissonance over human participant review of participatory research. *Qualitative Inquiry, 13*, 1060–1074.

Bosk, C. (2007). The new bureaucracies of virtue or when form fails to follow function. *PoLAR: Political and Legal Anthropology Review, 30*, 192–209.

Boswell, C., & Smith, K. (2017). Rethinking policy impact: Four models of research-policy relations. *Palgrave Communications 3*, 44.

Boyd, A., Geerling, T., Gregory, W. J., Kagam C., Midgley, G., Murray, P., et al. (2007). Systemic evaluation: A participative, multi-method approach. *Journal of the Operational Research Society, 58*, 1306–1320.

Boyte, H. (2007). Public work: Civic populism versus technocracy in higher education. In D. Brown & D. White (Eds.), *Agent of democracy* (pp. 79–102). Washington, DC: Kettering Foundation.

Boyte, H. C. (2013). Reinventing citizenship as public work. *Civic Engagement* 31. Retrieved from *https://digitalcommons.unomaha.edu/slceciviceng/31.*

Boyte, H. C. (2014). Deliberative democracy, public work, and civic agency. *Journal of Public Deliberation, 10*(1), Article 15. Retrieved from *www.publicdeliberation.net/jpd/vol10/iss1/art15.*

Boyte, H. C., & Kari, N. N. (1996). *Building America: The democratic promise of public work.* Philadelphia: Temple University Press.

Bozeman, B., Slade, C., & Hirsch, P. (2009). Understanding bureaucracy in health science ethics: Toward a better institutional review board. *American Journal of Public Health, 99*(9), 1549–1556.

Brall, C., Maeckelberghe, E., Porz, R., Makhoul, J., & Schröder-Bäck, P. (2017). Research ethics 2.0: New perspectives on norms, values, and integrity in genomic research in times of even scarcer resources. *Public Health Genomics, 20*, 27–35.

Brant Castellano, M. (1997, May). *Partnership: The key to ethical cross-cultural research.* Speech presented to the Canadian Evaluation Society, Ottawa, Ontario, Canada.

Breckon, J. (2016). *Using research evidence: A practice guide.* London: Nesta. Retrieved from *www.nesta.org.uk/toolkit/using-research-evidence-practice-guide.*

Bremmer, L. (2018). Creating new stories: The role of evaluation in truth and reconciliation. *Canadian Journal of Program Evaluation, 34,* 331–342.

Brinkerhoff, R. O. (2003). *The success case method: Find out quickly what's working and what's not.* San Francisco: Berrett-Koehler.

Brint, S. (1994). *In an age of experts: The changing role of professionals in politics and public life.* Princeton, NJ: Princeton University Press.

Brint, S. (2015). Professional responsibility in an age of experts and large organizations. In D. E. Mitchell & R. K. Ream (Eds.), *Professional responsibility* (pp. 89–107). New York: Springer.

Buckley, J., Archibald, T., Hargreaves, M., & Trochim, W. M. (2015). Defining and teaching evaluative thinking: Insights from research on critical thinking. *American Journal of Evaluation, 36,* 375–388.

Bunders, J. F. G., Broerse, J. E. W., Keil, F., Pohl, C., Scholz, R. W., & Zweekhorst, M. B. M. (2010). How can transdisciplinary research contribute to knowledge democracy? In R. J. in 't Veld (Ed.), *Knowledge democracy: Consequences for science, politics, and media* (pp. 125–152). New York: Springer.

Burbules, N. (2009). Privacy and new technologies: The limits of traditional research ethics. In D. M. Mertens & P. E. Ginsberg (Eds.), *The handbook of social research ethics* (pp. 537–549). Thousand Oaks, CA: SAGE.

Byrne, D., & Callaghan, G. (2014). *Complexity theory and the social sciences.* London: Routledge.

Cairney, P. (2019). *Fostering evidence-informed policymaking: Uncertainty versus ambiguity.* Montréal, Québec: National Collaborating Centre for Healthy Public Policy. Retrieved from *www.ncchpp.ca/docs/2019_ProcessPP_PCairney_EN.pdf.*

Campbell, D. T. (1969). Reforms as experiments. *American Psychologist, 24,* 409–429.

Campbell, D. T. (1971). Reforms as experiments. *Urban Affairs Quarterly, 7,* 133–171.

Carcasson, M. (2017). Deliberative pedagogy as critical connective: Building democratic mind-sets and skills for addressing wicked problems. In T. J. Shaffer, N. V. Longo, I. Manosevitch, & M. S. Thomas (Eds.), *Deliberative pedagogy: Teaching and learning for democratic engagement* (pp. 3–20). East Lansing: Michigan State University Press.

Carcasson, M., & Sprain, L. (2016). Beyond problem solving: Reconceptualizing the work of public deliberation as deliberative inquiry. *Communication Theory, 26,* 41–63.

Carden, F. (2017). Building evaluation capacity to address problems of equity. In S. Sridharan, K. Zhao, & A. Nakaima (Eds.), Building Capacities to Evaluate Health Inequities: Some Lessons Learned from Evaluation Experiments in China, India and Chile. *New Directions for Evaluation, 154,* 115–125.

Center for Community Health and Evaluation. (2020). Changing systems in community development: Lessons from the first three years of the Strong, Prosperous, and Resilient Communities Challenge (SPARCC). Retrieved from *www.sparcchub.org/wp-content/uploads/2020/04/sparcc-year-three-evaluation.pdf.*

Chambers, R. (2017). *Can we know better?: Reflections for development.* Warwickshire, UK: Practical Action.

Checkland, P. (1999). *Systems thinking, systems practice: Includes a 30-year retrospective.* Chichester, UK: Wiley.

Chelimsky, E. (2006). The purpose of evaluation in a democratic society. In I. F. Shaw, J. C. Greene, & M. M. Mark (Eds.), *Handbook of evaluation: Policies, programs, and practices* (pp. 33–55). London: SAGE.

Chelimsky, E. (2014). Public-interest values and program sustainability: Some implications for practice. *American Journal of Evaluation, 35,* 527–542.

Chen, H. T. (1990). *Theory-driven evaluations.* Thousand Oaks, CA: SAGE.

Child Protection Monitoring and Evaluation Reference Group. (2012). *Ethical principles, dilemmas and risks in collecting data on violence against children: A review of available literature.* New York: UNICEF, Statistics and Monitoring Section/Division of Policy and Strategy

Churchman, C. W. (1948). Statistics, pragmatics, induction. *Philosophy of Science, 15,* 249–268.

Churchman, C. W. (1967). Wicked problems. *Management Science, 14*(4), B-141–B-146.

Churchman, C. W. (1970). Operations research as a profession. *Management Science 17* (2), B-37–B-53.

Churchman, C. W. (1979). *The systems approach and its enemies.* New York: Basic Books.

Cilliers, P. (2005). Complexity, deconstruction and relativism. *Theory Culture and Society, 22*(5), 255–267.

Coady, C. A. J. (2008). *Messy morality: The challenge of politics.* Oxford, UK: Clarendon Press.

Coffman, J., Beer, T., Patrizi, P., & Thompson, E. H. (2013). Benchmarking evaluation in foundations: Do we know what we are doing? *The Foundation Review, 5*(2), Article 5, 36–51.

Consortium of Social Science Associations. (2019). Why social science? [Blog] Retrieved from *www.cossa.org/tag/why-social-science.*

Contandriopoulos, D., & Brousselle, A. (2012). Evaluation models and evaluation use. *Evaluation, 18,* 61–77.

Cordes, J. J. (2017). Using cost-benefit analysis and social return on investment to evaluate the impact of social enterprise: Promises, implementation, and limitations. *Evaluation and Program Planning, 64,* 98–104.

Coryn, C. L. S., Noakes, L. A., Westine, C. D., & Schröter, D. C. (2011). A systematic review of theory-driven evaluation practice from 1990 to 2009. *American Journal of Evaluation, 32,* 199–226.

Coryn, C. L. S., Ozeki, S., Wilson, L. N., Greenman, G. D., Schröter, D. C., Hobson, K. A., et al. (2016). Does research on evaluation matter?: Findings from a survey of American Evaluation Association members and prominent evaluation theorists and scholars. *American Journal of Evaluation, 37*(2), 159–173.

Coryn, C. L. S., Schröter, D. C., & Hanssen, C. E. (2009). Adding a time-series design element to the success case method to improve methodological rigor: An application for nonprofit program evaluation. *American Journal of Evaluation, 30*(1), 80–92.

Coryn, C. L. S., Wilson, L. N., Westine, C. D., Hobson, K. A., Ozeki, S., Fiekowsky, E. L., et al. (2017). A decade of research on evaluation: A systematic review of research on evaluation published between 2005 and 2014. *American Journal of Evaluation, 38*(3), 329–347.

Council for International Organizations of Medical Sciences, and the World Health Organization. (2009). International ethical guidelines for epidemiological studies. Retrieved from *https://cioms.ch/wp-content/uploads/2017/01/International_Ethical_Guidelines_LR.pdf*.

Cousins, J. B. (2019). *Collaborative approaches to evaluation: Principles in use.* Thousand Oaks, CA: SAGE.

Cousins, J. B., & Chouinard, J. (2012). *Participatory evaluation up close.* Charlotte, NC: Information Age.

Cousins, J. B., & Whitmore, E. (1998). Framing participatory evaluation. In E. Whitmore (Ed.), Understanding and practicing participatory evaluation. *New Directions for Evaluation, 80,* 5–23.

Cram, F., & Mertens, D. M. (2016). Negotiating solidarity between indigenous and transformative paradigms in evaluation. *Evaluation Matters—He Take Tō Te Aromatawai, 2,* 161–189.

Cronbach, L. J., Ambron, S. R., Dornbush, S. M., Hess, R. D., Hornik, R. C., Phillips, D. C., et al. (1980). *Toward reform of program evaluation.* San Francisco: Jossey-Bass.

Cullen, A., & Coryn, C. L. S. (2011). Forms and functions of participatory evaluation in international development: A review of the empirical and theoretical literature. *Journal of Multidisciplinary Evaluation, 7*(16), 32–47.

Curry, D., Waldman, R., & Caplan, A. (2014). *An ethical framework for the development and review of health research proposals involving humanitarian contexts.* Project Final Report prepared for the Department for International Development and the Wellcome Trust. Retrieved from *www.alnap.org/help-library/an-ethical-framework-for-the-development-and-review-of-health-research-proposals*.

Curtis, C., Vanstone, C., & Weinstein, L. (2019). Philanthropy, systems and change. The Australian Centre for Social Innovation. Retrieved from *www.tacsi.org.au/wp-content/uploads/2019/10/Philanthropy-systems-and-change.pdf*.

Dahler-Larsen, P. (2012). *The evaluation society.* Stanford, CA: Stanford University Press.

Dahler-Larsen, P. (2019). *Quality: From Plato to performance.* Cham, Switzerland: Springer.

Dalton, A. J., & McVilly, K. R. (2004). Ethics guidelines for international, multicenter research involving people with intellectual disabilities. *Journal of Policy and Practice in Intellectual Disabilities, 1*(2), 57–70.

Dart, J., & Davies, R. (2003). A dialogical, story-based evaluation tool: The most significant change technique. *American Journal of Evaluation, 24*(2), 137–155.

Datta, L.-E. (2011). Politics and evaluation: More than methodology. *American Journal of Evaluation, 32*(2), 273–294.

Davidson, E. J. (2005). *Evaluation methodology basics.* Thousand Oaks, CA: SAGE.

Davidson, E. J. (2014a). *Evaluative Reasoning, Methodological Brief Impact Evaluation No. 4.* Florence, Italy: UNICEF Office of Research. Retrieved from *www.unicef-irc.org/publications/pdf/brief_4_evaluativereasoning_eng.pdf*.

Davidson, E. J. (2014b). It's the very core of evaluation and makes or breaks our work: So why is it hardly in anyone's toolkit? *Evaluation Connections: Newsletter of the European Evaluation Society,* 4–5. Retrieved from *www. europeanevaluation.org/sites/default/files/ees_newsletter/ees-newsletter-2014-03-march-08.pdf*

Davies, R., & Dart, J. (2005). The most significant change (MSC) technique. Retrieved from *www.mande.co.uk/wp-content/uploads/2005/MSCGuide. pdf.*

Davis, J. E. (2013). Social science, objectivity, and moral life. *Society, 50*(6), 554–559.

Davis, M., & Feinerman, A. (2010). Assessing graduate student progress in engineering ethics. *Science and Engineering Ethics, 18*(2), 351–367.

de Maagt, S. (2017). Reflective equilibrium and moral objectivity. *Inquiry, 60*(5), 443–465.

De Munck, J., & Zimmermann, B. (2015). Evaluation as practical judgment. *Human Studies, 38*(1), 113–135.

Delli Priscoli, J. (2003). *Participation, consensus building and conflict management training course.* New York: UNESCO. Retrieved from *https://unesdoc. unesco.org/ark:/48223/pf0000133308.*

Deloitte Consulting GmbH. (2017). *Beyond the noise: The megatrends of tomorrow's world* (2nd ed.). Munich, Germany. Retrieved from *www2.deloitte. com/content/dam/Deloitte/nl/Documents/public-sector/deloitte-nl-ps-megatrends-2ndedition.pdf.*

Dewey, J. (1933). *How we think: A restatement of the relation of reflective thinking to the educative process* (rev. ed.). Boston: D. C. Heath.

Dickinson, P., & Adams, J. (2017). Values in evaluation—the use of rubrics. *Evaluation and Program Planning, 65,* 113–116.

Dietz, T. (2013). Bringing values and deliberation to science communication. *Proceedings of the National Academy of Sciences of the USA, 110*(Suppl. 3), 14081–14087.

Dockterman, D. (2018). Insights from 200+ years of personalized learning. *npj Science of Learning, 3*(1), 1–6.

Donaldson, S. I. (2007). *Program theory-driven evaluation science.* New York: Erlbaum.

Douglas, H. (2004). The irreducible complexity of objectivity. *Synthese, 138*(3), 453–473.

Douglas, H. (2007). Rejecting the ideal of value-free science. In H. Kincaid, J. Dupré, & A. Wylie (Eds.), *Value-free science?: Ideals and illusions* (pp. 120–139). New York: Oxford University Press.

Douglas, H. (2009). *Science, policy, and the value-free ideal.* Pittsburgh, PA: University of Pittsburgh Press.

Douglas, H. (2011). Facts, values, and objectivity. In I. C. Jarvie & J. Zamora-Bonilla (Eds.), *Handbook of the philosophy of the social sciences* (pp. 513–539). London: SAGE.

Douglas, H. (2014a). The moral terrain of science. *Erkenntnis, 79,* 961–979.

Douglas, H. (2014b). Values in social science. In N. Cartwright & E. Montuschi (Eds.), *Philosophy of social science: A new introduction* (pp. 162–182). Oxford, UK: Oxford University Press.

Douglas, H. (2016). Values in science. In P. Humphreys (Ed.), *Oxford handbook of philosophy of science* (pp. 609–632). Oxford, UK: Oxford University Press.

Drugge, A.-L. (Ed.). (2016). *Ethics in indigenous research: Past experiences, future challenges.* Umeå, Sweden: Vaarto-Centre for Sami Research, Umeå University. Retrieved from *www.diva-portal.org/smash/get/diva2:943266/FULL-TEXT03.pdf.*

Dryzek, J. (1993). Policy analysis and planning: From science to argument. In F. Fischer & J. Forester (Eds.), *The argumentative turn in policy analysis and planning* (pp. 213–253). Durham, NC: Duke University Press.

Duggan, C., & Bush, K. (2014). The ethical tipping points of evaluators in conflict zones. *American Journal of Evaluation, 35*(4), 485–506.

DuMont, K. (2015). *Leveraging knowledge: Taking stock of the William T. Grant Foundation's use of research evidence grants portfolio.* New York: William T. Grant Foundation. Retrieved from *http://wtgrantfoundation.org/library/uploads/2015/09/Leveraging-Knowledge-Taking-Stock-of-URE.pdf.*

Dunia, O. A., Baaz, M., Mwambari, D., Parashar, S., Oseema, A., Toppo, M., et al. (2020). The Covid-19 opportunity: Creating more ethical and sustainable research practices. Retrieved from *https://items.ssrc.org/covid-19-and-the-social-sciences/social-research-and-insecurity/the-covid-19-opportunity-creating-more-ethical-and-sustainable-research-practices.*

Dunne, J. (1993). *Back to the rough ground: 'Phronesis' and 'techne' in modern philosophy and Aristotle.* Notre Dame, IN: University of Notre Dame Press.

Dunne, J., & Pendlebury, S. (2003). Practical reason. In N. Blake, P. Smeyers, R. Smith, & P. Standish (Eds.), *The Blackwell guide to the philosophy of education* (pp. 194–212). Malden, MA: Blackwell.

Dussauge, I., Helgesson, C., Lee, F., & Woolgar, S. (2015). *Value practices in the life sciences and medicine.* Oxford, UK: Oxford University Press.

Dyck, M., & Allen, G. (2012). Is mandatory research ethics reviewing ethical? *Journal of Medical Ethics, 39*(8), 517–520.

Dynamics Model. (n.d.). Retrieved from *https://www.rethinkhealth.org/our-work/dynamics-model.*

Dzur, A. (2008). *Democratic professionalism.* University Park: University of Pennsylvania Press.

Eagleton, T. (2004). *After theory.* New York: Penguin Books.

Earl, S., Carden, F., & Smutylo, T. (2001). *Outcome mapping.* Ottawa, Ontario, Canada: International Development Research Centre.

Ecosystem Services for Poverty Alleviation. (2019). ESPA ethics principles and procedure. Retrieved from *www.espa.ac.uk/files/espa/Ethics%20Guidelines.pdf.*

Edmondson, R., & Hülser, K. (Eds.). (2012). *Politics of practical reasoning: Integrating action, discourse and argument.* Lanham, MD: Lexington Books.

Elliott, K. (2011). Direct and indirect roles for values in science. *Philosophy of Science, 78*(2), 303–324.

Elliott, K. (2013). Douglas on values: From indirect roles to multiple goals. *Studies in History and Philosophy of Science, 44*(3), 375–383.

Elliott, K. (2017a). *Rather than being free of values, good science is transparent about them* [Blog]. The Conversation. Retrieved from *http://theconversation.com/rather-than-being-free-of-values-good-science-is-transparent-about-them-84946.*

Elliott, K. (2017b). *A tapestry of values: An introduction to values in science.* Oxford, UK: Oxford University Press.

Elliott, K., & Resnik, D. (2014). Science, policy, and the transparency of values. *Environmental Health Perspectives, 122*(7), 647–650.

Engelhardt, T., Jr. (1992). Introduction. In J. L. Peset Reig & D. Gracia (Eds.), *The ethics of diagnosis* (pp. 1–10). Dordrecht, the Netherlands: Kluwer Academic.

Eoyang, G. H., & Berkas, T. H. (1999). Evaluating performance in a complex adaptive system. In M. Lissack & H. Gunz (Eds.), *Managing complexity in organizations* (pp. 1–21). Westport, CT: Quorum Books.

Eoyang, G., & Holladay, R. (2013). *Adaptive action: Leveraging uncertainty in your organization.* Stanford, CA: Stanford University Press.

Erickson, J., Milstein, B., Schafer, S., Pritchard, K. E., Levitz, C., Miller, C., et al. (2017). Progress along the pathway for transforming regional health: A pulse check on multi-sector partnerships. Retrieved from *www.rethinkhealth.org/wp-content/uploads/2019/09/2016-Pulse-Check-Narrative-Final.pdf.*

EvalPartners. (n.d.). International mapping of evaluation associations. Retrieved from *www.evalpartners.org/about/international-mapping-of-evaluation-associations.*

Fals-Borda, O., & Anisur Rahman, M. (1991). *Action and knowledge: Breaking the monopoly with participatory action research.* New York: Apex Press.

Feagin, J. R. (2013). *The white racial frame.* New York: Routledge.

Feinstein, O. (2019). Dynamic evaluation for transformational change. In R. D. van den Berg, C. Magro, & S. S. Mulder (Eds.), *Evaluation for transformational change: Opportunities and challenges for the sustainable development goals* (pp. 17–32). Exeter, UK: International Development Evaluation Association.

Fetterman, D. M., Kaftarian, S. J., & Wandersman, A. (Eds.). (2015). *Empowerment evaluation* (2nd ed.). Thousand Oaks, CA: SAGE.

Filipe, A., Renedo, A., & Marston, C. (2017). The co-production of what?: Knowledge, values, and social relations in health care. *PLOS Biology 15*(5), e2001403. Retrieved from *https://doi.org/10.1371/journal.pbio.2001403.*

Fischer, F. (1980). *Politics, values and public policy: The problem of methodology.* Boulder, CO: Westview Press.

Fischer, F. (1993). Citizen participation in the democratization of policy expertise: From theoretical inquiry to practical cases. *Policy Sciences, 26,* 165–187.

Fischer, F. (1999). *Evaluating public policy.* Chicago: Nelson-Hall.

Fischer, F. (2000). *Citizens, experts, and the environment.* Durham, NC: Duke University Press.

Fischer, F. (2003). Beyond empiricism: Policy analysis as deliberative practice. In M. Hajer & H. Wagenaar (Eds.), *Deliberative policy analysis: Understanding governance in the network society* (pp. 209–227). Cambridge, UK: Cambridge University Press.

Fischer, F. (2007). Deliberative policy analysis as practical reason: Integrating empirical and normative arguments. In F. Fischer, G. J. Miller, & M. S. Sidney (Eds.), *Handbook of public policy analysis* (pp. 223–236). New York: Taylor & Francis.

Fischer, F., & Forester, J. (Eds.). (1987). *Confronting values in policy analysis: The politics of criteria.* Thousand Oaks, CA: SAGE.

Fischer, F., & Forester, J. (Eds.). (1993). *The argumentative turn in policy analysis and planning.* Durham, NC: Duke University Press.

Fischer, F., & Gottweis, H. (2012). *The argumentative turn revisited: Public policy as communicative practice.* Durham, NC: Duke University Press.

Fisher, A., & Scriven, M. (1997). *Critical thinking: Its definition and assessment.* Norwich, UK: University of East Anglia, Center for Research in Critical Thinking.

Fitzpatrick, J. L., Sanders, J. S., & Worthen, B. R. (2011). *Program evaluation: Alternative approaches and practical guidelines* (4th ed.). Boston: Pearson.

Fleming, F. (2013). Evaluating methods for assessing value for money. Retrieved from *www.betterevaluation.org/en/resource/assessing-value-for-money.*

Flynn, L. R., & Goldsmith, R. E. (2013). *Case studies for ethics in academic research in the social sciences.* Thousand Oaks, CA: SAGE.

Flyvbjerg, B. (2001). *Making social science matter: Why social inquiry fails and how it can succeed again.* Cambridge, UK: Cambridge University Press.

Flyvbjerg, B. (2004). Phronetic planning research: Theoretical and methodological reflections. *Planning Theory and Practice, 5*(3), 283–306.

Foresight. (n.d.). Blog of the Rippel Foundation. Retrieved from *https://www.rippelfoundation.org/our-work/foresight.*

Forester, J. (1999). *The deliberative practitioner: Encouraging participatory planning processes.* Cambridge, MA: MIT Press.

Forrester, J. W. (1961). *Industrial dynamics.* Portland, OR: Productivity Press.

Forss, K. (2019). Getting value for money?: A critical analysis of the costs and benefits of evaluation. In J.-E. Furubo & N. Stame (Eds.), *The evaluation enterprise* (pp. 179–197). London: Routledge.

Fournier, D. M. (1995). Establishing evaluative conclusions: A distinction between general and working logic. In D. F. Fournier (Ed.), Reasoning in evaluation: Inferential links and leaps. *New Directions for Evaluation, 68,* 15–32.

Fox, R. W., & Westbrook, R. B. (1998). Introduction: Moral inquiry in American scholarship. *In face of the facts: Moral inquiry in American scholarship* (pp. 10–39). Cambridge, UK: Cambridge University Press.

Freire, P. (1970). *Pedagogy of the oppressed.* New York: Bloomsbury Academic.

Fricker, M. (2007). *Epistemic injustice: Power and the ethics of knowing.* Oxford, UK: Oxford University Press.

Friedmann, J. (1987). *Planning in the public domain: From knowledge to action.* Princeton, NJ: Princeton University Press.

Friedmann, J., & Abonyi, G. (1976). Social learning: A model for policy research. *Environment and Planning A: Economy and Space, 8,* 927–940.

Funnell, S. C., & Rogers, P. J. (2011). *Purposeful program theory: Effective use of theories of change and logic models.* New York: Wiley.

Funtowicz, S., & Ravetz, J. (1993). Science for the post-normal age. *Futures, 31,* 735–755.

Gamoran, A. (2018). Evidence-based policy in the real world: A cautionary view. *Annals of the American Academy of Political and Social Science, 678,* 180–191.

Gargani, J. (2017). The leap from ROI to SROI: Farther than expected? *Evaluation and Program Planning, 64,* 116–126.

Gasper, D. (2012). Development ethics—Why? What? How?: A formulation of the field. *Journal of Global Ethics, 8*(1), 117–135.

Gates, E. F. (2016). Making sense of the emerging conversation in evaluation about systems thinking and complexity science. *Evaluation and Program Planning, 59*, 62–73.

Gates, E. F. (2018). Toward valuing with critical systems heuristics. *American Journal of Evaluation, 39*, 201–220.

Gates, E. F., & Dyson, L. (2017). Implications of the changing conversation about causality for evaluators. *American Journal of Evaluation, 38*, 29–46.

Gates, E., & Fils-Aime, F. (in press). Evaluation about and for system change: Insights from the Rippel Foundation and its ReThink Health Initiative. In E. Gates, M. Walton, & P. Vidueira, P. (Eds.), Systems- and complexity-informed evaluation: Insights from practice. *New Directions for Evaluation.*

Gates, E., Walton, M., & Vidueira, P. (Eds.). (in press). Systems- and complexity-informed evaluation: Insights from practice. *New Directions for Evaluation.*

Gaventa, J. (2005). *Reflections on the uses of the "Power Cube" approach for analyzing the spaces, places and dynamics of civil society participation and engagement* (CFP evaluation series 2003–2006: no 4). Randwijk, the Netherlands: Learning by Design. Retrieved from *www.participatorymethods.org/ sites/participatorymethods.org/files/reflections_on_uses_powercube.pdf.*

Gaventa, J. (2006). Finding the spaces for change: A power analysis. *IDS Bulletin, 37*(6), 23–33.

Gerring, J., & Yesnowitz, J. (2006). A normative turn in political science? *Polity, 38*(1), 101–133.

Gertler, P. J., Martinez, S., Premand, P., Rawlings, L. B., & Vermeersch, C. M. J. (2016). The ethics and science of impact evaluation. In *Impact evaluation in practice* (2nd ed., pp. 231–246). Washington, DC: World Bank.

Gilad, S. (2019). Mixing qualitative and quantitative methods in pursuit of richer answers to real-world questions. *Public Performance and Management Review.* [Epub ahead of print]

Gilbert, N. (2008). *Agent-based models.* Thousand Oaks, CA: SAGE.

Gorski, P. S. (2013). Beyond the fact/value distinction: Ethical naturalism and the social sciences. *Society, 50*(6), 543–553.

Goulet, D. (1988). Tasks and methods in development ethics. *Cross Currents, 38*(2), 146–172.

Graham, A., Taylor, N., Fitzgerald, R., Powell, M. A., & Anderson, D. (2013). *Ethical research involving children.* Florence: UNICEF Office of Research–Innocenti.

Grantmakers for Effective Organizations and Management Assistant Group. (2016). Systems grantmaking resource guide. Retrieved from *http://systems. geofunders.org.*

Green, L. W. (2006). Public health asks of systems science: To advance our evidence-based practice, can you help us get more practice-based evidence? *American Journal of Public Health 96*(3), 406–409.

Green, L. W., Ottoson, J. M., Garcia, C., & Hiatt, R. A. (2009). Diffusion theory and knowledge dissemination, utilization, and integration in public health. *Annual Review of Public Health, 30*, 151–174.

Gregory, A. (2000). Problematizing participation: A critical review of approaches to participation in evaluation theory. *Evaluation, 6*, 179–199.

Guijt, I., & Artuso, F. (2020). *Global megatrends: Mapping the forces that affect us all* (Oxfam discussion paper). Oxford, UK: Oxfam GB for Oxfam International. Retrieved from *https://oxfamilibrary.openrepository.com/handle/10546/620942?show=full*.

Gunsalus, C., Bruner, E., Burbules, N., Dash, L., Finkin, M., Goldberg, J., et al. (2006). Mission creep in the IRB world. *Science, 312*(5779), 1441.

Guyatt, G. H., Oxman, A. D., Kunz, R., Falck-Ytter, Y., Vist, G. E., Liberati, A., et al. (2008b). GRADE: Going from evidence to recommendations. *British Medical Journal, 336*, 1049–1051.

Guyatt, G. H., Oxman, A. D., Vist, G. E., Kunz, R., Falck-Ytter, Y., Alonso-Coello, P., et al. (2008a). GRADE: An emerging consensus on rating quality of evidence and strength of recommendations. *BMJ, 336*, 924–926.

Haan, N., Bellah, R. N., Rabinow, P., & Sullivan, W. M. (1983). *Social science and moral inquiry*. New York: Columbia University Press.

Hacking, I. (1999). *The social construction of what?* Cambridge, MA: Harvard University Press.

Hacking, I. (2015). Let's not talk about objectivity. In F. Padovani, A. Richardson, & J. Y. Tsou (Eds.), *Objectivity in science* (pp. 19–33). Berlin: Springer.

Haggerty, K. (2004). Ethics creep: Governing social science research in the name of ethics. *Qualitative Sociology, 27*(4), 391–414.

Haidt, J. (2012). *The righteous mind: Why good people are divided by politics and religion*. New York: Vintage Books.

Hajer, M. A., & Wagenaar, H. (Eds.). (2003). *Deliberative policy analysis: Understanding governance in the network society*. Cambridge, UK: Cambridge University Press.

Hall, J. N., Ahn, J., & Greene, J. C. (2012). Values engagement in evaluation: Ideas, illustrations, and implications. *American Journal of Evaluation, 33*, 195–207.

Hammersley, M. (2000). *Taking sides in social research: Essays on partisanship and bias*. New York: Routledge.

Hammersley, M. (2001). Which side was Becker on?: Questioning political and epistemological radicalism. *Qualitative Research 1*(1), 91–110.

Hammersley, M. (2014). *The limits of social science: Causal explanation and value relevance*. Thousand Oaks, CA: SAGE.

Hammersley, M. (2017). On the role of values in social research: Weber vindicated? *Sociological Research Online, 22*(1), 1–12.

Hanrieder, T. (2016). Orders of worth and the moral conceptions of health in global politics. *International Theory, 8*(3), 390–421.

Harman, E., & Azzam, T. (2018). Incorporating public values into evaluative criteria: Using crowdsourcing to identify criteria and standards. *Evaluation and Program Planning, 71*, 68–82.

Harriman, S., & Patel, J. (2014). The ethics and editorial challenges of internet-based research. *BMC Medicine, 12*(1), 124.

Haskins, R. (2018). Evidence-based policy: The movement, the goals, the issues, the promise. *Annals of the American Academy of Political and Social Science, 678*, 8–37.

Haslam, N., & Loughnan, S. (2014). Dehumanization and infrahumanization. *Annual Review of Psychology, 65*(1), 399–423.

Hatry, H. (2014). *Transforming performance measurement for the 21st century.* Washington, DC: Urban Institute.

Hawkins, B., & Parkhurst, J. (2016). The "good governance" of evidence in health policy. *Evidence and Policy: A Journal of Research, Debate and Practice, 12*(4), 575–592.

Healy, S. (2003). Epistemological pluralism and the "politics of choice." *Futures, 35,* 689–701.

Healy, S. (2009). Toward an epistemology of participation. *Journal of Environmental Management, 90*(4), 1644–1654.

Heimer, C. A., & Petty, J. (2010). Bureaucratic ethics: IRBs and the legal regulation of human subjects research. *Annual Review of Law and Social Science, 6,* 601–626.

Helm, B. W. (2007). *Emotional reason: Deliberation, motivation, and the nature of value.* Cambridge, UK: Cambridge University Press.

Henry, G. T. (2000). Why not use? In V. J. Caracelli & H. Preskill (Eds.), The expanding scope of evaluation use. *New Directions for Evaluation, 88,* 85–98.

Henry, G. T., & Mark, M. M. (2003a). Beyond use: Understanding evaluation's influence on attitudes and actions. *American Journal of Evaluation, 24*(3), 293–314.

Henry, G. T., & Mark, M. M. (2003b). Toward an agenda for research on evaluation. In C. A. Christie (Ed.), The practice-theory relationship in evaluation. *New Directions for Evaluation, 97,* 69–80.

Hepi, M., Foote, J., Ahuriri-Driscoll, A., Rogers-Koroheke, M., Taimona, H., & Clark, A. (in press). Opportunities and challenges in cross-cultural evaluation: Reflections from New Zealand. In E. Gates, M. Walton, & P. Vidueira (Eds.), Systems- and complexity-informed evaluation: Insights from practice. *New Directions for Evaluation.*

Hicks, D. (2014). A new direction for science and values. *Synthese, 191*(14), 3271–3295.

Hinton, C., Fischer, K. W., & Glennon, C. (2013). Applying the science of how we learn. In R. Wolfe, A. Steinberg, & N. Hoffman (Eds.), *Anytime anywhere: Student-centered learning for schools and teachers* (pp. 153–170). Cambridge, MA: Harvard Education Press.

Hirschman, A. O. (1983). Morality and the social sciences: A durable tension. In N. Haan, R. N. Bellah, P. Rabinow, & W. M. Sullivan (Eds.), *Social science as moral inquiry* (pp. 19–32). New York: Columbia University Press.

Hoggan, J. (2016). *I'm right and you're an idiot: The toxic state of public discourse and how to clean it up.* Gabriola Isnad, British Columbia, Canada: New Society Publishers.

Homer, J., & Hirsch, G. (2006). System dynamics modeling for public health: Background and opportunities. *American Journal of Public Health, 96*(3), 452–458.

Homer, J., Milstein, B., Hirsch, G. B., & Fisher, E. (2016). Combined regional investments could substantially enhance health system performance and be financially affordable. *Health Affairs, 35*(8), 1435–1443.

Hood, S., Hopson, R., & Frierson, H. (Eds.). (2015). *Continuing the journey to reposition culture and cultural context in evaluation theory and practice.* Charlotte, NC: Information Age Press.

Hood, S., Hopson, R., & Kirkhart, K. (2015). Culturally responsive evaluation: Theory, practice, and future implications. In K. E. Newcomer, H. P. Hatry, & J. S. Wholey (Eds.), *Handbook of practical program evaluation* (4th ed., pp. 281–317). San Francisco: Jossey-Bass.

House, E. R. (2015). *Evaluating: Values, biases and practical wisdom.* Charlotte, NC: Information Age.

House, E. R. (2020). Evaluating in a fragmented society. *Journal of Multidisciplinary Evaluation, 16*(36), 26–37.

House, E. R., & Howe, K. (1999). *Values in evaluation and social research.* Thousand Oaks, CA: SAGE.

Howe, K. R., & MacGillivary, H. (2009). Social research attuned to deliberative democracy. In D. Mertens & P. E. Ginsberg (Eds.), *Handbook of social research ethics* (pp. 565–579). Thousand Oaks, CA: SAGE.

Howlett, M., & Geist, G. (2015). Policy cycle. In J. D. Wright (Ed.), *International encyclopedia of the social and behavioral sciences* (2nd ed., pp. 288–293). New York: Elsevier.

Hudson, M., & Russell, K. (2009). The treaty of Waitangi and research ethics in Aoteroa. *Journal of Bioethical Inquiry, 6*, 61–68.

Hummelbrunner, R. (2015). Learning, systems concepts and values in evaluation: Proposal for an exploratory framework to improve coherence. *IDS Bulletin 46*(1), 17–29.

Hummelbrunner, R., & Reynolds, M. (2013, June). Systems thinking, learning and values in evaluation. *Evaluation Connections: The European Evaluation Society Newsletter,* pp. 9–10. Retrieved from *http://oro.open.ac.uk/37718/1/Connections+613_Final+PrePub.pdf.*

Immediato, S. (2017, June 28). Leading with a value proposition: Making the case for change (Blogpost). Retrieved from *www.rethinkhealth.org/Resource/leading-with-a-value-proposition-making-the-case-for-change.*

Innes, J. E., & Booher, D. E. (1991). Consensus building and complex adaptive systems: A framework for evaluating collaborative planning. *Journal of the American Planning Association, 65*(4), 412–423.

Intezari, A., & Pauleen, D. (2014). Management wisdom in perspective: Are you virtuous enough to succeed in volatile times? *Journal of Business Ethics, 120*, 393–404.

Intezari, A., & Pauleen, D. (2019). *Wisdom, analytics, and wicked problems: Integrated decision making for the data age.* New York: Routledge.

Ison, R. (2010). *Systems practice: How to act in a climate-changed world.* London: Springer.

Ison, R. (2017). *Systems practice: How to act in situations of uncertainty and complexity in a climate-change world* (2nd ed.). London: Springer.

Ivaldi, S., Scaratti, G., & Nuti, G. (2015). The practice of evaluation as the evaluation of practices. *Evaluation, 21*, 497–512.

Jacobs, J. (2013). The fact/value distinction and the social sciences. *Society, 50*(6), 560–569.

Jahn, T., Bergmann, M., & Keil, F. (2012). Transdisciplinarity: Between mainstreaming and marginalization. *Ecological Economics, 79*(C), 1–10.

Jamieson, D. (2013). Constructing practical ethics. In R. Crisp (Ed.), *The Oxford handbook of the history of ethics* (pp. 843–866). Oxford, UK: Oxford University Press.

Jasanoff, S. (1990). *The fifth branch: Science adviser as policymakers.* Cambridge, MA: Harvard University Press.

Jasanoff, S. (2004). *States of knowledge: The co-production of science and the social order.* New York: Routledge.

Jenkins-Smith, H. (1982). Professional roles for policy analysts: A critical assessment. *Journal of Policy Analysis and Management, 2*(1), 88–100.

Johnson, C. E. (2018). *Meeting the ethical challenges of leadership* (6th ed.). Thousand Oaks, CA: SAGE.

Julnes, G., & Rog, D. J. (Eds.). (2007). Informing federal policies on evaluation methodology: Building the evidence base for method choice in government sponsored evaluation. *New Directions for Evaluation, 113.*

Kahan, D. M. (2016). The politically motivated reasoning paradigm: Part I. What politically motivated reasoning is and how to measure it. In R. Scott & S. Kosslyn (Eds.), *Emerging trends in the social and behavioral sciences* (pp. 1–16). New York: Wiley.

Kahneman, D. (2011). *Thinking fast and slow.* New York: Farrar, Straus & Giroux.

Kania, J., & Kramer, M. (2011, Winter). Collective impact. *Stanford Social Innovation Review,* pp. 36–41.

Kania, J., Kramer, M., & Senge, P. (2018). *The water of systems change.* FSG Reimagining Social Change. Retrieved from *www.fsg.org/publications/ water_of_systems_change.*

Kara, H. (2017). Identity and power in co-produced activist research. *Qualitative Research, 17*(3), 289–301.

Kendi, I. X. (2019). *How to be an antiracist.* New York: One World.

Kenter, J. O., Reed, M. S., & Fazey, I. (2016). The deliberative value formation model. *Ecosystem Services, 21,* 194–207.

Kimmel, A. J. (2015). Ethical issues in social influence research. In S. G. Harkins, K. D. Williams, & J. Burger (Eds.), *The Oxford handbook of social influence* (pp. 11–33). Oxford, UK: Oxford University Press.

King, J. (2016). *Value for money: A practical evaluation theory.* Auckland, New Zealand: Julian King & Associates. Retrieved from *www.julianking.co.nz/ wp-content/uploads/2014/09/160527-VFI-jk8-web.pdf.*

King, J. (2017). Using economic methods evaluatively. *American Journal of Evaluation, 38,* 101–113.

King, J. (2019). *Evaluation and value for money.* Doctoral dissertation, Centre for Program Evaluation, Melbourne Graduate School of Education, University of Melbourne, Australia.

King, J., & Alkin, M. (2018). The centrality of use: Theories of evaluation use and influence and thoughts on the first 50 years of use research. *American Journal of Evaluation, 40,* 431–458.

King, J., McKegg, K., Oakden, J., & Wehipeihana, N. (2013). Evaluative rubrics: A method for surfacing values and improving the credibility of evaluation. *Journal of Multidisciplinary Evaluation, 9*(21), 11–21.

King, J., & OPM VfM Working Group. (2018). *OPM's approach to assessing value for money.* Canberra, Australia: Oxford Policy Management. Retrieved from *www.opml.co.uk/publications/assessing-value-for-money.*

Kirkhart, K. E. (2010). Eyes on the prize: Multicultural validity and evaluation theory. *American Journal of Evaluation, 31,* 400–413.

Kitchener, K. S. (1984). Intuition, critical evaluation and ethical principles: The foundation for ethical decisions in counseling psychology. *The Counseling Psychologist, 12*(3), 43–55.

Kitchener, R. F., & Kitchener, K. S. (2012). Ethical foundations of psychology. In S. J. Knapp, M. C. Gottlieb, M. M. Handelsman, & L. D. VandeCreek (Eds.), *Handbook of ethics in psychology: Vol. 1. Moral foundations and common themes* (pp. 3–42). Washington, DC: American Psychological Association.

Klein, J. T. (2010). A taxonomy of interdisciplinarity. In R. Frodeman, J. T. Klein, & C. Mitcham (Eds.), *The Oxford handbook of interdisciplinarity* (pp. 15–30). Oxford, UK: Oxford University Press.

Knight, A. D., Lowe, T., Brossard, M., & Wilson, J. (2017). *A whole new world: Funding and commissioning complexity.* London: Collaborate. Retrieved from *http://wordpress.collaboratei.com/wp-content/uploads/A-Whole-New-World-Funding-Commissioning-in-Complexity.pdf.*

Koller, C. F. (2015). Non-partisan, but not neutral. Milbank Memorial Fund, President's Blog. Available at *www.milbank.org/2015/09/non-partisan-but-not-neutral.*

Kosar, K. (2015, January/February). Why I quit the Congressional Research Service. *Washington Monthly.* Available at *htps://washingtonmonthly.com/magazine/janfeb-2015/why-i-quit-the-congressional-reserch-service.*

Kuntz, M. (2012). The postmodern assault on science. *EMBO Reports, 13*(10), 885–889.

Lacey, H. (2002). The ways in which the sciences are and are not value free. In P. Gärdenfors, J. Woleński, & K. Kijania-Placek, (Eds.), *In the scope of logic, methodology and philosophy of science.* Dordrecht, the Netherlands: Springer.

Lackey, R. (2007). Science, scientists, and policy advocacy. *Conservation Biology, 21*(1), 12–17.

LaFrance, J., & Nichols, R. (2010). Reframing evaluation: Defining an indigenous evaluation framework. *Canadian Journal of Program Evaluation, 23*(2), 13–31.

Lake, R. W. (2014). Methods and moral inquiry. *Urban Geography, 35*(5), 657–668.

Lance, P., Guilkey, D., Hattori A., & Angeles, G. (2014). *How do we know if a program made a difference?: A guide to statistical methods for program impact evaluation.* Chapel Hill, NC: MEASURE Evaluation. Retrieved from *www.measureevaluation.org/resources/publications/ms-14-87-en.*

Lawrenz, F., & Huffman, D. (2006). Methodological pluralism: The gold standard of STEM evaluation. In F. Lawrenz & D. Huffman (Eds.), Critical issues in STEM evaluation. *New Directions for Evaluation, 109,* 19–34.

Leach, M., Scoones, I., & Wynne, B. (Eds.). (2005). *Science and citizens: Globalization and the challenge of engagement.* London: Zed Books.

Leithwood, K. A., & Montgomery, D. J. (1980). Evaluating program implementation. *Evaluation Review, 4*(2), 193–214.

Lemire, S., Nielsen, S. B., & Christie, C. A. (2018). Toward understanding the evaluation market and its industry—Advancing a research agenda. In S. B. Nielsen, S. Lemire, & C. A. Christie (Eds.), The evaluation marketplace: Exploring the evaluation industry. *New Directions for Evaluation, 160*, 145–163.

Levin, Y. (2006). The moral challenge of modern science. *The New Atlantis, 14*, 32–46.

Levin-Rozalis, M. (2015). A purpose-driven action: The ethical aspect and social responsibility of evaluation. In B. Rosenstein & H. Desivilya Syna (Eds.), Evaluation and social justice in complex sociopolitical contexts. *New Directions for Evaluation, 146*, 19–32.

Levine, P. (2014). Civic studies. *Philosophy and Public Policy Quarterly, 32*(1), 29–33.

Levine, P. (2019). *What is civic science?* (A blog for civic renewal). Retrieved from *https://peterlevine.ws/?p=21019*.

Lindblom, C. E. (1977). *Politics and markets*. New York: Basic Books

Lindblom, C. E. (1986). Who needs what social research for policymaking? *Science Communication, 7*(4), 345–366.

Lindblom, C. E. (1990). *Inquiry and change*. New Haven, CT: Yale University Press.

Lipsey, M. W., & Cordray, D. S. (2000). Evaluation methods for social intervention. *Annual Review of Psychology, 51*, 345–375.

Longino, H. (1990). *Science as social knowledge: Values and objectivity in scientific inquiry*. Princeton, NJ: Princeton University Press.

Longo, N. V., Manosevitch, I., & Shaffer, T. J. (2017). Introduction. In T. J. Shaffer, N. V. Longo, I. Manosevitch, & M. S. Thomas (Eds.), *Deliberative pedagogy: Teaching and learning for democratic engagement* (pp. xix–xxxv). East Lansing: Michigan State University Press.

Machamer, P., & Osbeck, L. (2004). The social in the epistemic. In P. Machamer & G. Wolters (Eds.), *Science, values and objectivity* (pp. 78–89). Pittsburgh, PA: University of Pittsburgh Press.

Majone, G. (1989). *Evidence, argument, and persuasion in the policy process*. New Haven, CT: Yale University Press.

Makau, J. M., & Marty, D. L. (2013). *Dialogue and deliberation*. Long Grove, IL: Waveland Press.

Mandel, D., & Tetlock, P. (2016). Debunking the myth of value-neutral virginity: Toward truth in scientific advertising. *Frontiers in Psychology, 7*, 451.

Mark, M. M., & Henry, G. (2006). Methods for policymaking and knowledge development evaluations. In I. Shaw, J. C. Greene, & M. M. Mark (Eds.), *Handbook of evaluation* (pp. 317–339). Thousand Oaks, CA: SAGE.

Mark, M. M., Henry, G., & Julnes, G. (2000). *Evaluation: An integrated framework for understanding, guiding, and improving policies and programs*. San Francisco: Jossey-Bass.

Mark, M. M., & Shotland, R. L. (1985). Stakeholder-based evaluation and value judgments. *Evaluation Review, 9*, 605–626.

Marsden, D., & Oakley, P. (1991). Future issues and perspectives in the evaluation of social development. *Community Development Journal, 26*, 315–328.

Martyn, C. (2003). The ethical bureaucracy. *QJM: An International Journal of Medicine, 96*(5), 323–324.

Mathison, S. (Ed.). (2005). *Encyclopedia of evaluation.* Thousand Oaks, CA: SAGE.

Mathison, S. (2008). What is the difference between evaluation and research and why do we care. In N. L. Smith & P. R. Brandon (Eds.), *Fundamental issues in evaluation* (pp. 183–196). New York: Guilford Press.

Mayne, J. (2001). Addressing attribution through contribution analysis: Using performance measures sensibly. *Canadian Journal of Program Evaluation, 16*(1), 1–24.

Mayne, J. (2011). Contribution analysis: Addressing cause and effect. In K. Forss, M. Marra, & R. Schwartz (Eds.), *Evaluating the complex* (pp. 53–96). New Brunswick, NJ: Transaction.

McBride, D., Casillas, W., & LoPiccolo, J. (2020). Inciting social change through evaluation. In L. C. Neubauer, D. McBride, A. D. Guajardo, W. D. Casillas, & M. E. Hall (Eds.), Examining issues facing communities of color today: The role of evaluation to incite change. *New Directions for Evaluation, 166,* 119–127.

McCoy, M. L., & Scully, P. L. (2002). Deliberative dialogue to expand civic engagement: What kind of talk does democracy need? *National Civic Review, 91*(2), 117–135.

McMillan, C., & Overly, J. (2016). Wicked problems: Turning strategic management upside down. *Journal of Business Strategy, 37,* 34–43.

Meadows, D. (1999). *Leverage points: Place to intervene in a system.* Hartland, VT: Sustainability Institute. Retrieved from *http://donellameadows.org/article-category/articles-papers.*

Mehrbani, R., Kinsella, M., & Weiser, W. (2019). *Proposals for reform.* New York: New York University School of Law, Brennan Center for Justice. Retrieved from *www.brennancenter.org/sites/default/files/2019-09/2019_10_TaskForce%20II_0.pdf.*

Menocal, A. R., Cassidy, M., Swift, S., Jacobstein, D., Rothblum, C., & Tservil, I. (2018). *Thinking and working politically through applied political economy analysis.* Washington, DC: USAID. Retrieved from *www.usaid.gov/documents/1866/thinking-and-working-politically-through-applied-political-economy-analysis.*

Mertens, D. M. (2009). *Transformative research and evaluation.* New York: Guilford Press.

Mertens, D. M. (2014). *Research and evaluation in education and psychology: Integrating diversity with quantitative, qualitative, and mixed methods* (4th ed.). Thousand Oaks, CA: SAGE.

Meyer, W., & Stockmann, R. (Eds.). (2016). *The future of evaluation: Global trends, new challenges, shared perspectives.* London: Palgrave/Macmillan.

Michelitch, K. (2018). Whose research is it?: Political scientists discuss whether, how, and why we should involve the communities we study. *PS: Political Science and Politics, 51,* 543–545.

Midgley, G. (2000). *Systemic intervention.* Dordrecht, the Netherlands: Kluwer Academic/Plenum.

Midgley, G., Cavana, R. Y., Brocklesby, J., Foote, J. L., Wood, D. R. R., & Ahuriri-Driscoll, A. (2013). Towards a new framework for evaluating systemic problem structuring methods. *European Journal of Operational Research, 229*, 143–154.

Miller, C. A., & Wyborn, C. (2020). Co-production in global sustainability: Histories and theories. *Environmental Science and Policy, 113*, 88–95.

Milstein, B. (2019). A brief history of stewarding health, wealth, and well-being. Retrieved from *www.rethinkhealth.org/wp-content/uploads/2020/04/A-Brief-History-of-Stewarding-Health-Wealth-and-Well-Being-Oct-6-2019.pdf*.

Mingers, J., & Rosenhead, J. (2002). Problem structuring methods in action. *European Journal of Operational Research, 152*, 530–544.

Morris, N. (2015). Providing ethical guidance for collaborative research in developing countries. *Research Ethics, 11*(4), 211–235.

Mowles, C. (2014). Complex, but not quite complex enough: The turn to the complexity sciences in evaluation scholarship. *Evaluation, 20*, 160–175.

Mt. Auburn Associates. (2019). Evaluation of the ReThink Health Ventures Project. Retrieved from *www.rethinkhealth.org/Resource/how-system-stewards-in-washingtons-king-county-are-turning-the-tide-toward-equitable-health-and-well-being*.

Mulkay, M. J. (1976). Norms and ideology in science. *Social Science Information, 15*(4–5), 637–656.

National Academies of Sciences, Engineering, and Medicine. (2017a). *Communicating science effectively: A research agenda*. Washington, DC: National Academies Press.

National Academies of Sciences, Engineering, and Medicine. (2017b). *Fostering integrity in research*. Washington, DC: National Academies Press.

National Academies of Sciences, Engineering, and Medicine. (2019). *Methodologies for evaluating and grading evidence: Considerations for public health emergency preparedness and response: Proceedings of a workshop in brief*. Washington, DC: National Academies Press.

National Research Council. (1996). *Understanding risk: Informing decision in a democratic society*. Washington, DC: National Academies Press.

National Research Council & Institute of Medicine. (2002). *Community programs to promote youth development*. Washington, DC: National Academies Press.

Nelson, M. C., Cordray, D. S., Hulleman, C. S., Darrow, C. L., & Sommer, E. C. (2012). A procedure for assessing intervention fidelity in experiments testing educational and behavioral interventions. *Journal of Behavioral Health Services and Research, 39*, 374–396.

Neubauer, L. C., & Hall, M. E. (2020). Is inciting social change something evaluators can do? Should do? In L. C. Neubauer, D. McBride, A. D. Guajardo, W. D. Casillas, & M. E. Hall (Eds.), Examining issues facing communities of color today: The role of evaluation to incite change. *New Directions for Evaluation, 166*, 129–135.

Neufeldt, R. C. (2016). *Wicked problems: Peacebuilding evaluation ethics, determining what is good and right*. The Peacebuilding Evaluation Consortium. Retrieved from *www.cdacollaborative.org/publication/wicked-problems-peacebuilding-evaluation-ethics-determining-good-right*.

Newcomer, K. E., Hatry, H. P., & Wholey, J. S. (2015). *Handbook of practical program evaluation.* Hoboken, NJ: Wiley.

Nielsen, S. B., Lemire, S., & Christie, C. A. (Eds.). (2018). The evaluation marketplace: Exploring the evaluation industry. *New Directions for Evaluation, 160.*

Niemi, P. (2016). Six challenges for ethical conduct in science. *Science and Engineering Ethics, 22*(4), 1007–1025.

Norman, C., Best, A., Mortimer, S., Huerta, T., & Buchan, A. (2011). Evaluating the science of discovery in complex health systems. *American Journal of Evaluation, 32,* 70–84.

Norström, A. V., Cvitanovic, C., Löf, M. F., West, S., Wyborn, C., Balvanera, P., et al. (2020, January 20). Principles for knowledge production in sustainability research. *Nature Sustainability.* Retrieved from *https://doi-org.proxy2.library.illinois.edu/10.1038/s41893-019-0448-2.*

Nussbaum, M. (1994). *The therapy of desire: Theory and practice in Hellenistic ethics.* Princeton, NJ: Princeton University Press.

Nutley, S. M., Walter, I., & Davies, H. T. O. (2007). *Using evidence: How research can inform pubic services.* Bristol, UK: Policy Press.

O'Connor, A. (2007). *Social science for what?: Philanthropy and the social question in a world turned right side up.* New York: Russell Sage Foundation.

O'Donnell, M. (2016). *Adaptive management: What it means for CSOs.* London: Bond. Retrieved from *www.bond.org.uk/sites/default/files/resource-documents/adaptive_management_-_what_it_means_for_csos_0.pdf.*

Office for Human Research Protections, U.S. Department of Health and Human Services. (2019). International compilation of human research standards. Retrieved from *www.hhs.gov/ohrp/sites/default/files/2019-International-Compilation-of-Human-Research-Standards.pdf.*

Ofir, Z. (2017). Updating the DAC evaluation criteria: Part 2. Why change the status quo? (Blog). Retrieved from *http://zendaofir.com/updating-the-dac-evaluation-criteria-part-2.*

Ofir, Z., Schwandt, T. A., Duggan, C., & McLean, R. (2016). *RQ+ Research Quality Plus: A holistic approach to evaluating research.* Ottawa, Ontario, Canada: International Development Research Centre. Retrieved from *www.idrc.ca/en/research-in-action/research-quality-plus.*

Ooms, G. (2015). Navigating between stealth advocacy and unconscious dogmatism: The challenge of researching the norms, politics and power of global health. *International Journal of Health Policy and Management, 4*(10), 641–644.

Organisation for Economic Co-operation and Development (OECD) Development Assistance Committee. (1991). *Principles for evaluation of development assistance.* Paris: Author. Available at *www.oecd.org/dac/evaluation/dcdndep/41029845.pdf.*

Orr, L. (2018). The role of evaluation in building evidence-based policy. *Annals of the American Academy of Political and Social Science, 678,* 51–59.

Ostrom, E. (1996). Crossing the great divide: Coproduction, synergy, and development. *World Development, 24,* 1073–1087.

Ostrom, E. (2015). *Governing the commons: The evolution of institutions for collective action* (6th ed.). New York: Cambridge University Press.

Parkhurst, J. O. (2017). *The politics of evidence: From evidence-based policy to the good governance of evidence.* London: Routledge.

Parkhurst, J. O., & Abeysinghe, S. (2016). What constitutes "good" evidence for public health and social policy-making?: From hierarchies to appropriateness. *Social Epistemology, 30* (5–6), 665–679.

Pasanen, T. (2020). Getting intentional about M&E: Choosing suitable approaches for adaptive programmes (Blog). Retrieved from *https://medium.com/glam-blog/getting-intentional-about-m-e-choosing-suitable-approaches-for-adaptive-programmes-f76c6b2790d9.*

Pasanen, T., & Barnett, I. (2019). Supporting adaptive management: Monitoring and evaluation tools and approaches (ODI working paper). Retrieved from *www.odi.org/publications/16511-supporting-adaptive-management-monitoring-and-evaluation-tools-and-approaches.*

Patton, M. Q. (1990). *Qualitative evaluation and research methods* (2nd ed.). Newbury Park, CA: SAGE.

Patton, M. Q. (2011). *Developmental evaluation: Applying complexity concepts to enhance innovation and use.* New York: Guilford Press.

Patton, M. Q. (2018). *Principles focused evaluation: The GUIDE.* New York: Guilford Press.

Patton, M. Q. (2019). Expanding futuring foresight through evaluative thinking. *World Futures Review, 11*(4), 296–307.

Patton, P. (2002). Postmodernism: Philosophical aspects. In N. J. Smelser & P. B. Baltes (Eds.), *International encyclopedia of the social and behavioral sciences* (pp. 11872–11877). New York: Elsevier.

Paul, R., & Elder, L. (2013). *The thinker's guide to ethical reasoning: Based on critical thinking concepts and tools* (2nd ed.). Lanham, MD: Rowman & Littlefield.

Pearson, J. (2016, September 2). The case for value neutrality in public administration. *PATimes.* Available at *https://patimes.org/case-neutrality-public-administration.*

Peersman, G. (2014). *Evaluative criteria, methodological brief impact evaluation No. 3.* Florence: UNICEF Office of Research. Retrieved from *www.unicef-irc.org/publications/748-evaluative-criteria-methodological-briefs-impact-evaluation-no-3.html.*

Pennock, R. T. (2015). Fostering a culture of scientific integrity: Legalistic vs. scientific virtue-based approaches. *Professional Ethics Report, 28*(2), 1–3.

Petticrew, M., & Roberts, H. (2003). Evidence, hierarchies, and typologies: Horses for courses. *Journal of Epidemiological Community Health, 57,* 527–529.

Picciotto, R. (2020). Towards a "New Project Management" movement?: An international development perspective. *International Journal of Project Management, 38,* 474–485.

Pielke, R. A., Jr. (2007). *The honest broker: Making sense of science and politics.* Cambridge, UK: Cambridge University Press.

Pierson, P. (2000). Increasing returns, path dependence, and the study of politics. *American Political Science Review, 94,* 251–267.

Pimple, K. (2002). Six domains of research ethics: A heuristics framework for the responsible conduct of research. *Science and Engineering Ethics, 8*(2), 191–205.

Polanyi, M. (1962). The republic of science: Its political and economic theory. *Minerva, 1*(1), 54–73.

Polk, M. (2014). Achieving the promise of transdisciplinarity: A critical exploration of the relationship between transdisciplinary research and societal problem solving. *Sustainability Science, 9*(4), 439–451.

Prewitt, K. (2019). Retrofitting social science for the practical moral. *Issues in Science and Technology, 36*(1), 180–187.

Prewitt, K., Schwandt. T. A., & Straf, M. (2012). *Using science as evidence in public policy.* Washington, DC: National Academies Press.

Proctor, R. N. (1991). *Value-free science?: Purity and power in modern knowledge.* Cambridge, MA: Harvard University Press.

Putnam, H. (1981). *Reason, truth, and history.* Cambridge, UK: Cambridge University Press.

Putnam, H. (2002). *The collapse of the fact/value dichotomy and other essays.* Cambridge, MA: Harvard University Press.

Ragin, C. C., & Amoroso, L. M. (2011). *Constructing social research: The unity and diversity of method.* Thousand Oaks, CA: SAGE.

Rawls, J. (1999). *A theory of justice* (rev. ed.). Oxford, UK: Oxford University Press.

Rebien, C. C. (1996). Participatory evaluation of development assistance: Dealing with power and facilitative learning. *Evaluation, 2*, 151–172.

Reeler, D. (2007). *A theory of social change and implications for practice, planning, monitoring and evaluation.* Capetown, South Africa: Community Development Resource Association. Retrieved from *www.mspguide.org/resource/theory-social-change-and-implications-practice-planning-monitoring-and-evaluation-0.*

Rein, M. (1983). Value-critical policy analysis. In D. Callahan & B. Jennings (Eds.), *Ethics, the social sciences, and policy analysis* (pp. 83–111). New York: Springer.

Reineke, R. A. (1991). Stakeholder involvement in evaluation: Suggestions for practice. *Evaluation Practice, 12*(1), 39–44.

Reiser, S. J. (1993). Overlooking ethics in the search for objectivity and misconduct in science. *Academic Medicine, 68*(9, Suppl.), 84.

Reiss, J., & Sprenger, J. (2017). Scientific objectivity. In E. N. Zalta (Ed.), *The Stanford encyclopedia of philosophy.* Retrieved from *https://plato.stanford.edu/archives/win2017/entries/scientific-objectivity.*

Resnik, D. (2008). Scientific autonomy and public oversight. *Episteme: A Journal of Social Epistemology, 5*(2), 220–238.

Resnik, D., & Elliott, K. (2016). The ethical challenges of socially responsible science. *Accountability in Research, 23*(1), 31–46.

Rest, J. (1986). *Moral development: Advances in research and theory.* New York: Praeger.

ReThink Health. (2015a). Public narrative: Story of self. Retrieved from *www.rethinkhealth.org/wp-content/uploads/2015/11/Story-of-Self-11-5.pdf.*

ReThink Health. (2015b). Summary of the ReThink Health dynamics model. Retrieved from *www.rethinkhealth.org/wp-content/uploads/2014/10/ReThink-Health-Model-Summary-v5.pdf.*

ReThink Health. (2019a). Essential practices. Retrieved from *www.rethinkhealth.org/wp-content/uploads/2019/01/RTH-10EssentialPractices_172019.pdf.*

ReThink Health. (2019b). Wellbeing portfolio. Retrieved from *www. rethinkhealth.org/wp-content/uploads/2019/07/RTH-WellBeingPortfolio_ InstructionsSummary_10222018-1.pdf.*

ReThink Health. (n.d.-a). Foundation website. Retrieved from *www.rethinkhealth. org.*

ReThink Health. (n.d.-b). Health dynamics model. Retrieved from *www. rethinkhealth.org/our-work/dynamics-model.*

ReThink Health. (n.d.-c). Health stewards' pathway. Retrieved from *www. rethinkhealth.org/stewards-pathway.*

ReThink Health. (n.d.-d). Pulse check. Retrieved from *www.rethinkhealth.org/ pulsecheck.*

ReThink Health. (n.d.-e). Stewards' resources. Retrieved from *www.rethinkhealth. org/stewards-resources/#t8.*

Reynolds, M. (2007, August 20–24). *Framing purposeful evaluation through critical systems thinking.* Paper presented at the XXIInd Congress of the European Society for Rural Sociology, Wageningen, the Netherlands.

Reynolds, M., Forss, K., Hummelbrunner, R., Marra, M., & Perrin, B. (2012, December). Complexity, systems thinking and evaluation—an emerging relationship? *Evaluation Connections: The European Evaluation Society Newsletter,* pp. 7–9.

Reynolds, M., Gates, E., Hummelbrunner, R., Marra, M., & Williams, B. (2016). Towards systemic evaluation. *Systems Research and Behavioral Science, 33*(5), 662–673.

Reynolds, M., & Holwell, S. (Eds.). (2020). *Systems approaches to making change: A practical guide* (2nd ed.). London: Springer.

Reynolds, M., & Schwandt, T. (2017). *Evaluation as public work: An ethos for professional evaluation praxis.* Paper presented at the UK Evaluation Society Annual Conference, London. Retrieved from *http://oro.open.ac.uk/50640.*

Richardson, R., & Patton, M. Q. (in press). Transformation-focused leadership for a transformational alliance: Infusing systems principles and complexity concepts through evaluative thinking. In E. Gates, M. Walton, & P. Vidueira (Eds.), Systems- and complexity-informed evaluation: Insights from practice. *New Directions for Evaluation.*

Rihoux, B., & Ragin, C. (Eds.). (2008). *Configurational comparative methods: Qualitative comparative analysis (QCA) and related techniques.* Thousand Oaks, CA: SAGE.

Rittel, H., & Webber, M. M. (1973). Dilemmas in a general theory of planning. *Policy Sciences, 4*(2), 155–169.

Robert, C., & Zeckhauser, R. (2011). The methodology of normative policy analysis. *Journal of Policy Analysis and Management, 30*(3), 613–643.

Rockefeller Philanthropy Advisors. (2019). Scaling solutions toward shifting systems (A Funder's workshop report). Retrieved from *https://www.rockpa. org/wp-content/uploads/2019/10/Assessing-Systems-Change-A-Funders-Workshop-Report-Rockefeller-Philanthropy-Advisors-August-2019.pdf.*

Rog, D. J. (2012). When background becomes foreground: Toward context-sensitive evaluation practice. In D. J. Rog, J. L. Fitzpatrick, & R. F. Conner (Eds.), Context: A framework for its influence on evaluation practice. *New Directions for Evaluation, 135,* 25–40.

Rogers, P. (2014). *Overview: Strategies for causal attribution, methodological briefs, impact evaluation No. 6.* Florence: UNICEF Office of Research. Retrieved from *www.unicef-irc.org/publications/pdf/brief_6_overview_strategies_causal_attribution_eng.pdf.*

Rogers, P. J., & Williams, B. (2006). Evaluation for practice improvement and organizational learning. In I. F. Shaw, J. C. Greene, & M. M. Mark (Eds.), *Handbook of evaluation* (pp. 76–97). London: SAGE.

Rogerson, M. D., Gottlieb, M. C., Handelsman, M. M., Knapp, S., & Younggren, J. (2011). Nonrational processes in ethical decision making. *American Psychologist, 66*(7), 614–623.

Rose, N. (1991). Governing by numbers: Figuring out democracy. *Accounting, Organizations, and Society, 16,* 673–692.

Rossi, R. H., Lipsey, M. W., & Henry, G. T. (2019). *Evaluation: A systematic approach* (8th ed.). Thousand Oaks, CA: SAGE.

Rudner, R. (1953). The scientist qua scientist makes value judgements. *Philosophy of Science, 20,* 1–6.

Rule, J. B. (1971). The problem with social problems. *Politics and Society, 2*(1), 47–56.

Sanderson, I. (2009). Intelligent policy making for a complex world: Pragmatism, evidence and learning. *Political Studies, 57,* 699–719.

Saran, A., & White, H. (2018). *Evidence and gap maps: A comparison of different approaches.* Oslo, Norway: Campbell Collaboration. Retrieved from *www.campbellcollaboration.org.*

Sarewitz, D. (2016, Spring/Summer). Saving science. *The New Atlantis, 49,* 5–36. Retrieved from *www.thenewatlantis.com/publications/saving-science.*

Sastry, A., & Penn, K. (2014). *Fail better: Design smart mistakes and succeed sooner.* Boston: Harvard Business School Publishing.

Sayer, A. (2011). *Why things matter to people: Social science, values and ethical life.* Cambridge, UK: Cambridge University Press.

Scally, C. P., Lo, L., Pettit, K. L. S., Anoll, C., & Scott, K. (2020). *Driving systems change forward: Leveraging multisite, cross-sector initiatives to change systems, advance racial equity, and shift power.* Washington, DC: Urban Institute. Retrieved from *www.urban.org/research/publication/driving-systems-change-forward-leveraging-multisite-cross-sector-initiatives-change-systems-advance-racial-equity-and-shift-power/view/full_report.*

Schön, D. A. (1983). *The reflective practitioner: How professionals think in action.* New York: Basic Books.

Schön, D. A. (1992). The crisis of professional knowledge and the pursuit of an epistemology of practice. *Journal of Interprofessional Care, 6*(1), 49–63.

Schön, D. A. (1995). The new scholarship requires a new epistemology. *Change, 27*(6), 26–34.

Schorr, L. B. (2012, Fall). Broader evidence for bigger impact. *Stanford Social Innovation Review,* pp. 50–55.

Schorr, L. B., & Farrow, F. (2011). *Expanding the evidence universe: Doing better by knowing more.* Washington, DC: Center for the Study of Social Policy. Retrieved from *https://cssp.org/resource/expanding-the-evidence-universe.*

Schwandt, T. A. (1997). The landscape of values in evaluation: Charted terrain and unexplored territory. In D. J. Rog & D. Fournier (Eds.), *Progress and future* directions in evaluation: Perspectives on theory, practice and methods. *New Directions for Evaluation, 76,* 25–39.

Schwandt, T. A. (2002). *Evaluation practice reconsidered.* New York: Peter Lang.

Schwandt, T. A. (2005). The centrality of practice to evaluation. *American Journal of Evaluation, 26*(1), 95–105.

Schwandt, T. A. (2008). Educating for intelligent belief in evaluation. *American Journal of Evaluation, 29,* 139–150.

Schwandt, T. A. (2015). *Evaluation foundations revisited: Cultivating a life of the mind for practice.* Stanford, CA: Stanford University Press.

Schwandt, T. A. (2017). Professionalization, ethics, and fidelity to an evaluation ethos. *American Journal of Evaluation, 38,* 546–553.

Schwandt, T. A. (2018). Acting together in determining value: A professional ethical responsibility of evaluators. *Evaluation, 24,* 306–317.

Schwandt, T. A. (2019a). Post-normal evaluation? *Evaluation, 25,* 317–329.

Schwandt, T. A. (2019b). The concerted effort to professionalize evaluation practice: Whither are we bound? In J.-E. Furubo & N. Stame (Eds.), *The evaluation enterprise: A critical view* (pp. 221–242). New York: Taylor & Francis.

Schwandt, T. A., & Dahler-Larsen, P. (2006). When evaluation meets the "rough ground" in communities. *Evaluation, 12,* 496–505.

Schwandt, T. A., & Gates, E. F. (2016). What can evaluation do?: An agenda for evaluation in service of an equitable society. In S. I. Donaldson & R. Picciotto (Eds.), *Evaluation for an equitable society* (pp. 67–81). Charlotte, NC: Information Age.

Schwartz, B., & Sharpe, K. (2010). *Practical wisdom.* New York: Riverhead Books.

Scriven, M. (1959). The logic of criteria. *Journal of Philosophy, 56*(22), 857–868.

Scriven, M. (1972). The exact role of value judgments in science. In K. F. Schaffner & R. S. Cohen (Eds.), *PSA: Proceedings of the Biennial Meeting of the Philosophy of Science Association* (Vol. 1972, pp. 219–247). New York: Springer.

Scriven, M. (1976). Evaluation bias and its control. In G. V Glass (Ed.), *Evaluation studies review annual* (pp. 119–139). Beverley Hills, CA: SAGE.

Scriven, M. (1991). *Evaluation thesaurus* (4th ed.). Newbury Park, CA: SAGE.

Scriven, M. (1994a). Evaluation as a discipline. *Studies in Educational Evaluation, 20,* 147–166.

Scriven, M. (1994b). The final synthesis. *Evaluation Practice, 15*(3), 367–382.

Scriven, M. (2003). Evaluation theory and metatheory. In T. Kellaghan & D. L. Stufflebeam (Eds.), *International handbook of educational evaluation* (pp. 15–30). Dordrecht, the Netherlands: Kluwer Academic.

Scriven, M. (2005). The logic of evaluation. In S. Mathison (Ed.), *Encyclopedia of evaluation* (pp. 236–239). Thousand Oaks, CA: SAGE.

Scriven, M. (2007). The logic of evaluation. In H. V. Hansen, C. W. Tindale, A. A. Blair, & R. H. Johnson (Eds.), *Dissensus and the search for common ground* [CD-ROM] (pp. 1–16). Windsor, ON, Canada: Ontario Society for the Study of Argumentation. Retrieved from *https://scholar.uwindsor.ca/ossaarchive/OSSA7/papersandcommentaries/138.*

Scriven, M. (2009). Probative inference. OSSA Conference Archive. Paper 147. Retrieved from *https://scholar.uwindsor.ca/cgi/viewcontent.cgi?referer=&httpsredir=1&article=1232&context=ossaarchive.*

Scriven, M. (2012). The logic of valuing. In G. Julnes (Ed.), Promoting valuation in the public interest: Informing policies for judging value in evaluation. *New Directions for Evaluation, 133*, 17–28.

Scriven, M. (2016a). Roadblocks to recognition and revolution. *American Journal of Evaluation, 37*, 27–44.

Scriven, M. (2016b). The last frontier of evaluation: Ethics. In S. Donaldson & R. Picciotto (Eds.), *Evaluation for an equitable society* (pp. 11–48). Charlotte, NC: Information Age.

Scudder, M. F. (2020). The ideal of uptake in democratic deliberation. *Political Studies, 68*, 504–522.

SDG Transformations Forum. (2018). Manifesto and first initiatives of Working Group #1: Transformational Evaluation for Transformational Development. Retrieved from *www.transformationsforum.net/wp-content/uploads/2018/08/TE-TD-WG-Manifesto-Pre-final-31-July-2018.pdf.*

Segone, M. (2012). *Evaluation for equitable development results.* New York: UNICEF. Retrieved from *www.clear-la.cide.edu/sites/default/files/Evaluation_for_equitable%20results_web.pdf.*

Selznick, P. (2008). *A humanist science: Values and ideals in social inquiry.* Stanford, CA: Stanford University Press.

Senge, P. M. (1990). *The fifth discipline: The art and practice of the learning organization.* New York: Doubleday/Currency.

SenGupta, S., Hopson, R., & Thompson-Robinson, M. (2004). Cultural competence in evaluation: An overview. *New Directions for Evaluation, 102*, 5–19.

Sensoy, Ö., & DiAngelo, R. (2017). "We are all for diversity, but . . .": How faculty hiring committees reproduce whiteness and practical suggestions for how they can change. *Harvard Education Review, 87*, 557–580.

Shadish, W. R., Cook, T. D., & Leviton, L. C. (1991). *Foundations of program evaluation: Theories of practice.* Newbury Park, CA: SAGE.

Shamoo, A. E., & Resnik, D. B. (2015). *Responsible conduct of research* (3rd ed.). Oxford, UK: Oxford University Press.

Shaw, I., Greene, J. C., & Mark, M. M. (Eds.). (2006). *Handbook of evaluation.* Thousand Oaks, CA: SAGE.

Shipman, S. (2012). The role of context in valuing federal programs. In G. Julnes (Ed.), Promoting valuation in the public interest: Informing policies for judging value in evaluation. *New Directions for Evaluation, 133*, 53–61.

Shouten, G., & Brighouse, H. (2015). The relationship between philosophy and evidence in education. *Theory and Research in Education, 13*(1), 5–22.

Shulha, L. M., Whitmore, E., Cousins, J. B., Gilbert, N., & al Hudib, H. (2016). Introducing evidence-based principles to guide collaborative approaches to evaluation: Results of an empirical process. *American Journal of Evaluation, 37*, 193–215.

Sieber, J. E. (1982). *The ethics of social research.* Berlin: Springer-Verlag.

Smith, C. M., & Shaw, D. (2019). The characteristics of problem structuring methods: A literature review. *European Journal of Operational Research, 274*, 403–416.

Smith, L. (2012). *Decolonizing methodologies: Research and indigenous peoples* (2nd ed.). London: Zed Books.

Smith, T. (2004). "Social" objectivity and the objectivity of values. In P. Machamer

& G. Wolters (Eds.), *Science values and objectivity* (pp. 143–171). Pittsburgh, PA: University of Pittsburgh Press.

Snilstveit, B., Bhatia, R., Rankin, K., & Leach, B. (2017). *3ie evidence gap maps: A starting point for strategic evidence production and use* (3ie Working Paper 28). New Delhi: International Initiative for Impact Evaluation (3ie). Retrieved from *www.3ieimpact.org/sites/default/files/2019-01/wp28-egm.pdf.*

Snilstveit, B., Vojtkova, M., Bhavsar, A., Stevensen, J., & Gaarder, M. (2016). Evidence gap maps: A tool for promoting evidence informed policy and strategic research agendas. *Journal of Clinical Epidemiology, 79,* 120–129.

Spector, M., & Kitsuse, J. I. (1977). *Constructing social problems.* Menlo Park, CA: Cummings.

Sphere Association. (2018). *The Sphere handbook: Humanitarian charter and minimum standards in humanitarian response.* Geneva, Switzerland: Author. Retrieved from *www.spherestandards.org/handbook.*

Stake, R. E. (1975). *Evaluating the arts in education: A responsive approach.* Columbus, OH: Merrill.

Stake, R. E. (1995). *The art of case study research.* Thousand Oaks, CA: SAGE.

Sterman, J. D. (1994). Learning in and about complex systems. *System Dynamics Review, 10*(2–3), 291–330.

Sterman, J. D. (2006). Learning from evidence in a complex world. *American Journal of Public Health, 96,* 505–514.

Stern, E., Stame, N., Mayne, J., Forss, K., Davies, R., & Befani, B. (2012). *Broadening the range of designs and methods for impact evaluation* (Working Paper No. 38). London: UK Department for International Development. Retrieved from *www.gov.uk/dfid-research-outputs/dfid-working-paper-38-broadening-the-range-of-designs-and-methods-for-impact-evaluations.*

Sternberg, R. J. (2012). A model for ethical reasoning. *Review of General Psychology, 16*(4), 319–326.

Stone, D. (2002). *The policy paradox: The art of political decision making* (rev. ed.). New York: Norton.

Stufflebeam, D. L. (2001a). Evaluation checklists: Practical tools for guiding and judging evaluation. *American Journal of Evaluation, 22,* 71–79.

Stufflebeam, D. (2001b). Evaluation values and criteria checklist. Retrieved from *https://wmich.edu/sites/default/files/attachments/u350/2014/values_criteria.pdf.*

Sugiura, L., Wiles, R., & Pope, C. (2017). Ethical challenges in online research: Public/private perceptions. *Research Ethics, 13*(3–4), 184–199.

Suhay, E. (2015). The politics of science: Political values and the production, communication, and reception of scientific knowledge. *Annals of the American Academy of Political and Social Science, 658*(1), 6–15.

Systems in Evaluation Topical Interest Group of the American Evaluation Association. (2018). Principles for effective use of systems thinking in evaluation (rev.). Retrieved from *www.systemsinevaluation.com/wp-content/uploads/2018/10/SETIG-Principles-FINAL-DRAFT-2018-9-9.pdf.*

Talbert, M. (2019). Moral responsibility. In E. N. Zalta (Ed.), *The Stanford encyclopedia of philosophy.* Retrieved from *https://plato.stanford.edu/archives/win2019/entries/moral-responsibility.*

Taylor, C. (1995). Overcoming epistemology. In *Philosophical arguments* (pp. 34–60). Cambridge, MA: Harvard University Press.

Taylor, D., & Balloch, S. (2005). *The politics of evaluation: Participation and policy implementation*. Bristol, UK: Policy Press.

Teasdale, R. (2019). *How do you define success?: Selecting criteria in evaluations of informal science, technology, engineering, and mathematics education*. Doctoral dissertation, University of Illinois, Urbana–Champaign, IL.

Tetlock, P. (2002). Social functionalist frameworks for judgment and choice: Intuitive politicians, theologians, and prosecutors. *Psychological Review, 109*(3), 451–471.

Thacher, D. (2006). The normative case study. *American Journal of Sociology, 111*(6), 1631–1676.

Thacher, D. (2015). Perils of value neutrality In M. S. Kraatz (Ed.), *Institutions and ideals: Philip Selznick's legacy for organizational studies* (pp. 317–352). Bingley, UK: Emerald Group.

Thacher, D. (2016). The perception of value: Adam Smith on the moral role of social research. *European Journal of Social Theory, 19*(1), 94–110.

Tilley, N., & Clarke, A. (2006). Evaluation in criminal justice. In I. F. Shaw, J. C. Greene, & M. M. Mark (Eds.), *The SAGE handbook of evaluation* (pp. 513–535). London: SAGE.

Toulmin, S. (2003/1958). *The uses of argument* (updated ed.). Cambridge, UK: Cambridge University Press.

Tripathi, S., Kingra, J. J., Rathinam, F., Tyrrell, T., & Gaarder. M. (2019). *Social protection: A synthesis of evidence and lessons from 3ie-supported impact evaluations* (Working Paper 34). New Delhi: International Initiative for Impact Evaluation (3ie). Retrieved from *https://doi.org/10.23846/WP0034*.

Ulrich, W. (1983). *Critical heuristics of social planning: A new approach to practical philosophy*. Bern, Switzerland: Verlag Paul Haupt.

Ulrich, W. (1987). Critical heuristics of social systems design. *European Journal of Operational Research, 31*, 276–283.

Ulrich, W. (1988a). Churchman's process of unfolding—its significance for policy analysis and evaluation. *Systems Practice, 1*(4), 415–428.

Ulrich, W. (1988b). Systems thinking, systems practice, and practical philosophy: A programme of research. *Systems Practice, 1*(2), 137–163.

Ulrich, W. (1996/2014). *A primer to critical systems heuristics for action researchers*. Hull, UK: University of Hull, Centre for Systems Studies. Retrieved from *http://wurich.com/downloads.html*.

Ulrich, W. (2000). Reflective practice in the civil society: The contribution of critically systemic thinking. *Reflective Practice, 1*(2), 247–268.

Ulrich, W. (2001). The quest for competence in systemic research and practice. *Systems Research and Behavioral Science, 18*, 3–28.

Ulrich, W. (2011). What is good professional practice? Retrieved from *www.wulrich.com/downloads/bimonthly_march2011.pdf*.

Ulrich, W. (2017). If systems thinking is the answer, what is the question?: Discussions on research competence (expanded and updated version of Working Paper No. 22, Lincoln School of Management, University of Lincoln, Lincoln, UK, 1998). Available on Werner Ulrich's Homepage: *Ulrich's Bimonthly*,

May–June 2017 (Part 1/2) and July–August 2017 (Part 2/2). Retrieved from *https://wulrich.com/downloads.html.*

Ulrich, W., & Reynolds, M. (2010). Critical systems heuristics. In M. Reynolds & S. Holwell (Eds.), *Systems approaches to managing change: A practical guide* (pp. 243–292). London: Springer.

United Nations Evaluation Group. (2016). *Norms and standards for evaluation.* New York: Author. Retrieved from *www.unevaluation.org/document/detail/1914.*

United Nations Research Institute for Social Development. (2016). *Policy Innovations for Transformative Change: Implementing the 2030 Agenda for Sustainable Development.* Geneva: Author. Retrieved from *www.unrisd.org/UNRISD/website/document.nsf/(httpPublications)/92AF5072673F924DC125804C0044F396?OpenDocument.*

U.S. Agency for International Development (USAID). (2016). Evaluation: Learning from experience. USAID Evaluation Policy. Retrieved from *www.usaid.gov/sites/default/files/documents/1870/USAIDEvaluationPolicy.pdf.*

U.S. Department of Health and Human Services. (n.d.). Definition of research misconduct. Retrieved from *https://ori.hhs.gov/definition-misconduct.*

U.S. Department of Health and Human Services, Centers for Disease Control and Prevention. (2011). *Introduction to program evaluation for public health programs: A self-study guide.* Atlanta, GA: Author.

U.S. Department of Health and Human Services Office for Human Research Protections. (2019). Revised Common Rule. Retrieved from *www.hhs.gov/ohrp/regulations-and-policy/regulations/finalized-revisions-common-rule/index.html.*

Valters, C. (2015). *Theories of change: Time for a radical approach to learning in development.* London: Overseas Development Institute. Retrieved from *www.odi.org/publications/9883-theories-change-time-radical-approach-learning-development.*

Valters, C., Cummings, C., & Nixon, H. (2016). *Putting learning at the centre: Adaptive development programming in practice.* London: Overseas Development Institute. Retrieved from *www.odi.org/publications/10367-putting-learning-centre-adaptive-development-programming-practice.*

Vedung, E. (1997). *Public policy and program evaluation.* New York: Routledge.

Wadsworth, Y. (2011). *Everyday evaluation on the run* (3rd ed.). New York: Routledge.

Wagenaar, H., & Noam Cook, S. D. (2003). Understanding policy practices: Action, dialectic and deliberation in policy analysis. In M. A. Hajer & H. Wagenaar (Eds.), *Deliberative policy analysis* (pp. 139–171). Cambridge, UK: Cambridge University Press.

Walton, D. (2008). *Informal logic: A pragmatic approach* (2nd ed.). Cambridge, UK: Cambridge University Press.

Walton, M. (2014). Applying complexity theory: A review to inform evaluation design. *Evaluation and Program Planning, 45,* 119–126.

Webler, T. (1998). Beyond science: Deliberation and analysis in public decision making. *Human Ecology Review, 5*(1), 61–62.

Weimer, D. (2005). Institutionalizing neutrally competent policy analysis:

Resources for promoting objectivity and balance in consolidating democracies. *Policy Studies Journal, 33*(2), 131–146.

Weiss, C. H. (1972). *Evaluation research: Methods for assessing program effectiveness.* Englewood Cliffs, NJ: Prentice-Hall.

Weiss, C. H. (1973). Where politics and evaluation research meet. *Evaluation, 1,* 37–45.

Weiss, C. H. (1978). Improving the linkage between social research and policy. In L. E. Lynn (Ed.), *Knowledge and policy: The uncertain connection* (pp. 23–81). Washington, DC: National Academies Press.

Weiss, C. H. (1980). Knowledge creep and decision accretion. *Knowledge: Creation, Diffusion, Utilization, 1,* 381–404.

Weiss, C. (1998). *Evaluation* (2nd ed.). New York: Prentice-Hall.

Weiss, C. H. (1999). The interface between evaluation and public policy. *Evaluation, 5*(4), 468–486.

Weiss, C. H., & Bucuvalas, M. J. (1980). *Social science research and decision-making.* New York: Columbia University Press.

Weiss, R. S., & Rein, M. (1970). The evaluation of broad-aim programs: Experimental design, its difficulties, and an alternative. *Administrative Science Quarterly, 1*(15), 97–109.

Westheimer, J., & Kahne, J. (2004). What kind of citizen?: The politics of educating for democracy. *American Educational Research Journal, 41*(2), 237–269.

White, L., & Taket, A. (1994). The death of the expert. *Journal of the Operational Research Society, 45,* 733–748.

Whitmore, E., Guijt, I., Mertens, D. M., Imm, P. S., Chinman, M., & Wandersman, A. (2006). Embedding improvements, lived experience, and social justice in evaluation practice. In I. F. Shaw, J. C. Greene, & M. M. Mark (Eds.), *Handbook of evaluation* (pp. 340–359). Thousand Oaks, CA: SAGE.

Williams, B. (1985). *Ethics and the limits of philosophy.* Cambridge, MA: Harvard University Press.

Williams, B. (2015). Prosaic or profound: The adoption of systems ideas by impact evaluation. *IDS Bulletin, 46*(1), 7–16.

Williams, B., & Hummelbrunner, R. (2011). *Systems concepts in action.* Stanford, CA: Stanford University Press.

Williams, B., & van't Hof, S. (2016). Wicked solutions: A systems approach to complex problems. Retrieved from *www.researchgate.net/publication/263110523_Wicked_Solutions_A_Systems_Approach_to_Complex_Problems.*

Williams, D. R., Lawrence, J. A., & Davis, B. A. (2019). Racism and health: Evidence and needed research. *Annual Review of Public Health, 40*(1), 105–125.

Wilson, E., Kenny, A., & Dickson-Swift, V. (2018). Ethical challenges in community-based participatory research: A scoping review. *Qualitative Health Research, 28*(2), 189–199.

Wilson-Grau, R., & Britt, H. (2012). *Outcome harvesting.* New York: Ford Foundation. Retrieved from *www.managingforimpact.org/sites/default/files/resource/wilsongrau_en_outome_harvesting_brief_revised_nov_2013.pdf.*

Wolfe, R., Steinberg, A., & Hoffman, N. (Eds.). (2013). *Anytime anywhere: Student-centered learning for schools and teachers.* Cambridge, MA: Harvard Education Press.

World Health Organization. (2013). *WHO evaluation practice handbook.* Geneva, Switzerland: WHO Press.

World Health Organization. (2019). *Ethical consideration for health policy and systems research.* Geneva: Author. Retrieved from *https://apps.who.int/iris/bitstream/handle/10665/330033/9789241516921-eng.pdf?ua=1.*

World Health Organization Department of Gender and Women's Health. (2001). *Putting women first: Ethical and safety recommendations for research on domestic violence against women.* Geneva, Switzerland: World Health Organization. Retrieved from *www.who.int/gender/violence/womenfirtseng.pdf.*

Zuberi, T., & Bonilla-Silva, E. (2008). *White methods: Racism and methodology.* Lanham, MD: Rowman & Littlefield.

Author Index

Subject Index

Note: Page numbers in **bold** indicate glossary terms;
page numbers followed by *f* or *t* indicate a figure or a table.

About the Authors

Thomas A. Schwandt, PhD, is Emeritus Professor of Educational Psychology at the University of Illinois, Urbana–Champaign. He has written extensively about evaluation theory and practice. Dr. Schwandt is a recipient of the Paul F. Lazarsfeld Award from the American Evaluation Association for his contributions to evaluation theory. He is editor emeritus of the *American Journal of Evaluation*; serves on the editorial board of *Evaluation: The International Journal of Theory, Research and Practice*; and is a member of the Evaluation Advisory Panel of the Independent Evaluation Office of the United Nations Development Programme.

Emily F. Gates, PhD, is Assistant Professor in the Department of Measurement, Evaluation, Statistics, and Assessment in the Lynch School of Education and Human Development at Boston College. She has extensive experience conducting mixed methods evaluations of programs, primarily in K–12 and higher education; science, technology, engineering, and mathematics (STEM) education; and public health. Dr. Gates's research examines the intersecting areas of systems thinking and approaches, values and valuing, and equity in evaluation theory and practice. She was an evaluation fellow in the Office on Smoking and Health at the U.S. Centers for Disease Control and Prevention.